P9-AOL-584

Robbie Ross

Oscar Wilde's devoted friend

Robbie Ross

Oscar Wilde's devoted friend

~~~~~

Jonathan Fryer

Carroll & Graf Publishers, Inc.
NEW YORK

Carroll & Graf Publishers, Inc.
19 West 21st Street
New York
NY 10010-6805

First published in the UK by Constable,
an imprint of Constable & Robinson Ltd 2000

First Carroll & Graf edition 2000

Copyright © Jonathan Fryer 2000

The right of Jonathan Fryer to be identified as the author
of this work has been asserted by him in accordance
with the Copyright, Designs and Patents Act, 1988.

CIP data available from the Library of Congress

ISBN 0-7867-0781-X

Printed and bound in the EU

Contents

Acknowledgements

A biographical enterprise such as this invariably depends to a large extent on the goodwill and co-operation of the families and estates of the main protagonists. Given the bitter feuds that existed between some of the characters here portrayed, it is little short of miraculous that their descendants should work so well together in encouraging and furthering research into Oscar Wilde's circle. My previous study of the friendship between Oscar and André Gide had already made me familiar with many of them. But focussing more intently on Robbie Ross has opened new doors, for which I am truly grateful.

In particular, I would like to thank, from Robbie's side, John-Paul Ross, Oliver Ross, Carolyn Gould and the estate of Prof. G. Robertson. In Bosie's corner, my dear friend, his executor Sheila Colman. And last but not least, Oscar Wilde's grandson, Merlin Holland, who not only is an eminent Wildean scholar in his own right, but also heartily endorsed the need for an up-to-date, accessible account of Robbie's extraordinary role in Oscar's life. To all of them, sincere thanks for related information and permissions. Similarly the late Rupert Hart-Davis, and the estates of William Rothenstein, Siegfried Sassoon and Aubrey Beardsley.

Don Mead and other members of the Oscar Wilde Society have been both a source of inspiration and convivial company, as have Matthew Sturgis and the 1890s Society. Both groups do so much to keep interest in the era alive, as well as producing journals and other publications of considerable interest and use.

As usual, the London Library and its staff have been of enormous assistance, ably supplemented, in this instance, by: King's College, Cambridge; the Bodleian Library, Oxford; Canada House Library, London; the Henry Ransom Foundation, University of Texas; the William Andrews Clark Memorial Library, Los Angeles. Greg Gatenby and the Harbourfront Literary Festival, Toronto, enabled me to get to Canada during the course of my research, for which I am indebted.

All shortcomings should be laid at my own door. Any omissions or misattributions there might be relating to copyright matters are purely unintentional and will be corrected in future editions.

J.F.
London, September 2000

Illustrations

For my chum
Michael Bloch

Prologue

ON 12 NOVEMBER 1895, Oscar Fingal O'Flahertie Wills Wilde was brought from Wandsworth Prison in London to a bankruptcy court, to attend the public examination of his case that had been adjourned seven weeks previously. A scandalously indisciplined sale of the effects in his marital home in Tite Street, Chelsea, at the end of April, had failed to raise sufficient funds to satisfy his creditors, despite Thomas Carlyle's writing desk being put under the hammer, along with drawings by Whistler and Burne-Jones, exquisite Chinese porcelain and dedication copies of books by Swinburne, Morris, Whitman, Hugo, Mallarmé and Verlaine, amongst others. Even an appeal to those few friends who had remained loyal to him fell short of the sum required when the Marquess of Queensberry, to whom Oscar Wilde had presented the opportunity to bring about his downfall, pursued the matter with all the manic vindictiveness of a man on a moral mission.

Attending the bankruptcy hearing, a reporter from the *Labour Leader* noted that the prison authorities had 'cut his hair in a shocking way and parted it down the side and he wears a short, scrubby, unkempt beard'. Such sartorial shortcomings were the least of Wilde's suffering. As his twenty-six-year-old Canadian friend Robbie Ross recounted in a letter to his former Cambridge tutor Oscar Browning, after Robbie had been excep-

1

tionally granted a half-hour interview meeting with Wilde in a private room at the court, after his bankruptcy was declared: 'Physically he is much worse than anyone had led me to believe. Indeed I really should not have known him at all . . . His clothes hung about him in loose folds and his hands are like those of a skeleton. The colour of his face is completely changed, but this cannot be altogether attributed to his slight beard. The latter only hides the appalling sunken cheeks . . . I cannot understand how any human nation, the English being Protestant of course are not Christians, can keep him in this condition.'

The private meeting Robbie Ross had been granted with Wilde was in recognition for the months of hard work he had spent, along with Wilde's official trustee, Arthur Clifton, in trying to avoid the very outcome now confirmed – bankruptcy – yet one more humiliation for the man who had not unfairly described himself as the Lord of Life, and who had been toppled from his pedestal on conviction of various acts of gross indecency. For Ross personally, it was also a bitter defeat. But at least at this stage, Oscar believed that Robbie could have done nothing more. In fact, he had been reassured of Robbie's selfless love at the first bankruptcy hearing on 24 September, when Wilde had appeared in public for the first time since his disgrace. As he later recalled in *De Profundis*:

When I was brought down from my prison to the Court of Bankruptcy between two policemen, Robbie waited in the long dreary corridor, that before the whole crowd, whom an action so sweet and simple hushed into silence, he might gravely raise his hat to me as handcuffed and with bowed head I passed by him. Men have gone to heaven for smaller things than that. It was in this spirit, and with this mode of love that the saints knelt down to wash the feet of the poor, or stooped to kiss the leper on the cheek.[1]

This was an act not just of Christian compassion, but of bravery. For in the climate of that age, to show sympathy for Oscar Wilde's plight was to risk opprobrium. Wilde had discovered that Britain's ruling classes were not, as W. H. Auden so brilliantly put it, a giant Lady Bracknell, to be laughed at, but rather a snake-haired gorgon whose glare could turn one to stone. Wilde had discovered, in the most painful way, that it was not possible to be in society and at the same time to flout its rules in the way he did. He could not have it both ways. Yet, as Robbie Ross was to demonstrate so intriguingly in his own life, if one handled things differently, one could.

ONE

A Legacy to Live Up To

THE RESIDENTS OF TOURS have long been proud of the fact that they are reputed to speak the finest French in the world. Moreover, as Robbie Ross liked to remind people, the town gave birth not only to him, but also to that great chronicler of French life in the first half of the nineteenth century, Honoré de Balzac. Though as a young man Balzac abandoned the respectable confines of Tours for the greater human comedy of Paris, he remained susceptible to the physical charms of his birthplace, writing in an early epistolary novel, *Sténie*:

> The city is round, and its western edge has the finest view in the world, equal to that of Naples . . . As you follow the hill, gradually the cottages with their smoking chimneys grow more sparse and in the curves and angles of the hillside, country houses catch your eye . . . And then one's gaze is lost in the bluish distance, which leaves you wanting still more. Nature, in these parts, resembles those flirtatious women who conceal their treasures so that imagination may increase them.[1]

In earlier centuries, Tours had been the favourite residence of several French kings. Yet for the numerous foreigners who were

5

drawn to live in this historic town in the Loire valley, in the years after Balzac's death in 1850, it was the gentle climate and the healthy air which were the major attractions. Many of these immigrants were English, who had fled the pollution and stress of London and other cities that were undergoing the rapid transformations brought about by science, industrialization and an unshakeable belief in progress. The newcomers liked to remind themselves that the area of France where they were now settled had actually been in a union with England under Henry II, as well as having intimate links to Mary, Queen of Scots.

A prosperous town of about 50,000 inhabitants, with a particularly high reputation for silk manufacture, Tours was able to trace its origins back to pre-Roman times, though the Romans shifted the settlement from one side of the river to the other. Moreover, it was at what became known as the Battle of Tours – the fighting actually taking place half way between Tours and Poitiers – that the Moors' northwards penetration into Europe was stopped in 732, thus saving Tours' many ecclesiastical treasures from destruction and half of Western Europe from Arab domination. By the second half of the nineteenth century, such was the town's renown for culture, civility and sanitary excellence that it even received migrants from the other side of the Atlantic, including one particularly distinguished Canadian family: John and Augusta Elizabeth (usually called Eliza) Ross, with their three children, Mary Jane (known as Mary, and born in 1855), John (Jack, 1859) and Alexander Galt (Aleck, 1860[2]). While living in Tours, Eliza Ross produced two more babies: Maria Elizabeth (Lizzie) in 1867, and Robert Baldwin (initially known as Bobby) on 25 May 1869.

There had in fact been two earlier Ross children, both of whom had died in their infancy in Canada: Maria-Louisa (1852) and a first Robert Baldwin (1854–6). Memories of this double tragedy were doubtless one reason why John Ross decided in 1866 to remove his pregnant wife and young family from the still relatively arduous living and travelling conditions of the British North American colonies and the rigours of Canadian winters, though his own declining health was an important consideration. He was only in his late forties at the time of the move to France, but a busy career in law, business and politics had taken its toll.

In a sense, moving to Europe was a kind of homecoming for John Ross, as he had been born in County Antrim in Ulster, in March 1818, and was a firm believer in the superiority of European civilization, however tirelessly he may have worked for the advancement of his adopted homeland. His parents, Alexander and Jane Ross, of Scots lineage, like so many Ulster Protestants, had been part of the great migration of 800,000 people from the British Isles to the colonies in Canada between 1815 and 1850. They settled in Upper Canada (as Ontario was then known), which was still largely a pioneer's land. John Ross proved to be a good student, and in 1839, at the age of twenty-one, he was called to the Bar of Upper Canada. Within a matter of months, by an Act of the British Parliament, Upper Canada was united with Lower Canada (Quebec), though the other colonies of the eastern British North America – Nova Scotia, New Brunswick and Prince Edward Island – remained separate entities.

John Ross practised law successfully in Toronto, which was then a town of well under 20,000 inhabitants. Indeed, he made such an impression on the local hierarchy that in 1848 he was appointed a member of the united Canada's Legislative Council. Over the next fifteen years, he held a variety of offices in the government of Canada, including Solicitor-General for Upper Canada (1851–3), Attorney General (1853–4), Speaker of the Legislative Council (1854–6), Receiver-General (1858) and lastly, concurrently, President of the Legislative Council and

Minister of Agriculture (1858–62). He played an important role in the opening up of the province during the great railway-building boom of the 1850s, being a government director of the Grand Trunk Railway from 1852 to 1857, and even its president for a while. In 1862, he cut down his political activities, concentrating more on his legal practice and his family, though he remained a member of the Legislative Council, and was 'on call' at times of public need.

In keeping with such an energetic and successful political career, John Ross married well, even brilliantly. In 1851, the same year he became Solicitor-General, at the age of thirty-three, he wed Augusta Elizabeth Baldwin (Eliza), much-loved daughter of the Honourable Robert Baldwin, the man largely credited with introducing what is known as 'responsible government' to Canada. This was to have profound implications for the development of Britain's attitude to its overseas possessions, as it gave credence to the notion that the more 'mature' colonies could govern their internal affairs and yet still remain loyal to the Crown.

Despite his commitment to responsible government, Robert Baldwin was shy, introverted and prone to depression; he was a politician almost despite himself. Called to the Bar in 1825, at the age twenty-one, he worked in his father's law practice and entered politics four years later, as a Reformer, winning a seat in the Assembly in a by-election. He was thrown out by his electors the following year and withdrew to the security of his home life. He adored his wife, his cousin Augusta Elizabeth Sullivan, whom he had married in 1827, and they produced four children – two sons and two daughters. It was therefore an almost unbearable blow when his wife died in January 1836. Robert experienced an acute emotional breakdown, depending heavily on his children for support, not least his daughter, Eliza, whose very name daily reminded him of his late wife. Yet only weeks after the bereavement, citing Christian duty as his motive, Robert Baldwin accepted an appointment to Upper Canada's Legislative Assembly. Not long afterwards the question arose whether it would not be better for Canada to declare independence from Britain, as the United States had done. In Lower Canada, there was the added dangerous element of the grievances of French Canadians who felt they were being treated as second-class citizens. Things came to a head in 1837, with outright rebellion, notably in Lower Canada, which lasted into the following year. It was an alarming initiation into the complexities of colonial rule for the young Queen Victoria, who ascended the throne while the insurrection was still being put down.

Wisely, the British despatched to Canada the Earl of Durham, who had been instrumental in framing the Great Reform Bill, and who was now charged with the task of making a report on the situation in the two Canadas. It was he who recommended the union of the two, and opened the door to the possibility of responsible government, though it took Robert Baldwin and his allies almost a decade to bring it to fruition, thanks to the reluctance, even hostility, of successive Governors. Baldwin doggedly kept on raising the issue, so much so that even some of his fellow Reformers made use of the nickname his political enemies had given him: the Man with One Idea. He was much abetted in his efforts by his partnership with the French Canadian, Louis Hippolyte LaFontaine. To the disgust of some of his colleagues, Robert Baldwin insisted that the French language should be recognized as an official language of the territory, not just English.

Baldwin was joint Premier of the united Canada with LaFontaine twice from 1842–3 and 1848–51 – in recognition of which the Queen made him a Companion of the Bath. His constituents were less generous, as they rejected him when he presented himself for election again, and he retired to Spadina, dejected and moody, becoming ever more preoccupied with the cult of his dead wife. His daughter Eliza's happy marriage and the appearance of grandchildren were among his few consolations, though the death of the grandson who had been named after him, only days after the child's second birthday, must have been singularly hard to bear. Robert Baldwin himself died in December 1858, shortly after John Ross had become President of the Legislative Council.

It was a matter of great pride to Eliza that her husband had picked up the baton of constitutional reform from her father and run with it. In this, he had a close, formidable associate, Alexander Galt (after whom Robbie Ross's brother Aleck was named). The son of the Scottish novelist and biographer John Galt, who was instrumental in chartering land for settlement in Canada, Alexander Galt was Commissioner of the British American Land Company from 1844 to 1855, and was one of the promoters of the Grand Trunk Railway, with which John Ross was so involved. Galt was elected to the Legislative Assembly, and in 1858 became Minster of Finance, alongside John Ross as Minister of Agriculture. The two were part of a heavyweight delegation that went to London to lobby the British government in favour of making Canada a confederation, bringing in New Brunswick and Nova Scotia, to which could later be added the northern territories administered by the Hudson Bay Company, the new colony of British Columbia and the huge central plains, which were only just starting to be opened up. The mission was a failure and both Galt and Ross resigned office in 1862. Their concern for Canada's future did not die, however. During the American Civil War, which had broken out in 1861, there were fears that the North might try to annex Canada in the name of 'liberation', though these proved groundless.

By 1866, the year John Ross and his family left for France, the tide of opinion in London had turned, and a successful third and last Confederation Conference was held there. This led to the passing of the British North American Act in March, and the creation of the new Canadian Dominion. By royal proclamation, John Ross was called to be a member of the new Canadian Senate, a position he would initially have to fill largely in absentia. In 1869, the year of Robbie's birth, however, John was chosen as the Senate Speaker, making a return to Canada inevitable.

However, it was the Prussians who finally forced the decision on the Ross family as a whole. In July 1870, the Emperor Napoleon III foolishly declared war on Prussia. Outnumbered and outskilled, the French were quite easily beaten in the East. On 2 September, Napoleon surrendered; the Second Empire was over. Among the proclaimers of a new French Republic in Paris was the young radical lawyer and politician Léon Gambetta. Far from laying down their arms, the Prussians meanwhile marched deeper into France. When Paris came under siege, Gambetta flew to Tours in a balloon, believing the town would be safe from the Prussian advance. The Rosses – quite rightly, as it turned out – did not have such faith, and had long since packed their bags and left.

As the infant Robbie was still only one year old, it is doubtful that he could have had much awareness of the dramatic events going on around him, though maybe over the coming months in Canada he would have been able to sense that papa was an important person. However, the strain of an active public life on John Ross was all too much, especially as he discovered on his return to Canada that a business associate had been misappropriating clients' funds in order to make disastrous speculative investments. He had thereby run up great debts which John Ross felt obliged to try to cover. In January 1871 he died, leaving Eliza not only as a young widow with five small children, but also with a moral burden to pay off the debts. Fortunately, her father's estate had left her a comparatively wealthy woman in her own right, so she was able to clear outstanding obligations, although this took considerable organization. She had no wish to stay in Canada, however. Without parents or husband, there was nothing to keep her there. Yet there was no question of returning to France for the time being, much as she loved that country, given ongoing political turmoil there. England therefore seemed the obvious choice, not least as it could offer good educational opportunities for the children. Accordingly, in April 1871, she and her brood set sail for England and headed for London, where the fame of her relations would guarantee her a warm welcome in Liberal circles.

As the last child of the union of John and Eliza Ross, Bobby would perhaps be expected to have a special place in his mother's affection. As he had in addition been given her beloved father's name, that place was guaranteed. A strong, imposing and extremely practical woman, she was used to dealing with men who had emotional or physical weaknesses, and who looked to her to be a pillar of support. When it soon became clear that little Bobby was a rather small and frail child, her protectiveness became all the more pronounced. This infuriated his sisters, Mary and Lizzie, who began to see him as a mummy's boy. Interestingly, though, his two brothers, Jack and Aleck – ten and nine years older than him respectively – both displayed a rather paternal attitude towards him. Presumably their mother had told them to keep an eye on him, but both seem to have done so willingly. In Jack's case, this took on the nature of a serious commission, whereas Aleck – a far more laid-back character – regarded his little brother with a high degree of amusement as well as affection.

Indeed, in North American parlance, Bobby was a very cute kid. 'Puck-like' was the term most often applied to him, even into his early twenties. It wasn't just his slight frame and funny little nose that gave that impression; he was also cheeky, without being rude. At times, his sister Lizzie found him positively nauseating, especially when he was dressed up in a little kilt in homage to the Rosses' seventeenth-century Scottish ancestry. In later life, Robbie Ross looked back on this fancy-dress garb with horror, recalling that it made him look a sissy, though it did catch the eye of a very distinguished neighbour, when Eliza Ross and her children were living in one of a series of rented houses in Kensington and Chelsea, namely, the Scottish historian and essayist Thomas Carlyle. In an article in *The Bystander* in 1910, Robbie wrote:

> The Ross tartan is particularly hideous, and wounded my nascent Aesthetic sense. We were not even entitled to wear it, having no connection with the noble family that bears our name . . . However, [the kilt] must have attracted the attention of the author of *Sartor Resartus*. He patted my head on several occasions, and addressed me in language generally incomprehensible to my little Cockney ears. One day he inquired my name. I replied that it was *Bobby*. He animadverted thereon, in words I do not profess to remember, and urged that it should be *Robbie* – a reminiscence, no doubt, of Burns.[3]

In fact, Robbie was still frequently called 'Bobby' by his family and friends, well into his late teens. Like many of his printed and spoken recollections, the above extract should be treated with a healthy degree of scepticism. Robbie Ross understood instinctively how truth could sometimes be enhanced with a little embellishment. By no stretch of the imagination could he justifiably be called a cockney, even though he chose London as his main residence for much of his life. Indeed, as he spent so much time with his mother during his formative years, he always spoke with a pronounced Canadian accent. As she was especially keen that he treasure the legacy of his father and grandfather, this would not have displeased Eliza.

In keeping with the practices of the time, Robbie spent much of his earlier years at home in the nursery in London with Lizzie and a nanny. The older boys had been sent to Cheltenham College – from which they both progressed to Cambridge University – while Mary went to finishing school. Suitably 'finished' in less than two years, she then married, aged nineteen, a fellow Canadian, Major Charles Jones, with whom she settled happily in the north of England. Meanwhile, as Eliza had plans for her own life, which included travel on the Continent, as well as finding a place in London society she soon despatched Robbie to a prep school within easy striking distance of London: Sandroyd, at Cobham in Surrey. A well-equipped school, set in forty acres of grounds in pine and heather country near Fairmile Common, Sandroyd was designed to prepare young boys for future study at major public schools such as Eton, Harrow and Winchester or, in some cases, the Royal Navy. Quite small and intimate, it gave boys a good grounding in both sports and academic subjects. Robbie appears to have participated quite cheerfully in both, although his small size and rather weak constitution did not really equip him for the sportsfield, where he was once felled when one of his kidneys was struck by a cricket ball. He was more adept at academic lessons, though not a swot. He rarely mentioned his schooldays in later life; or if he did, his comments were not recorded. It is highly likely, though, that with his looks he would have attracted quite a lot of amorous attention from older boys, or indeed, some of the masters. While any such experience, physically consummated or not, need not necessarily affect the sexual development of an individual, something certainly happened somewhere, either at school or on his travels abroad, to make him not just enthusiastically but contentedly homosexual by his late teens.

At the age of thirteen, he won a classical scholarship to Clifton College near Bristol, having shown a particular aptitude for Greek and Roman literature and art. It was a well-informed choice of secondary school by Eliza Ross. Founded only in 1862, its progressive tenor had been set by its first headmaster, the Reverend John Percival, an anti-Tory radical who outraged his counterparts in more conservative establishments by arguing that teachers' relations with pupils should be 'not so much professional, but as that of friends'. Robbie never got to experience this West Country version of ancient Greek mentorship, however, as Eliza changed her mind and decided that he really was not robust enough to cope with secondary school at all. One can imagine how his sister Lizzie must have gritted her teeth.

For the next four years, therefore, Robbie's education was in the hands of his mother and a series of tutors, sometimes individually, sometimes with a small group of selected friends. This involved repeated and extended continental tours, not just to France and Italy, but Germany, Austria and Switzerland as well, sometimes with a tutor, sometimes with his mother. Robbie was a good companion for Eliza; unlike many teenage boys, Robbie was genuinely interested in the historic sites, churches and galleries that they visited. He was also spiritually seduced by Catholic ritual and imagery, and by the time he and his mother returned to London after a particularly long continental sojourn, sometime in early 1886, he had a knowledge and understanding of art rare amongst people twice his age, as well as a leaning towards Rome that would have appalled his Ulster forebears.

His brother Aleck had by now graduated from Caius College, Cambridge, and had launched himself as a modest gentleman of letters on the London scene. He was delighted by Robbie's newly-acquired sophistication, and began to introduce him to some of his literary friends. Aleck was working as Secretary to the Incorporated Society of Authors, which put him in daily contact with writers of distinction. It also enabled him easily to gain membership of the Savile Club, which was probably the most literary of London's gentlemen's clubs. Several Savilians, including Rudyard Kipling, Justin M'Carthy and Walter Besant, were on the Society of Authors' management committee.

Founded in 1868 as the 'New Club' by the Honourable Aubrey Herbert (who was elected the Liberal/Radical MP for Berkshire that same year), together with his brother the Earl of Carnarvon and various friends and relations, the Savile acquired the name it retains to this day by moving into premises in Savile Row in 1871. Conviviality was its watchword from the beginning. But another of the aims of its founders was to provide a suitable meeting place for congenial young men of promise but of slender means. In fact, as the Candidates' Book of the Club shows, it immediately attracted a rather larger number of well-established middle-aged gentlemen, keen to encounter such congenial young men, though not necessarily with any scabrous intent. For example, the intake of 1871 included the brilliant conversationalist, the Revd Dr John Pentland Mahaffy, Professor of Ancient History at Trinity College Dublin, amongst whose freshmen students that very autumn was a certain Oscar Wilde. Although the Savile quickly acquired a reputation in some of the more staid corners of London's clubland as a queer sort of place that required its members either to be atheists or to have written a book, its popularity grew to such an extent that the premises in Savile Row became too small. Accordingly, in 1881, a lease was negotiated, not without difficulty, with the Liberal Under-Secretary for the Home Department, Lord Rosebery, for a splendid, stuccoed eighteenth-century house that he owned at 107 Piccadilly. This has long since been demolished and the site subsumed into the Park Lane Hotel.

On the ground floor was an elongated but elegant dining room, with two communal tables that were almost invariably full, as members savoured their half-crown table d'hôte lunch. Afterwards, many would retire to the rather cramped billiard room at the back, not just to play or to watch a game, but to carry on impassioned conversations. The distinguished men of letters who were members of the Savile during its forty-five-year occupancy of 107 Piccadilly were legion, and many spent countless hours there engaged in banter or more serious debate, or reading in the Book Room on the second floor, which offered a fine prospect over Green Park to Buckingham Palace, as well as a bird's eye view of Piccadilly itself. In 1887, Thomas Hardy was among a group who watched Queen Victoria's Golden Jubilee procession from the club's windows. Perhaps Aleck Ross was present on the same occasion, as he was successfully elected to membership in January of that year. Once a member of the Savile, of course, he was then entitled to invite Robbie as a guest, which he willingly did.

Fearing that Robbie had little chance of making much of his life in London without a university education, preferably at Cambridge, his family persuaded him to attend a well-known crammer's in Covent Garden – W. B. Scoone's – on his return from his travels. The idea was that in just two years, he could acquire sufficient qualifications and skills to be accepted for a university course. For the first few months, he lived at home with his mother. But she began to get itchy feet and was anxious to return to warmer climes. Unwilling to let her young son live alone, yet not wanting to take him away from the crammer's, she decided that it would be best if he lodged as a paying guest with a family, who would ensure that he ate well and kept out of trouble. Thus it was, that for several months in 1887, Robbie went to stay at 16 Tite Street, Chelsea, with Mr and Mrs Oscar Wilde. Little did Eliza Ross or Constance Wilde suspect, when they finalized this arrangement, that some time the previous year, the thirty-two-year-old Oscar and the seventeen-year-old Robbie had become lovers.

There has been endless speculation about how Robbie Ross and Oscar Wilde first met. The contention made by one of Wilde's earliest biographers, the magazine editor, entrepreneur and notorious rake, Frank Harris, that it was in a public lavatory almost certainly hails from the wilder shores of that writer's fabulous imagination. It is far more likely that the original encounter was perfectly innocent, even if the outcome was not. Certainly, the Wildes and various members of the Ross family had several friends in common in London, who might have effected an introduction. And Aleck Ross would have known of Oscar Wilde, even if he had not met him. What seems far more likely, however, is that Eliza Ross first met either Oscar's mother, Lady Wilde, at one of that flamboyant lady's salons, or else knew Constance Wilde through Women's Liberal Federation events. Constance, unlike Oscar, was a committed Liberal and played an active part at bazaars and other social functions organized by the Chelsea Women's Liberal Association, some of which Eliza Ross would have been likely to have patronized. Whatever the precise circumstances of the contact being forged, it would appear that young Robbie seduced Oscar some time in 1886, and that this was Oscar's first experience of a homosexual act. Oscar told his friend, the journalist and wit Reggie Turner, that this was the case. Robbie himself later confirmed it to one of Wilde's earliest biographers, Arthur Ransome.

In an irony that would not have been lost on Robbie, a major contributing factor to his seduction of Oscar Wilde was Oscar's as yet unborn second son, Vyvyan. There is no doubt that Oscar was sexually attracted to Constance at the time of their marriage in 1884, as well as being deeply in love with her. She was indeed a very beautiful woman: slim, elegant and refined. Moreover, although Oscar had expressed an appreciation of handsome youths while he was at Oxford University, this was considered perfectly normal in the Hellenic hot-house environment of that establishment, and did not necessarily have overtly sexual connotations. Similarly, his pose as a languid aesthete, notably on his year-long tour of the United States and Canada in 1882, was not intended (or indeed seen by most people) as a manifestation of sexual inversion.

Oscar's passion for his wife seems to have survived her first pregnancy, and the birth of their son Cyril in June 1885. But when, in early 1886, Constance became pregnant again with Vyvyan, Oscar observed her increasingly bloated body with little short of revulsion. His idolization of her as the physical manifestation of feminine grace was over. Instead, how much more aesthetically pleasing were the narrow-waisted working-class boys he saw in the streets; how much more appealing the puckish, cheeky Robbie Ross.

The physical attractions of Oscar Wilde himself were less obvious. The socialite Lady Colin Campbell once rather bitchily described him as 'a great white caterpillar'. Even at school in Ireland he had been ungainly, and as he matured he took on a quite alarming resemblance to his mother. But he more than overcame his physical deficiencies by his brilliant conversation and quick wit – even if some of the supposedly spontaneous gems had in fact been laboriously polished. He loved to entertain mature society ladies and comely youths with his verbal flights of fancy, pithy epigrams and disquieting paradoxes. Robbie Ross – who seems to have sought out father figures for much of his early life – was by no means the only young man charmed. But he was the first to externalize his fascination with Oscar Wilde by making a pass.

Professionally, Oscar was going through rather a low period. Having confounded some of his critics at Oxford by graduating brilliantly, as well as carrying off the much-coveted Newdigate Prize for poetry, he at first found it difficult to find a medium for the expression of his genius, other than in conversation and as a 'personality'. His volume of *Poems*, published in 1881, was largely uninspiring and highly derivative. The satirical publication *Punch* summed up the disappointment felt by those who had expected better: 'Aesthete of Aesthetes! What's in a name? The poet is WILDE. But his poetry's tame.' To add insult to injury, the Oxford Union rejected a presentation copy for its library on grounds of plagiarism.

Even Wilde's first ventures into drama were damp squibs. His first play *Vera* did finally get performed, in New York in 1883, but the reception was cool and it closed after a week. His second work, *The Duchess of Padua*, fared even less well. He was able to obtain journalistic commissions from the London evening newspaper *The Pall Mall Gazette* and others, but in the year preceding his meeting with Robbie Ross, he was obliged to sing for his supper by giving lectures on fashion, interior design and other such topics in provincial towns and cities around Britain. In April 1887, he acknowledged the need for greater financial security by agreeing to edit the magazine *Lady's World* (which he had renamed *Woman's World*), but he was not really cut out for a job of that nature, despite an initial burst of enthusiasm and procuring contributions from his mother, his wife and several notable friends. The encouragement and emotional support he received from Constance, as well as the real joy he evinced in being with the infant Cyril, must have been much-needed consolations at a time when he knew he was not fulfilling his great promise.

It was indeed a strange ménage that existed in what the press had dubbed 'The House Beautiful' in Tite Street during those months of 1887 when Robbie was the Wildes' lodger. Immaculately conceived in white, the house's interior décor had created quite a stir, even in artistic Chelsea. Against this incongruous backdrop, Constance was nursing baby Vyvyan, while Cyril was a toddler in the upstairs nursery. Oscar, not for the first or last time in his life desperately short of money, would sit for hours in his study, trying to dream up other means of gainful employment. For example, he unsuccessfully lobbied Dr Mahaffy to try to get him an appointment as an Inspector of Schools. Although Constance had a small income of her own, Oscar did not have the means to maintain their lifestyle, let alone live up to his aspirations. His mother was unable to give significant help; indeed, she had started discreetly selling off her library, including many signed volumes by Irish authors she had entertained in Dublin, just to keep up a modicum of appearances on London's social scene. So even Eliza Ross's modest financial contribution, to cover Robbie's board and lodging, would have been very welcome.

Meanwhile, Robbie went back and forth each day to the crammer's in Covent Garden. One wonders what was going through each of the main protagonists' minds as they sat down to dinner together in the evening, on those occasions when Oscar was not out on the town. It should not be assumed, however, that Oscar and Robbie conducted a passionate, clandestine affair on the premises. On the contrary, it is unlikely that they did, and not only for reasons of propriety. Despite the initial seduction, and the huge bond of affection between them, neither was physically each other's 'type'. Robbie was bedazzled by Oscar's wit and brilliance, and rightly predicted huge future success. But he was far more interested sexually in youths of his own age than in the rather portly, flabby, albeit fascinating Oscar Wilde. Moreover, once Robbie had opened the floodgates of Oscar's homoerotic imagination, Oscar was consciously or unconsciously on the look-out for somebody far more exciting, challenging and even dangerous than nice, sweet, safe Robbie. Yet Robbie's relationship with Oscar Wilde, in all the many transformations to come, was to be the most significant of his life, leading literally to the grave.

TWO

Reckless Youth

THE TIMING OF Oscar Wilde's conversion to practising homosexuality was singularly unfortunate, as it was only in 1885 that 'acts of gross indecency' between males – including consenting adults in private – became a crime in England. The architect of the measure that was to cause so much misery over nearly eight decades, until the decriminalization of male homosexuality under the Labour Home Secretary Roy Jenkins in 1967, was a campaigning journalist and Liberal-Radical politician, Henry Du Pré Labouchere, popularly known as 'Labby'. A former diplomat who had been educated at Eton and Trinity College, Cambridge, Labouchere had won fame as a journalist during the Franco-Prussian War. In 1876, he had become the founder-editor and owner of a weekly magazine called *Truth*, which aimed to expose corruption and hypocrisy in Britain.

Nowhere in late Victorian society was hypocrisy more evident than in its attitudes to sexual morality. In stark contrast to the libertarianism and bawdiness of Regency England, the country had by the mid-1880s been swept by a stifling and unforgiving puritanism. Muscular Christianity went hand in hand with a condemnatory approach to all sexual activity outside marriage, and a considerable amount of distaste or guilt regarding sexual desire in general. Yet in London, tens of thousands of women and girls survived through prostitution, many of them working as highly visible streetwalkers. Young girls were particularly sought after by clients, often in the misplaced belief that they would be less likely to be infected with venereal disease. Such juvenile prostitution and the related issue of white slavery became a particular concern of the Liberal journalist and reformer W. T. (William Thomas) Stead, editor of *The Pall Mall Gazette*, who highlighted the practice of buying child prostitutes as virtual slaves by purchasing one himself and then writing about it – an act of principled bravado which landed him with a three-month prison sentence.

As a direct result of the Stead exposé, the Government drafted a measure designed to give greater protection to women and girls, as well as to suppress brothels. At its core was a raising of the female age of consent from thirteen to sixteen. Originally introduced in the House of Lords, the Criminal Law Amendment Bill, as it was called, at first made no mention of homosexual acts, but during the bill's committee stage in the House of Commons, Henry Labouchere introduced an amendment to insert a new clause, viz.:

> Any male person who, in public or private, commits, or is a party to the commission of, or procures or attempts to procure the commission by any male person of, any act of gross indecency with another male person, shall be guilty of a misdemeanour, and being convicted thereof, shall be liable, at the discretion of the court, to be imprisoned for any term not exceeding one year with or without hard labour.[1]

The Attorney-General, Sir Henry James, readily accepted the Labouchere amendment on behalf of the Government, with one alteration, namely the raising of the maximum penalty from one year's imprisonment to two. The matter was uncontroversial, though a few dissident voices, such as the writer John Addington Symonds, pointed out that the vague wording about 'gross indecency' and the inclusion of acts in private made it a far more sweeping measure than Labby perhaps intended. Undoubtedly conceived largely to protect boys and young men from indecent assault, it was soon identified, both by more enlightened members of the legal profession and by sections of the criminal fraternity, as a blackmailer's charter. Any and every homosexual was at risk once the Act took effect on 1 January 1886, just months before Robbie Ross and Oscar Wilde started their relationship. By making practising homosexuals criminals, the Act helped drive many of them underground, or indeed abroad. Others became adept at leading double lives, often marrying, while precariously satiating their homosexual appetites with working-class rent-boys.

It has to be said that the Labouchere amendment was passed at a time when conventional morality in Britain viewed homosexual acts as unspeakably vile. Yet here again there was a large element of hypocrisy. Many of the men in Parliament who voted on the measure, being products of the public school system, would have experienced intense same-sex relationships, though not necessarily overtly carnal ones. 'Spooning', as passionate friendships between boys, and sometimes between pupils and members of staff, was known, was rampant in several of the country's most elevated educational establishments, though, as with all aspects of public school life, it had its own strict code of conduct, one element of which was that boys from one House in a school should not become intimately involved with boys in another. 'Crushes' were quite openly discussed between friends, and at Eton, for example, some boys would exchange perfumed Valentine cards.

In many cases, intense schoolboy relationships were legitimized, even idealized, as 'Greek love', which was meant to be platonic – in other words not involving sex, though hand-holding, a comforting embrace and the odd stolen kiss were generally deemed acceptable. Such love would, however, be corrupted if a sexual act took place – or so many boys convinced themselves. Moreover, particularly from the mid-1880s onwards, schoolmasters were in general determined to prevent it happening. Just as bourgeois Victorian parents would monitor their sons' bedsheets for any trace of self-abuse, so schoolmasters would be on the lookout for evidence of unhealthy relationships. A prime motivation for the cult of strenuous physical exercise and cold baths, which took hold of several schools in this period, was to curb the juvenile libido and to send boys to bed so physically exhausted that they would fall asleep straight away, their purity undefiled.

As youths from public schools made up the vast bulk of the undergraduate intake of the universities of Oxford and Cambridge, their imaginations partly shaped by the study of the civilizations of Ancient Greece and Rome, these two institutions also fostered passionate friendships, as well as being the stage for confrontations between sports-oriented 'hearties' and intellectual aesthetes. Aesthetes abhorred the vulgarity of the philistine hearties, who in turn considered the aesthetes unmanly. Assaults on aesthetes' rooms in college by groups of hearties were quite common, as Oscar Wilde had experienced at Oxford. He had proved more than able physically to hold his own in the circumstances, which Robbie Ross would never be able to do so in a similar situation. Nonetheless, Oscar was delighted when Robbie was accepted to go up to King's College, Cambridge, in the autumn of 1888, as he was sure university life would open up significant new horizons for his young friend.

My dear Bobbie, I congratulate you. University life will suit you Admirably, though I shall miss you in town . . . Are you in

College or lodgings? I hope in College; it is much nicer. Do you know Oscar Browning? You will find in him everything that is kind and pleasant.

I have been speaking at Stratford about Shakespeare, but in spite of that enjoyed my visit immensely. My reception was semi-royal, And the volunteers played God Save the Queen in my honour. Ever yours[2]

Robbie had chosen King's College as he wished to study history, which was a comparatively recent academic discipline at Cambridge. King's College had become an acknowledged centre of excellence for the subject, thanks largely to the Vice-Provost Augustus Austen Leigh and the history don G. W. Prothero, though both were overshadowed as personalities in the college by the larger-than-life Oscar Browning mentioned in Oscar Wilde's letter. Browning's academic credentials were not espe-cially impressive; in fact, he was never awarded a doctorate, as his fellow academics had little respect for his scholarship. He was a prolific author of books, as well as of historical and travel articles, many of which were riddled with factual errors, but became popular with the wider reading public because of their subjectivity and verve. By 1888, 'the O. B.', as Browning was usually referred to, was one of Cambridge's most famous charac-ters. Squat, fat, balding and possessing a nose of singular ugliness, he reminded many people of Mr Punch. He was often to be seen riding through the streets of the town on a large tricycle, emphasizing his absurdity. He was noisy and gregarious, and a snob of Olympian proportions, collecting royal friends and acquaintances rather as more humble souls might collect cigarette cards. Name-dropping and social pretension became an art form in the O. B.'s hands, at times lightened by an element of self-parody. This was nicely illustrated by his often quoted remark that the German Emperor was about the pleasantest emperor he had ever met. University vacations, which he almost invariably spent abroad, were an opportunity for Browning to maintain his huge network of contacts, as well as to ensnare new, prestigious recruits for his address book.

What's more, he had a penchant for barrow-boys, soldiers, sailors, and waifs and strays, whom he would pick up in the streets of Cambridge or on his travels. The proud possessor of one of the first private bathrooms in the university, he would lure some of his new young friends in for a scrubbing. Undoubtedly sex did play a part in some of these encounters, but often Oscar Browning's relationships with boys were based on a genuine desire to educate them and give them a helping hand in life. The many thousands of letters he received from former protégés, as well as from their grateful parents – all neatly filed and boxed and kept for posterity – bear witness to the philanthropic side to his activities. Often he assisted lads with money, or found them work, or gave them other useful introductions. Similarly, he took a huge personal interest in his students, many of whom adored him, although Browning's colleagues in the senior common room at King's noted sourly how it was usually the most comely youths who received most of the O. B.'s attention.

Paradoxically, it was the ambiguous nature of Browning's dealings with his academic charges that had resulted in his teaching at King's in the first place. After graduating from that same college, he had in 1860 gone to teach at his old school, Eton. He was a schoolmaster of brilliance, inspiring hundreds of boys with his enthusiasm and avuncular concern, though his tendency to have 'pets' – who might suddenly be dropped when they fell out of favour or began to bore him – caused considerable consternation. He was warned strongly about the passionate interest he took in one particular boy at Eton, the future Viceroy of India, George Curzon, who was not even in his

House, yet got invited by the O. B. to travel with him on the Continent. When, in 1875, Browning was dismissed from Eton, on the pretext of exceeding the quota of pupils he was allowed to tutor, it was widely assumed that the real reason was impropriety. Certainly, he took a prurient interest in his pupils' physical development, zealously warning them about the dangers of masturbation, as well as explaining the facts of life to them.

Under the peculiar regulations in force at King's College, Cambridge at the time, Browning was able to claim an automatic fellowship there, after which he established a niche for himself tutoring in history. The links between Eton and King's were strong; indeed, until the 1850s, all King's students came from Eton. There were only seventy of them at one time, living a charmed existence in the magnificent surroundings of what was and remains one of the most beautiful colleges in Cambridge, with its famous chapel and choir and its stately residential buildings. By the time Robbie Ross went there (incidentally, living in lodgings in Mill Lane, not in college rooms), many of the rules had been changed, to widen the intake. Heated debates were taking place – with Oscar Browning as one of the main protagonists – regarding further reforms. Even so, a significant number of Robbie's fellow students were from Eton, and almost all were imbued with the public school ethos.

At Oscar Wilde's suggestion, Oscar Browning took Robbie under his wing. The two hit it off immediately, to Wilde's delight.

> . . . I knew you would like Bobbie Ross. He is charming, and as clever as can be, with excellent taste and sound knowledge. I am so glad he is with you. I know no one who has a more intellectual influence than yourself: to be ranked amongst your friends is, for anyone, a liberal education.[3]

Some of Robbie's fellow undergraduates were not so enthusiastic about the young Canadian, however. It was not just that he had not been to a top public school, or indeed to any secondary school at all. His worldliness grated. He had seen so much more of life than his fellows, and he put their backs up with his rapturous accounts of continental travels, the superiority of Roman Catholic ritual over Protestant liturgy, and his antecedents' contribution to Canada's development as a nation. His pose as a young man-about-town, who already had a tenuous foothold on the London literary and political scenes, was hardly likely to endear him to those whose horizons had so far been little wider than the playing fields of Eton and weekend parties at houses in the country. Though Robbie did not go in for the sort of name-dropping Oscar Browning indulged in, nonetheless he could not refrain from letting it be known that various eminent men in London were taking a personal interest in his future advancement.

Indeed, a few weeks prior to Robbie's arrival in Cambridge, the well-known but cantankerous poet, playwright and critic W. E. (William Ernest) Henley had, perhaps on Aleck Ross's suggestion, proposed Robbie for membership of the Savile Club. His name duly went into the Candidates' book, where the novelist and social reformer Sir Walter Besant and half a dozen others recorded their support. W. E. Henley, who had just published his idiosyncratic collection *A Book of Verses*, was obviously in a mood to make his mark on the Savile's membership, as he suggested to Oscar Wilde that he propose him as well.

Wilde's star was in the ascendant at last, with the publication of *The Happy Prince and Other Tales* in May 1888. The book was well received and Wilde ensured that it was widely noticed; among the complimentary copies he despatched was one to the bibliophile, former and future Prime Minister William Gladstone, who was one of a number of senior Liberal politicians Constance and he occasionally met. At this stage, Wilde and Henley got on famously, and Henley had just introduced Oscar to his great countryman, the poet W. B. (William Butler) Yeats. However, Wilde wondered presciently whether he was perhaps a little too raffish for the Savile.

> My dear Henley, It will give me great pleasure to lunch with you at the Savile on Saturday, though I am afraid that I shall be like a poor lion who has rashly intruded into a den of fierce Daniels. As for proposing me for the Savile, that is of course one of your merry jests . . .
>
> Pray remember me to Mrs Henley, and believe me, ever yours.[4]

In fact, within a matter of weeks, Oscar's name was indeed inscribed in the Club's Candidates' Book, just a few entries below Robbie's, though his proposer was actually the Revd W. J. (William John) Loftie, author of the somewhat cumbersomely titled *A Plea for Art in the House, with special reference to the Economy of Collecting Works of Art and the importance of Taste in Education and Morals* – a detail that Robbie surely savoured. W. E. Henley of course supported Oscar's candidacy, as did Aleck Ross, along with nearly thirty other members, including such luminaries as Henry James, Walter Besant, Edmund Gosse and the bestselling author of *King Solomon's Mines*, Henry Rider Haggard, who spent part of this year yomping across Iceland with Aleck.

Robbie was determined to prove his own literary credentials, and during his first term at Cambridge sought an outlet for his writing. He quickly found it in a new publication called *The Gadfly*, which was edited by W. M. (Walter Murray) Guthrie, a student at Trinity Hall. As its title would suggest, *The Gadfly* was intended to irritate or harass the powers that be, in a spirit of exuberant youthful iconoclasm, but it was unfortunate that the first (and indeed only) issue made Oscar Browning a target for satire, deriding the O. B.'s intellectual capacities and social pretensions. Browning was used to appearing in student publications, but not in this derogatory way, and he was most offended. The authorities rallied to his support and *The Gadfly* was closed down. Given the friendly patronage Robbie was receiving from his tutor, it seems unlikely that he was the author of the critical article, but nevertheless came under suspicion and was certainly tarred with the same brush as the actual offender. It was not an auspicious beginning to his time at King's College.

After a short break with his sister Mary, her husband and seven children at their substantial northern home, Jesmond Hill in Newcastle-upon-Tyne – where he fell off a horse while out riding and injured his hand – Robbie spent Christmas in London, at the house his mother had taken at 85 Onslow Square. The Wildes were also at home in London, and indeed had W. B. Yeats round for Christmas dinner. It was then that Wilde read out to Yeats an essay he had just completed, entitled 'The Decay of Lying'. Written in the form of a dialogue, the essay champions Art's preference for lies and masks over sincerity and accuracy. At its heart is the paradox that Life imitates Art. And within it are several of Wilde's most memorable aphorisms (some later recycled in his comedies), including the statement that 'if one tells the truth, one is sure, sooner or later, to be found out!' Viewed from the standpoint of conventional morality, 'The Decay of Lying' was highly subversive, and it marked a key stage in the development of Wilde's distinctive philosophy and aesthetics. Yeats was suitably impressed, though he might have been surprised to learn that much of the inspiration for the essay had come from conversations Oscar had been having with the young Robbie Ross almost from the first day they met.

In fact, Robbie was already, at the age of nineteen, much more than a disciple and sometime lover for Oscar. The two could talk frankly, despite the difference in their ages, and bounce ideas off each other. Oscar could evolve his theories about Life and Art out loud with Robbie, who was ready not just to listen, but to challenge and criticize. Thus Oscar was able to share with Robbie the thrill he had gained from studying the life and work of the early nineteenth-century artist, forger and convicted murderer Thomas Wainewright, who was the subject of another essay by Wilde, written in 1888, 'Pen, Pencil and Poison'. This was published by Frank Harris in the *Fortnightly Review* in January 1889. Wilde was mesmerized by the conjunction of Art and criminality in Wainewright's persona, declaring in his essay that 'there is no essential incongruity between crime and culture'. One can imagine the relish with which Oscar shared with Robbie Wainewright's remark, when he was reproached about a murder he had committed: 'Yes; it was dreadful thing to do, but she had very thick ankles.'

It must have been something of an anti-climax for Robbie to return to Cambridge after the Christmas vacation, especially as the unfavourable echoes of *The Gadfly* article about the O. B. were still reverberating. He decided to close that unfortunate chapter by using the occasion of a speech he made in the Cambridge Union Society (of which Oscar Browning had been Treasurer for over twenty years) to apologize for his part in the publication. In the main body of his speech, however, Robbie guaranteed further ructions by presuming to recommend to the Fellows of King's, including Browning, who they should support to fill the vacancy of Vice-Provost of the College to replace Augustus Austen Leigh, who had been made Provost when his nonagenarian predecessor Richard Okes had died the previous November.

Robbie followed up his Union speech with a long and at times intemperate article in a new publication started up by *The Gadfly*'s editor, Walter Guthrie, named *Granta*. The magazine proved a useful platform for Robbie's youthful journalism, much of which was imbued with the sort of reformist zeal his ancestors would have appreciated. In one article, for example, he applauded ongoing reforms at King's, including the partial severance of its connection with Eton:

> For, however much the lovers of Eton, and those whose conservative prejudices are something more than mere sentiment, may regret the admission of non-Etonians into the place, we believe it was the salvation of the college, for in these advanced days an exclusively Etonian college is impossible for Cambridge. The change naturally brought evil with good, and among those who battered at the doors for admission under the new regulations, there came some of the most undesirable Undergraduates that could well be imagined. Not only long-haired, but the short-haired and the no-haired came – the purely social and the socially pure.[5]

Such feeble wit was hardly likely to endear Robbie, either to the Old Etonians in his college, or to those King's men who hailed from other schools. He seems to have been blissfully unaware of the growing antagonism against him, however, and even took part in the Bump Races that term, as one of the rowers in King's second boat. If this was a strategy to ingratiate himself with his fellow students, it failed.

As a result of the *Granta* articles, a group of half a dozen undergraduates plotted to teach the upstart Ross a lesson. The group included E. F. ('Fred') Benson, son of the Archbishop of Canterbury (and future author of the Mapp and Lucia novels), a young man called Arthur Bather, and John Tilley, whose elder brother Arthur was a junior tutor at the college. On the evening of Friday, 8 March as Robbie emerged from dining in Hall, he was set upon by the six conspirators and thrown into the ornamental fountain in the college's front quad. It was a chilly night and Robbie was enraged by his icy dousing. Provost Austen Leigh was not amused either, when he learnt about it, especially when it became known that the young tutor Arthur Tilley had known of the plan to duck Robbie and maybe had even encouraged it. The Provost decided a full investigation was warranted.

Anxious to defuse the situation – and avoid the possibility of their being sent down – Fred Benson and Arthur Bather asked for a meeting with the Provost that Sunday evening, to explain their conduct. Austen Leigh requested Oscar Browning to sit in on the meeting, not just because the attack on him in *The Gadfly* had been one of the contributing factors leading up to the assault, but because several people, including fellow historian George Prothero, suspected that the O.B. had also had prior knowledge of the students' intent. Browning professed outrage at this suggestion and when an extraordinary meeting of the King's College Council was convened the following day, he proposed a motion condemning the six plotters for a serious breach of discipline and asking for them to be punished accordingly. However, the case was so complex, not least because of the involvement of Arthur Tilley, that no precise conclusion was reached. It was noted that the assailants had indeed broken college discipline, but then so too had Robbie Ross by his ill-considered articles.

Being thus found to be amongst the guilty caused Robbie to seethe with injustice to such a degree that he had a minor nervous breakdown. In one bout of hysteria he wrote to his family threatening suicide, which brought Aleck up to Cambridge post-haste, to take him back to the reassuring comforts of Onslow Square. Distressed by the turn of events, Oscar Browning urged Mrs Ross to keep him regularly informed of Robbie's state of health. This she did, with daily telegrams. She was alarmed by what she called Robbie's attacks, while on the sidelines his sister Lizie simmered with contempt for what she saw as his pathetic over-reaction to undergraduate horseplay.

By 29 March, though, Robbie was returning to a semblance of normality, and Oscar Browning came to London to visit him. It would have been immediately obvious to the O.B. that domestic tensions in Onslow Square were hardly helping the invalid's recuperation, so he suggested Robbie accompany him to stay for the weekend at his mother's home in Windsor. While the O.B. had been a master at Eton, Mrs Browning had lived in his House, supervising the boarders, and she had stayed on in the town after he had left. She helped her daughter – like herself named Mariana, but usually referred to as 'Dick' – run a small girls' school called The Beehive, in Osborne Road. The Browning household was busy the particular weekend that Robbie visited, as Biscoe Wortham, a clergyman married to Oscar Browning's other sister, Mina, was visiting from Bruges, where he ran a boys' school. The Revd Wortham had brought with him his young son Philip, who was aged about fourteen at the time. In a written confession extracted from Philip Wortham by his father four years later, the boy recalled:

> When I first knew Mr Ross, at Windsor, at the Beehive in my Grandmother's lifetime he behaved in an indecent manner. I was in his room alone with him early one morning, before breakfast. I was in my nightshirt, he was in his pyjamas: he put me on the bed. He had me between the legs. He placed his **** between my legs.[6]

When confronted with this document by Biscoe Wortham in 1893, Robbie flatly denied that the incident had taken place. But in Mandy Rice-Davies's immortal phrase during the

Profumo case in the 1960s, he would, wouldn't he? If it did happen – and Philip Wortham maintained that this was only the first of three sexual experiences with Robbie, the others allegedly occurring later in London – then it was a singularly irresponsible thing to do. Oscar Browning would certainly not have approved, though a high degree of complicity on sexual matters had developed between the tutor and his currently mentally unstable pupil. Indeed, after Windsor, the two of them repaired to the Isle of Wight, where Browning had an assignation with one of his Cambridge sailor boys, a certain Matthew Oates.

A youth of humble origins, like most of the O.B.'s pick-ups, Oates had recently been apprenticed to the Shaw Savill shipping line. Robbie found him as appealing as Browning did, dubbing him 'the fair sailor' and declaring him very beautiful and very charming. Both Browning and Robbie showered the lad with presents and attention, for which they were doubtless amply rewarded. The fair sailor's mother later wrote to Browning saying that 'words cannot express how much I thank you for your great kindness to Matt. It will never be in my power to reward you on earth but God I know will fully do it, if not here in the next world.' Sadly, Matthew Oates's character failed to live up to his beauty, as he jumped ship twice over the coming months, later doing a runner without paying the rent when Browning arranged a room for him in London. As Robbie learnt at Browning's side, one had to become inured to such behaviour when one took up feckless boys.

Back in London, the Ross family were becoming increasingly concerned that Robbie was going completely off the rails. Presumably with Aleck's approval, on 3 April 1889 someone scored two thick, black ink lines through Robbie's entry in the Savile Club's Candidates' book and wrote 'Withdrawn at request of proposer'. Aleck then took Robbie off to Naples, in the hope that some sun and a change of air would do him good, but the trip was not a success, as Aleck – as accident-prone as his brother – injured himself on the outward journey by ship, and Robbie's moods fluctuated alarmingly. His humiliation at King's still distressed him greatly, and he had got Aleck to seek a legal opinion about whether criminal charges could be brought against his attackers – a clear indication how the ducking incident had indeed been blown out of all proportion in his mind.

Nonetheless, when the new university term began at the end of April, Robbie returned to King's, as much to continue his fight for justice as to pursue his studies, which seem to have been sorely neglected. A number of his fellow undergraduates, disturbed by the impact the affair had had on him, petitioned the college authorities and senior dons, including Oscar Browning, begging them to take action on his behalf. In the middle of May, another don, John Nixon, duly filed a formal report to the University's Congregation, despite his distaste at the ructions the case was causing in the King's senior common room. In the report, Nixon opined that the disgust many people felt at the sort of highly personalized journalism Robbie had been publishing in Cambridge should not blind them to the offensiveness and harm of retaliation through physical violence. 'Lynch law cannot be tolerated in civilized society,' he declared, 'and any encouragement of it by a responsible officer seems to be inexcusable.' The 'responsible officer' of course, was the young don Arthur Tilley, who was finally prevailed upon to bring the matter to a reasonably acceptable close by standing up in Hall one dinner-time to offer Robbie a public apology. This was a fearful humiliation for Tilley, who reportedly never dined in Hall again. Yet it did not satisfy Robbie's thirst for revenge. Over the following weeks, nevertheless, he developed a friendship with none other than one of his former tormentors, E. F. Benson, thereby ensuring, in a move of which Oscar Browning would have heartily approved, that he could widen his London social base with an entrée to Lambeth Palace.

All the stress of the preceding couple of months had taken its toll on Robbie's constitution, however, and he now succumbed to measles. Once again he had to be taken home to his mother's house in South Kensington for some tender, loving care. Lying in bed, as spring turned to summer, he had plenty of time to ruminate about his first year at Cambridge. It was hard not to see the experience as almost entirely negative. He had evinced little interest in his studies, and his sorties into journalism had only brought opprobrium and worse upon him. The thought of going back to King's in the autumn held no attraction whatsoever; even the friendships he had made there could easily be maintained in London. Besides, London was where everything was happening, and where he was impatient to make his mark. Accordingly, he decided to abandon Cambridge, and none of the many contrary arguments Oscar Browning produced could dissuade him.

The other Oscar in Robbie's life at least had encouraging news that lifted Robbie's spirits. In the course of some of their long conversations over the past three years, they had analysed the theory that Shakespeare was homosexual, and that the object of his greatest, anonymous passion in the sonnets was a boy. It was not an especially original idea; neither was it one that was openly discussed in respectable literary circles. But it greatly appealed to Oscar Wilde, who was by now an increasingly zealous convert to homosexual passion and the supposedly noble ideal of boy-love. The product of Wilde's deliberations on the subject was a long story entitled 'The Portrait of Mr W. H.', the W. H. being a boy actor, Willie Hughes. In the story, Wilde imagines the married Shakespeare being captivated by Willie Hughes, as he had himself been by Robbie. He had originally thought of writing the piece as an essay, but Frank Harris had strongly advised him against it, on the grounds that he would set himself up as an

Aunt Sally, given the prevailing homophobia. In fact, choosing a fictional form gave Wilde far more scope for subtlety and ambiguity. The borders between reality and invention in 'The Portrait of Mr W. H.' are in a constant state of flux. Yet the almost proselytizing message in favour of Platonic love between males is clear. Oscar became hugely enthusiastic about the story as it progressed and in May 1889 called on his neighbours, the artists Charles Ricketts and Charles Shannon, who lived together in a ménage, to persuade Ricketts – successfully, as it turned out – to produce a portrait of the supposed 'onlie begetter' of Shakespeare's sonnets, Willie Hughes.

Oscar had hoped that Frank Harris might publish the story in the *Fortnightly Review*, but Harris was abroad when he sent in the manuscript, and an assistant who was holding the fort rejected it curtly. Instead, the story appeared in *Blackwood's Magazine* in July. Robbie was one of the first to send Oscar a telegram of congratulations, to which Oscar replied, acknowledging that if Robbie was not quite the story's 'onlie begetter', he was certainly instrumental in its production.

> Your telegram (of course it was *yours*) has just arrived. So many thanks for it: it was really sweet of you to send it, for indeed the story is half yours, and but for you would not have been written. Are you well again? Terror for Cyril* kept me away, but now I may come, may I not?
>
> Write me a letter. Now that Willie Hughes has been revealed to the world, we must have another secret.[7]

One of Wilde's clear intentions as a writer was to be noticed. Though that is true of most writers, the craving for fame as a result of literary output was especially strong in his case. What

---

*Oscar was worried that he could inadvertently transmit Robbie's measles to his adored elder son, whose health was at this time anyway a cause for concern.

he achieved with 'The Portrait of Mr W. H.', however, was not so much fame as a writer as notoriety, which was in many ways just as satisfying for Oscar's vanity, but far more dangerous. W. E. Henley was appalled by the story, declaring that it should not have been published anywhere, let alone in a magazine as prestigious as *Blackwood's*. Henceforth, Henley made sure Oscar would never be a member of the Savile Club, and he missed few opportunities of attacking Wilde's work in print. The predominantly hostile reaction to 'The Portrait of W. H.' should have come as no surprise to Wilde. When he had read it out loud to one of his friends, Herbert Asquith, the Liberal MP for East Fife, Asquith had urged him not to publish it, as it could have an unhealthy influence on young people. Typically, Oscar's response to such criticism was to work on a longer and even more explicit version. As Robbie and Frank Harris later agreed, it was at this moment that the seeds of Wilde's downfall were sown.

For much of the late summer of 1889, Robbie and Oscar saw little of each other, partly because Oscar was busy with a number of projects – travelling to Germany, for example, to discuss the possibility of his play *The Duchess of Padua* being staged. But another reason was that a new passion had entered Oscar's life: a young man by the name of John Gray. The twenty-three-year-old son of a carpenter, John Gray had had to leave school at the age of thirteen to earn a living as a metal-turner. But from an early age, he had had literary ambitions and was determined to improve himself. Through hard study, he managed to pass the civil service examinations at the age of sixteen and went on to work as a government clerk, first in the Post Office, then in the Foreign Office. He was a good friend of the two Charleses, Ricketts and Shannon, who published a couple of pieces by him in the first issue of a magazine they produced called *The Dial*. Oscar was enthusiastic about John Gray's work, particularly after he had met him and seen how handsome the young man was. He started to court him assiduously, informing him that the lead character in a novel he was now working on would be named after him.

Robbie seems to have felt no jealousy towards John Gray. Indeed, he was remarkably generous and understanding when it came to Oscar's other lovers. Of course, he himself was enjoying various encounters with youths, though none at this stage held any claim to his affections, let alone to the sort of love he felt for Oscar. As Oscar's notoriety began to grow, however, the subject of homosexuality was broached in the Ross household. Robbie made no attempt to hide his sexuality from his family; it was something he was perfectly at ease with. Aleck – who remained a lifelong bachelor, but was not gay – was not particularly fussed about the matter, and Mrs Ross was prepared not to be judgemental about her favourite offspring. Robbie's sister Lizzie, on the other hand, was another matter. The long-standing antagonism between the two siblings became even more acute, to the point at which a family council decided that it would be better if Robbie left home. Mrs Ross would pay him an allowance to cover basic living costs. However, there was no question of his staying in London, where he would be prey to myriad temptations, including Oscar Wilde. In the family's view, he needed to be somewhere much more sedate, preferably where there was someone who could keep an eye on him. As W. E. Henley still took a fatherly interest in Robbie, and had recently gone to work in Edinburgh as Literary Editor of the *Scots Observer*, it was to the beautiful but strait-laced Edinburgh that Robbie was sent.

THREE

In Oscar's Shadow

ROBBIE EVINCED NO JOY at the prospect of going to live in the land of his distant ancestors. What is more, the reality was even worse than his fears. He found lodgings in Rutland Square, in Edinburgh's West End, an agreeable walk away from the *Scots Observer*'s offices in Thistle Street, New Town. But any pleasure he might have gained from the fine architecture around him, or the view of the mighty castle as he emerged from Rutland Street into Princes Street on his way to work, paled in comparison with the drudgery of the job he was doing. It was quite usual for youngsters being apprenticed into journalism to be given the humblest of tasks by their bosses; for many, being the tea-boy was but the first rung on a career ladder that would lead forever upwards. But Robbie was even more impatient than most beginners in the trade. He had mixed socially with leading journalists and editors in London, which made it all the more difficult for him to accept the role of anonymous underling in Edinburgh.

The real problem, though, was the personality of W. E. Henley, with whom Robbie was now in daily contact. The fifty-year-old Henley's notoriously bad temper may well have resulted from his being crippled by tuberculosis as a child. As a young teenager, he spent nearly two years in the Edinburgh Infirmary and it was in hospital that he started to write poems, characterized by their esoteric vocabulary and unusual rhymes, which attracted the attention and admiration of his contemporary and fellow invalid, Robert Louis Stevenson. Together, Henley and Stevenson wrote a series of plays in the early 1880s until a spectacular falling-out terminated their collaboration. This was a pattern often repeated in Henley's relationships, in which friends would be turned into enemies, who then became targets for his wrath. Like many men with fierce tempers, however, Henley also had a sentimental side, which in his case was almost entirely shown to his young daughter, about whom he was positively mawkish. He had a range of nicknames for her, one of which was 'The Emperor'.

Deprived of the sort of companionship and conversation he had enjoyed in London, Robbie was lonely and bored. Moreover, with nothing to excite his imagination in Edinburgh, he kept mulling over his débâcle at Cambridge. His vindictiveness against Arthur Tilley had not abated. As Robbie informed Oscar Browning in a letter dated September 1889, if Tilley were ever appointed a Lecturer in Classics, he would publish a fully documented account of the 'Outrage', as he referred to the ducking incident. The declared purpose of this would be to provoke Tilley to sue him for libel.

> ... I shall act in such a way as to make it incumbent on Tilley to bring an action against me. You can tell the [King's College] Council that you know (privately) that if any attempt to bring Tilley back is successful, then I shall make the whole thing public. It is perfectly disgraceful that he should be allowed to remain in Cambridge at all.[1]

It is astonishing that the twenty-year-old Robbie should have been thinking seriously of a libel action, even if he believed he could win one with a plea of justification. This was also to prove a worrying portent of his life ahead, as the litigious side to his nature would result in considerable expense and stress. What was at this stage, with regard to Tilley, perhaps little more than a juvenile threat would in future develop into an obsessive trait.

Christmas provided a respite from exile in the gloomy North, as Robbie was able to go back home to London. But W. E. Henley was determined that he should not consider himself merely on holiday, writing somewhat unctuously:

> My dear Bobby, It's awful good of you to look after our interests. We've bullied our London agent as he deserves about the late supply, and we've writ to him about the Remington books. You might see in respect of the former matter, if there's any improvement; and let us know.
>
> I should like you, if you've time, to go to the Reading Room [in the British Museum], and do a bit of devilling for me and the Tudor Translations. I want to know approximately the length *in words* of the First Part of Shelton's *Don Quixote* and *in stanzas* of Harington's *Orlando Furioso*. You know what I mean: take the rough guess at the words in a page and multiply by the number of pages. Also I should like you to copy me out half a dozen stanzas (octaves) of the *Orlando*: textually. Will you? It will be a good turn that I won't forget. I shall look forward to the sight of the unpublished Wordsworth with satisfaction.[2]

These little commissions can hardly have pleased Robbie, who would far rather have been spending his precious days in London seeing friends, though to his frustration, the most important of those friends, Oscar Wilde, was not often available. Oscar had been unwell for some weeks, and was struggling with the competing demands of finishing his novel, playing the role of devoted father to his two boys over Christmas and finding time to be with his new paramour, John Gray. Oscar's magic had certainly worked on the young man, as Gray was becoming quite besotted with him. Bernard Shaw once aptly described him as the most abject of all Oscar's lovers.

A shock was waiting for Oscar in the New Year. On 2 January 1890 Labouchere's magazine *Truth* published a long, stinging letter from the painter James McNeill Whistler, with whom Oscar had long enjoyed a competitive friendship spiced with sparkling epigrams and bitchy put-downs. The venomous tone of Whistler's letter in *Truth* put things on an entirely different level, as the beginning and end of the letter amply demonstrate:

> Among your ruthless exposures of the shams of today, nothing, I confess, have I enjoyed with keener relish than your late tilt at that arch-impostor and pest of the period – the all-pervading plagiarist!
>
> I learn, by the way, that in America he may, under the 'Law of '84,' as it is called, be criminally prosecuted, incarcerated and made to pick oakum, as he has hitherto picked brains – and pockets!
>
> How was it that, in your list of culprits, you omitted that fattest of offenders – our own Oscar? . . .
>
> . . . I acknowledge that 'Oscar has the courage of opinions of others!'
>
> My recognition of this, his latest proof of open admiration, I send him in the following little note, which I fancy you may think *à propos* to publish, as an example to your readers, in similar circumstance, of noble generosity in sweet reproof, tempered, as it should be, to the lamb in his condition:
>
> Oscar, you have been down the area again, I see! I had forgotten you, and so allowed your hair to grow over the sore

place. And now, while I looked the other way, you have stolen *your own scalp*! And potted it in more of your pudding.

Labby has pointed out that, for the detected plagiarist, there is still one way to self-respect (besides hanging himself, of course), and that is for him boldly to declare, '*Je prends mon bien là où je le trouve.*'

You, Oscar, can go further, and with fresh effrontery, that will bring you the envy of all criminal *confrères*, unblushingly boast, '*Moi, je prends* son *bien là où je le trouve!*'[3]

Whistler's specific charge of plagiarism against Wilde related to a lecture Oscar had given to art students of the Royal Academy nearly seven years previously, and which was supposedly based on many of Whistler's own theories. But it was not the detail of the charge that was of interest, rather the ferocity of assault. Oscar was, of course, obliged to reply: *Truth* duly published his response in the following week's edition.

Sir, I can hardly imagine that the public are in the very smallest degree interested in the shrill shrieks of 'Plagiarism' that process from time to time out of the lips of silly vanity or incompetent mediocrity.

However, as Mr James Whistler has had the impertinence to attack me with both venom and vulgarity in your columns, I hope you will allow me to state that the assertions contained in his letter are as deliberately untrue as they are deliberately offensive.

The definition of a disciple as one who has the courage of the opinions of his master is really too old even for Mr Whistler to be allowed to claim it, and as for borrowing Mr Whistler's ideas about art, the only thoroughly original ideas I have ever heard him express have had references of his own superiority over painters greater than himself. It is a trouble for any gentleman to have to notice the lucubrations of so ill-bred and ignorant a person as Mr Whistler, but your publication of his insolent letter left me no option in the matter.[4]

W. E. Henley found this exchange greatly entertaining, believing that Oscar was getting the come-uppance he so richly deserved. Robbie, now back in Edinburgh, took the opposite point of view, feeling that Oscar had been the subject of Whistler's spite purely out of jealousy. The difference of opinion over Wilde soured relations between the two, at least from Robbie's point of view, making the prospect of a prolonged stay in Edinburgh even more unbearable. Fortunately, his feeble health once more intervened in his favour, as in February he collapsed with acute peritonitis. Whatever it was that caused the inflammation of his abdominal organs, the case was serious enough for him to be transported back to London by ambulance and train once he was fit enough to travel. A room at 85 Onslow Square was converted into a sickroom again, and Eliza Ross once more became his nurse. Oscar Browning, who liked to keep tabs on all his favourite former charges, was duly informed.

Oscar Wilde, meanwhile, was able to capitalize on his growing notoriety by welcoming more attractive young men into his circle of acolytes. His ability to sweep them off their feet was breathtaking. On a visit to Oxford in mid-February, for example, he called on one of his aesthetic mentors, the critic and scholar Walter Pater, and from him heard about a young poet of beauty and brilliance at New College, named Lionel Johnson. Oscar promptly set off for New College, where he discovered that Mr Johnson was still in bed, though it was already noon. He sent in a pathetically worded note, begging to be received and, once admitted, set about charming the young poet with his wit and gentle malice. As Lionel Johnson wrote to his friend Arthur Galton, 'He discourses, with infinite flippancy, of everyone:

lauded the *Dial*: laughed at Pater: and consumed all my cigarettes. I am in love with him.'

The danger with acquiring too many young admirers was that not all of them were as broad-minded as Robbie. Both John Gray and Lionel Johnson would later turn against Wilde, dismayed by his infidelity. Whereas for Robbie, flirtation and seduction were savoured as part of the spice and variety of life – something which Oscar Wilde was now determined to enjoy, with the energy of one who was making up for lost time.

Obviously W. E. Henley had something of a soft spot for people physically more disadvantaged than himself, albeit temporarily through illness, as by the end of the month, he wrote to Robbie engagingly:

> We are glad indeed to have so good an account of you. I hope that Bell* will contrive to get a sight of his young contributor – 'the Youngest gentleman of the Company,' so to speak – and confirm the report upon experience.
>
> I send you one parcel more. One item, *Merin*, is really *indecent*. Also it shows what you may come to on a mixed diet of Shelley and Lord T[ennyson].
>
> I've given you a very brilliant number this week. See that you admire it duly. And tell me what you think of the Kiplings. Up here we are all mashed on 'em.
>
> The Emperor hath a slight cold in the nose, but is otherwise blooming. When next you see her, she will hold you in conversation and probably take you for a walk. Get well soon for we all wish it.[5]

It would appear from the above that Henley was still quite fond of Robbie, in a rather paternal way, despite their disagreement over Oscar Wilde. But Henley was not the sort of father-figure

*A colleague on the *Scots Observer*.

Robbie was looking for. It was a relief that his state of health gave him a valid reason not to return to Edinburgh, but his link with Henley and the *Scots Observer* was not severed. Henley continued to write to him from Edinburgh, and when the editorial offices were later moved down to London, with Henley as Editor – soon changing the name of the publication to *The National Observer* – Robbie continued to collaborate on a part-time basis. At this stage in his journalistic career, he could hardly afford to do otherwise. Moreover, the link with the periodical gave him a certain standing at the Savile Club, which he had begun to frequent again, thanks to Aleck's forebearance and his circle of friends and contacts. Aleck had resigned his position as Secretary of the Society of Authors at the beginning of 1889, but he still served on its management committee. And Walter Besant, a key figure in the Society of Authors, as well as a leading light in the Savile, was as determined as Aleck to engineer Robbie's rehabilitation. Once fully recovered from his peritonitis, Robbie moved out of his mother's house into rented rooms in Bury Street, St James, a respectable address that was just a short amble away from the Savile, as well as offering him the greater independence that he craved.

Oscar Wilde's mother, who had recently had her financial worries relieved by the award of a modest civil pension, once startled a visitor by informing him that the word 'respectable' was not something she wished to hear uttered in her household; like mother, like son, for Oscar, too, found the concept at best ridiculous, at worst oppressive. Robbie's quest for respectability (whatever his marginal private life) was therefore a source of constant amazement and amusement for Oscar. He himself guaranteed that he would never, ever attain such a state, with the publication at the end of June, in the July edition of *Lippincott's Monthly Magazine*, of his short novel, *The Picture of Dorian Gray*. In the magazine version (altered when the work later appeared in book form) Oscar made a veiled reference to the moment when he had first met Robbie, and thereby had his life transformed. But Robbie was not the model for Dorian Gray, the beautiful, bisexual young man who manages to retain his looks and cuts an amoral swathe through London in a life of pure selfishness, pleasure and debauchery, while a portrait that had been painted of him, long hidden in an attic, becomes ever more hideous with each passing day. Nor was John Gray, despite the use of his surname, and the fact that he had started to sign some of his letters 'Dorian'. Though Wilde claimed that the character was based partly on himself, the model for Dorian Gray was really an ideal, though a demonic one. Fate had not yet introduced to Oscar Wilde the ideal's incarnation, though it would not keep him waiting long.

The publication of *The Picture of Dorian Gray* caused an immediate sensation. Robbie was thrilled, but frankly he judged the mood of the novel's reception wrongly:

Dear Oscar, Even in the precincts of the Savile nothing but praise of Dorian Gray though of course it is said to be very dangerous. I heard a clergyman extolling it he only regretted some of the sentiments of Lord Henry [Wotton] as apt to lead people astray. Spriggie* tells me Lippincotts has had a phenomenal sale. 80 copies were sold in one day at a Strand booksellers, the usual amount being about 3 a week in that part. I hope you will consent to speak tomorrow night at the [Society of] Authors. My brother is particularly anxious that you should. Your article in the 19th Century if possible eclipses the Decay of Lieing [sic] but it seems a pity it should have come out in the same month as Dorian Gray. Perhaps it is as well that you should be in every magazine to correct the

*Samuel Squire Sprigge, who succeeded Aleck Ross as Secretary of The Society of Authors.

note of tediousness in all the other articles. Will you come to dinner some night this week. Yrs always[6]

Constance Wilde was a more reliable witness to the effect the novel had when she remarked plaintively that 'Since Oscar wrote *Dorian Gray*, no one will speak to us.' The critics were not so reticent. Many of them, including several members of the Savile, were repelled by the Faustian tale. It was to no avail that Oscar could claim that it was a highly moral work, in that the decadent anti-hero comes to a sticky end. As far as many of the reviewers were concerned, the novel was immoral.

The *St James's Gazette* was one of the first to weigh in with a stinging unsigned review under the headline 'A Study in Puppydom'. Wilde immediately composed and sent off a letter to the Editor, Sidney Low, whom he had known at Oxford, declaring that 'the sphere of art and the sphere of ethics are absolutely distinct and separate'. He tartly observed that 'the English public, as a mass, takes no interest in a work of art until it is told that the work in question is immoral, and your *réclame* will, I have no doubt, largely increase the sale of the magazine'. The criticism clearly rankled, however, as Oscar sent off another letter to Low the following day, a third the day after that, and then a fourth, each time refuting comments that had appeared in the paper. He followed up this epistolary barrage with a visit to the Editor's office, where Sidney Low summoned his assistant Samuel Henry Jeyes, who was the author of the offending review. Far from being cowed by the irate author, Jeyes asked him aggressively, 'What is the use of writing of, and hinting at, things that you do not mean?' 'I mean every word I have said,' Wilde replied, 'and everything at which I have hinted in *Dorian Gray*.' Jeyes retorted, 'Then all I can say is that if you do mean them, then you are very likely to find yourself at Bow Street [Magistrates' Court] one of these days.'

This was indeed the crux of the matter, and the cause of all the bile. For *Dorian Gray* confronted the reading public with the existence of homosexual emotions and hinted at homosexual acts, and in doing so, offended public decency. Its publication paradoxically acted as a clarion call to the righteous, to man the barricades against immorality. Not surprisingly, the *Scots Observer* was in the vanguard. Its unsigned review demanded:

Why go grubbing in muck heaps? The world is fair, and the proportion of the healthy-minded men and honest women to those that are foul, fallen or unnatural is great. Mr Oscar Wilde has again been writing stuff that were better unwritten; and while *The Picture of Dorian Gray*, which he contributes to *Lippincott's*, is ingenious, interesting, full of cleverness, and plainly the work of a man of letters, it is false art – for its interest is medico-legal; it is false to human nature – for its hero is a devil; it is false to morality – for it is not made sufficiently clear that the writer does not prefer a course of unnatural iniquity to a life of cleanliness, health, and sanity. The story – which deals with matters only fitted for the Criminal Investigation Department or a hearing *in camera* is discreditable alike to author and editor. Mr Wilde has brains, and art, and style; but if he can write for none but outlawed noblemen and perverted telegraph-boys, the sooner he takes to tailoring (or some other decent trade) the better for his own reputation and the public morals.[7]

The mention of outlawed noblemen and perverted telegraph-boys, which would have provoked some appreciative chuckles from some of the men ensconced in the leather armchairs of their London clubs, referred to the Cleveland Street scandal, which had exploded the previous year. A male brothel had been operating at number 19 Cleveland Street in London's West End, where telegraph-boys and others could supplement their income by entertaining gentlemen clients, who included not only several senior military officers, but also members of the nobility, including Lord Arthur Somerset, son of the Duke of Beaufort, as well as, allegedly, the Prince of Wales's elder son, the Duke of Clarence. When the authorities realized how many distinguished people were involved, there was a cover-up, and Lord Arthur Somerset was allowed to escape to the Continent. It was impossible to keep the whole affair secret, however, especially when there were crusaders such as Henry Labouchere, who thundered in the House of Commons, 'What is this case but a criminal conspiracy by the very guardians of morality and law, with the Prime Minister at their head, to defeat the ends of justice?'

The accusation stung, which was why many in the Establishment, including the press, were keen to be seen to be standing up for morality, as the *Scots Observer* did on the publication of *Dorian Gray*. Oscar Wilde assumed that W. E. Henley himself had written the hostile review, though in fact the author was his younger editorial assistant, Charles Whibley. Predictably, Wilde demanded to exercise his right of reply, penning a lengthy letter, of which perhaps the most telling passage reads:

> Your critic . . ., sir, commits the absolutely unpardonable crime of trying to confuse the artist with his subject-matter. For this, sir, there is no excuse at all. Of one who is the greatest figure in the world's literature since the Greek days Keats remarked that he had as much pleasure conceiving the evil as he had in conceiving the good. Let your reviewer, sir, consider the bearings of Keats's fine criticism, for it is under these conditions that every artist works. One stands remote from one's subject-matter. One creates it, and one contem-

plates it. The further away the subject-matter is, the more freely can the artist work. Your reviewer suggests that I do not make it sufficiently clear whether I prefer virtue to wickedness or wickedness to virtue. An artist, sir, has no ethical sympathies at all.[8]

Quite apart from the fact that such an artistic doctrine struck many contemporary men of letters as being dangerously subversive, Wilde's protestation of distance from his subject-matter was deeply unconvincing, not least to those who knew a little of the reality behind the façade of his marriage and House Beautiful. A ferocious correspondence then developed in the pages of the *Scots Observer*, like a table-tennis match between Wilde and various irate readers; one of Oscar's missives, dated 13 August, ran to several thousand words. It was perhaps then that Robbie decided, over dinner one evening, to save his friend further labour by revealing that the supposed readers' letters had all been false, concocted by Charles Whibley as a sort of game, to liven up the correspondence columns. It says much for Robbie's mischievous sense of humour that he should go along with such a deception, and much for Oscar's forebearance that he treated it as a good joke at his expense. 'A comedy ends when the secret is out,' Wilde then wrote to W. E. Henley, who was miffed that Robbie had let the cat out of the bag.

Like a child playing with a new toy, Oscar actually relished his notoriety and the pompous, self-righteous condemnation from his critics. All those close to him, though, with the exception of his wife, were enthusiastic about the novel. Lady Wilde declared, with her habitual theatricality, 'it is the most wonderful piece of writing in all the fiction of the day . . . I nearly fainted at the last scene.' And Lionel Johnson wrote a witty Latin verse in its praise.

Perhaps inspired by Oscar's fecundity, Robbie decided that he, too, needed to start producing written work that would give some substance to his vision of himself as a budding man of letters. In this he was greatly helped by Walter Besant who, among his many responsibilities, was Editor of the Society of Authors' journal, *The Author*. By January 1891, Robbie was reviewing books for that publication, and the following month, placed a short story there, 'How We Lost the Book of Jasher'. A slight tale, with some humorous twists, set in the FitzTaylor Museum at Oxbridge (an amalgam of the Fitzwilliam Museum at Cambridge and the Taylorian at Oxford), it provides an interesting foretaste of both the style and content of the slim body of fictional work he would produce over the coming years. The approach is elitist, yet gently mocking. He clearly already loves the dusty environment of connoisseurship that would become his home, yet he is not blind to its foibles and petty jealousies. Interestingly, when the experts at the FitzTaylor take their professional feuds into print, the narrator comments, '. . . the London press animadverted on our conduct. It became a positive scandal. We were advised to wash our dirty linen at home, and though I have often wondered why the press should act as a voluntary laundress on such occasions, I suppose the remark is a just one.'

In introducing the story's main character, the mysterious philanthropist Dr Groschen, Robbie employed several of what Max Beerbohm came to refer to as 'Bobbyisms': absurd details, false pomposity and caricatures of received ideas, which gently deflate the world he is describing.

America, it has been wisely said, is the great land of fraud. It is the Egypt of the modern world. From America came the spiritualists, from America bogus goods, and cheap ideas and pirated editions, and from America I have every reason to believe came Dr Groschen. But if his ancestors came from

Rhine or Jordan, that he received his education on the other side of the Atlantic I have no doubt. Why he came to Oxbridge I cannot say. He appeared quite suddenly, like a comet. He brought introductions from various parts of the world – from the British Embassy at Constantinople, from the British and German Schools of Archaeology at Athens, from certain French Egyptologists at Alexandria, and a holograph letter from Archbishop Sarpedon, Patriarch of Hermaphroditopolis, Curator of the MSS in the Monastery of St Basil, at Mount Olympus. It was this last that endeared him, I believe, to the High Church Party in Oxbridge.[9]

Compared with *The Picture of Dorian Grey*, this was pretty tame stuff. Of course, it is unfair to compare the output of a novice with the work of a man in his prime, as Oscar Wilde incontrovertibly was; the biographer Richard Ellmann was not alone in describing 1891 as Wilde's *annus mirabilis*. But the difference is more than a matter of literary competence. Wilde was striking out into the new, defining himself, through his writing as well as through his lifestyle, as a truly modern figure, one who was in fact ahead of his time. British society would only catch up with him well after his death, in the second half of the twentieth century. Hence Wilde's revolutionary nature in the Victorian context, and inevitable martyrdom. Robbie Ross, on the other hand, could speak with a voice that was within the acceptable parameters of his age, while nevertheless following a reformist agenda.

He also knew how to ingratiate himself with men at the heart of the literary establishment, in a way that Wilde would never have attempted or aspired to. He could be useful, and enjoyed being useful, knowing that those whom he helped would be likely to be useful to him, as a quid pro quo. The sort of relationship he established with men like Walter Besant, for example, is nicely reflected in a letter Besant sent about a forthcoming Society of Authors dinner.

> My dear Robert, If you would give me your assistance tomorrow afternoon in placing our kind friends so as to make as few mortal enemies as possible I should be deeply grateful. Yours ever
>
> W. B.
>
> [P.S.] The true placing of a Society of Authors should [be] imitated from the Chapel of a prison where no guest is able to see anybody but the parson-person.[10]

A few weeks prior to this dinner, Lionel Johnson took a visitor to see Oscar Wilde at his Tite Street home. The book version of *The Picture of Dorian Gray*, amended and expanded, had appeared in April, to a renewed chorus of disapproval from the reviewers. The booksellers W. H. Smith refused to stock it, on the grounds that it was 'filthy'. But Johnson thought the novel was even more wonderful than in its original version. He lent a copy to a cousin of his at Magdalen College, Oxford, Lord Alfred Douglas, who was a son of the belligerent Marquess of Queensberry, originator of the boxing rules that bear his name. Alfred Douglas was so taken with the book that he read it fourteen times over, or so he later told one of Wilde's biographers, A. J. A. Symons. He was therefore keen for Lionel Johnson to effect an introduction with the book's author, which probably took place some time during June 1891.

It was a short encounter, at which Oscar can only have got a very superficial impression of the handsome but haughty young aristocrat, who bore quite a strong resemblance to John Gray. Nonetheless, Oscar was intrigued enough to offer to give Douglas some private tutoring when he learnt that Douglas was not only at his old college, but was also studying Greats. A few weeks later, Alfred Douglas returned to Tite Street, where Oscar gave him an inscribed deluxe edition of *Dorian Gray*. According to the account Douglas gave his biographer H. Montgomery Hyde, forty years later, 'From the second time he saw me, when he gave me a copy of *Dorian Gray*, which I took with me to Oxford, he made overtures to me. It was not until I had known him for at least six months and after I had seen him over and over again and he had twice stayed with me in Oxford that I gave in to him.'

Alfred Douglas was often an extremely unreliable auto-biographer; for years he denied, despite the existence of considerable evidence, that he had ever had any sort of physical relationship with Wilde at all. But the recollections he related to H. Montgomery Hyde have the ring of truth. They also underline an essential difference between the relationship Oscar had with Alfred Douglas and anything that had happened before. With Robbie, it had been Robbie who had taken the initiative. John Gray and Lionel Johnson had not played hard to get. But with Alfred Douglas, Oscar was a supplicant, and the more he fell under the young Lord's spell, the less he was master of his own destiny. Dorian Gray had indeed come to life.

However, Oscar saw little of Alfred Douglas, or indeed of Robbie, during the latter part of 1891, as he was working intensively. Not content with having published a novel, two volumes of stories and a long political essay (*The Soul of Man under Socialism*) during the year, he was simultaneously at work on two plays: his first comedy, *Lady Windermere's Fan*, and a tragedy on a biblical theme, written in French, *Salomé*. Partly for inspiration for the latter, but also to raise his profile on the French literary scene, he went to stay in Paris for a couple of months. There he met the young André Gide, who was so bulldozed by Oscar's energy and perverse monologues, spread over a period of several days, that he could no longer distinguish truth from falsehood, and felt he had been spiritually raped. Others, such as Gide's heterosexual friend Pierre Louÿs, were entranced by the garrulous phenomenon from the other side of the Channel. The *Echo de Paris* acknowledged the impact he had had by declaring on 19 December, shortly before Oscar returned to England, that he had been the 'great event' of the Paris salons.

Robbie could not compete with Oscar's catalogue of successes when Wilde returned to London to spend Christmas with his family. But he did have a little victory of his own to trumpet. At the beginning of December, Walter Besant had written to him, offering him an opening at the Society of Authors.

> My dear Robert, Would you like to undertake definitely with a table and a room to yourself the sub-editing of the *Author*? It would mean two fixed days every week and a constant cadging about to get good stuff and accumulations of notes etc. It isn't one quarter as good as it might be: I have not the time to do it. I believe you would be all the better for regular work. If you think of it, I would make it a paid and salaried post beginning at 2/- a quarter. You could draw it weekly if you pleased.[11]

The proposed remuneration was, of course, a joke, but the offer of this modest responsibility at the heart of the Society of Authors was not. Robbie leapt at the chance. The allowance from his mother meant that pecuniary matters were not uppermost in his mind. He now had a foot firmly in the door of literary London, not just as Aleck Ross's charming younger brother, but in his own right.

FOUR

Catastrophe Averted

THE OPENING NIGHT OF *Lady Windermere's Fan*, on 20 February 1892, at the (now long since demolished) St James's Theatre in London's West End, was a brilliant affair, with the audience being as carefully stage-managed as the sets and the players. Apart from habitual first-nighters and the critics – most of whom, with some notable exceptions such as George Bernard Shaw, were unimpressed with the comedy itself – the theatre was full of Oscar's friends. Oscar had invited not just his wife Constance and the first woman he had fallen in love with, the actress Florence Balcombe (by this time married to the Irish writer Bram Stoker), but also most of the other past and present objects of his affection and desire, from Lillie Langtry to Robbie and a young clerk at the Bodley Head publishers, Edward Shelley, whom Oscar was actively courting. Robbie and other members of Oscar's young male coterie were asked by the author to wear green carnations, bought from the florists Goodyear's in the Royal Arcade. When the artist Graham Robertson asked what the significance of this was, Oscar replied that there was none, but that is not how Robbie and his companions saw the unnatural blooms they were sporting. The buttonholes, in their studied artificiality, were a symbol of defiance, while the colour green echoed Wilde's observation in 'Pen, Pencil and Poison', regarding Thomas Wainewright's 'curious

61

love of green, which in individuals is always the sign of a subtle artistic temperament, and in nations is said to denote a laxity, if not a decadence, of morals'.

Pierre Louÿs, who had come over specially from Paris, and was seated next to young Edward Shelley, reported back enthusiastically to André Gide about the unconventionality of the behaviour of Oscar's circle of admirers, who gathered in the bar during the intervals. Blind to the erotic overtones of the gesture, Louÿs singled out the way some of the young men would light a cigarette and then pass it from their own mouth to that of a friend. But it was Oscar's own nonchalant flouting of social conventions which captured the attention of the audience, and the censure of its more decorous members. At the end of the performance, to tumultuous initial applause, the playwright walked right out onto the front of the stage, a lit cigarette in one outstretched hand. He looked down at the rows of the now hushed and expectant theatre-goers in their evening finery and – if the account given by the actor-manager George Alexander is to be believed – declared with studied accentuation: 'Ladies and gentlemen, I have enjoyed this evening *immensely*. The actors have given us a *charming* rendering of a *delightful* play, and your appreciation has been *most* intelligent. I congratulate you on the *great* success of your performance, which persuades me that you think *almost* as highly of the play as I do myself.'

Three years later, Oscar justified this departure from the usual convention of thanking 'kind friends' for their patronage by telling Robbie, in an interview published in the *St James's Gazette*, that 'the artist cannot be degraded into the servant of the public. While I have always recognized the cultural appreciation that actors and audience have shown for my work, I have equally recognized that humility is for the hypocrite, modesty for the incompetent. Assertion is at once the duty and privilege of the artist.' As if to prove the point, as the audience dispersed after the first performance of *Lady Windermere's Fan*, Oscar further asserted his artistic privilege by sending Constance back to the children in Tite Street, bidding farewell to Robbie and the green carnationed claque, and taking the bedazzled publishers' clerk Edward Shelley off to the Albemarle Hotel to spend the night with him. As was the case with some of the characters in his play, Oscar was living out what he described as the 'doctrine of sheer individualism', challenging society's assumed right to dictate to people how they should behave. 'It is not for anyone to censure what anyone else does,' he proclaimed at a meeting of the Royal General Theatrical Fund after *Lady Windermere's Fan* had been running for a few weeks, 'and everyone should go his own way, to whatever place he chooses, in exactly the way he chooses.'

Such anarchism was both appealing and troubling to Robbie, who was more prepared than Oscar to conform to society's norms in his everyday demeanour. He was still in awe of Oscar and in his hero-worship subconsciously allowed his personality and interests to be overshadowed by those of the playwright. He further strengthened his links with Oscar by co-authoring with an art connoisseur friend, William More Adey, an anonymous preface to a reissue of a long-forgotten novel by Wilde's great-uncle, the Revd Charles Maturin, entitled *Melmoth the Wanderer*. Earlier in the century, the book's demonic hero had acquired a certain cult status, not least in France, where the book had been a bestseller; Charles Baudelaire identified strongly with Melmoth, and Honoré de Balzac wrote a fantastic sequel to *Melmoth the Wanderer* called *The Centenarian or the Two Beringhenns*, in which a 400-year-old monster maintains his vitality by murdering young women. Gothic horror stories and romances were much to Robbie's taste; he was also a fan of the novels of Ann Radcliffe, to whom he referred in a letter to the influential critic Edmund Gosse, to explain why a complimentary copy of *Melmoth the Wanderer* had been despatched to him:

> Being responsible for part of the introduction I ventured to
> send it to you. I fear you have not much sympathy for the
> *école prestige* but I believe you will find *Melmoth* amusing
> enough for holiday reading. Though many people imagine it
> is a mere repetition of Mrs Radcliffe it has little in common
> with the work of that estimable lady. In saying this I merely
> wish to spare you from reading the preface.[1]

Despite the typically self-deprecating final remark, Robbie very
much wanted Edmund Gosse to take an interest in his writing,
and indeed Gosse was the first literary figure of any standing to
take Robbie's tentative first efforts seriously. Yet with its lurid
content and its Oscar Wilde connection, Maturin's novel was
perhaps an inauspicious book to send to a man who had been
brought up as a member of the strict Plymouth Brethren, and
believed that anyone who had not been 'born again' in their
narrow Non-conformist way was damned to eternal fire and
brimstone. Still, Gosse had mellowed considerably since his reli-
giously fervent youth, when he had still been living in the
shadow of his famous naturalist father, Philip Henry Gosse, so
memorably depicted, in all his hideous rectitude, in Edmund
Gosse's autobiography, *Father and Son*. Edmund Gosse nevertheless retained a sense of propriety, which could easily be
offended, and Oscar Wilde was not someone he particularly
esteemed. Indeed, he had greeted Wilde's *Poems* a decade earlier
with fierce derision, describing the volume in a letter to an
American friend as 'a curious toadstool, a malodorous parasitic
growth' put forth by 'the fat young gentleman in the long hair,
whose portrait appears in *Punch*'.

Though Edmund Gosse never completely overcame his
distaste for Oscar Wilde – as much for the man as for his literary

output – the two men became complementary poles in Robbie's existence. While Oscar fired Robbie with his revolutionary ideas and his zest for life, Edmund Gosse provided a valuable link to the literary establishment, as well as a firm shoulder to lean on. He was among those who supported Robbie's second attempt to join the Savile Club, which ended with his election to membership in March 1893. Twenty-five years his senior, Gosse quickly became the most satisfactorily paternal of all the surrogate fathers in Robbie's life. He regularly proffered advice, including trying, unsuccessfully, to get Robbie to cut down on his cigarette-smoking. Both Gosse and his wife Nellie were truly fond of the young man, and regularly invited him to their Sunday afternoon 'At Homes' at their comfortable canal-side home in Delamere Terrace, Maida Vale, at which would be gathered many of the great writers of the day, thronging the rooms of the house and the balconies that overlooked the water and the surrounding poplars. The setting was quite a contrast to the grim offices of the Board of Trade, where Gosse earned the bedrock of his income as a translator, notably from Scandinavian languages. His interest in northern European cultures had developed early and was profound. Tall, pale and blond, Gosse looked increasingly Nordic himself as the years went by. He was proud of the fact that once while on a visit to Norway, he had accidentally been introduced in a bookshop to the work of Henrik Ibsen, whose name he made familiar to the English-speaking world. Ibsen's work soon found other champions in England, not least George Bernard Shaw, and it was in counterpoint to Ibsen's dark dramas and spare dialogue that Wilde's bright and witty comedies would appear on the London stage over the next four years.

More Adey – Robbie's co-author of the preface to *Melmoth the Wanderer* – was one of the rare people who succeeded in making a bridge between the two, by being both a close friend of Wilde's and the translator (under the pseudonym William Wilson) of Ibsen's *Brand*. Adey became more than just a friend and collaborator to Robbie, as the two of them shared lodgings for several years at 24 Hornton Street, Kensington, not as lovers, but as two bachelor friends with a common interest in art, literature, companionship, gossip and sitting around in armchairs for hours on end smoking cigarettes. They made an odd couple when they walked out together. Though only eleven years Robbie's senior, Adey looked considerably older, with his receding hair, his beard, bushy eyebrows and dark, almost Eastern looks. A Roman Catholic, who aided Robbie's definitive shift towards the Church of Rome, he startled many people by his intensity and eccentricity. Even Oscar Wilde at times found him unsettling.

Far more disturbing and exciting, however, were the demands made on Oscar by Lord Alfred Douglas that spring of 1892. They had had little contact since their first brief meetings, despite Oscar's interest in the young aristocrat. But then Douglas turned to him in a moment of crisis. He was being blackmailed over an indiscreet letter sent to a boy; although still an undergraduate at Oxford, he was already well acquainted with working-class 'renters'. He did not have access to funds to satisfy the blackmailer and, although his father was rich, under the circumstances he could hardly approach him. Oscar was flattered that he should turn to him for help, and rather like a gallant knight setting off to rescue a damsel in distress, he went to Oxford, where he stayed the weekend in Douglas's rooms. By the end of the stay, Oscar was calling Alfred Douglas by the nickname his family had given him, 'Bosie'. He arranged through his solicitor George Lewis to acquire the incriminating document and to pay off the blackmailer with £100. Out of gratitude, or at least a sense of obligation, Bosie then succumbed to Oscar's advances. Within weeks, Wilde was totally smitten. He inscribed a copy of his *Poems* to Bosie, with the words 'To the

Gilt-mailed Boy at Oxford in the heart of June, Oscar Wilde'. The intensity of the infatuation was clear in a letter he wrote to Robbie:

> My dearest Bobbie, Bosie has insisted on stopping here for sandwiches. He is quite like a narcissus – so white and gold. I will come either Wednesday or Thursday night to your rooms. Send me a line. Bosie is so tired: he lies like a hyacinth on the sofa, and I worship him.[2]

Oscar was quite comfortable talking to Robbie about his new passion, though he did not let the two young men meet until the following year. Perhaps he feared Bosie would be jealous of Robbie's prior claim; certainly Robbie himself was by no means proprietorial. Or maybe at this stage Oscar wanted to keep Bosie to himself. As yet, he found no thrill in showing Bosie off in public, or of flaunting their relationship. Besides, he had other things on his mind. He had persuaded Sarah Bernhardt to star in his play *Salomé*, for which, he was convinced, she was ideally suited. She was equally enthusiastic, and the play went into rehearsal at the Palace Theatre in London in the second week in June. But later that month, the Lord Chamberlain banned the production, invoking an ancient law forbidding the depiction of biblical characters on stage. Oscar should have known about the prohibition, but he was incensed. It seemed to him particularly unjust that his tragedy of the princess who asks for the head of John the Baptist when he rejects her advances should be deemed unsuitable, while a vulgar burlesque of *Lady Windermere's Fan* called *The Poet and the Puppets*, written by Charles Brookfield, was permitted, despite the fact that the poet in it was played by an actor who cruelly aped Wilde's dress, voice and mannerisms. As far as Oscar was concerned, such double standards only confirmed the philistine nature of England. Unwisely, he announced that he was thinking of emigrating to France, where everything was so much more civilized. This threat prompted one cartoonist to imagine what Oscar would look like as a plump common soldier, were he called up to do French military service. In the end, Oscar accepted the fact that if he was to pursue his new career as a dramatist, he would need to be in England. However, he did go to a spa in Germany to try to lose some weight.

There was no let-up in the attacks upon him in the more conservative British press, which provoked a rebuke to fellow critics from Edmund Gosse. His sense of fair play offended, Gosse wrote in the *New Review* that 'to peck at one another is not the business of humming-birds and nightingales. Daws do it best, and are kept for that very purpose, in large numbers in the aviaries of Grub Street. Mr Oscar Wilde (with whom I seldom find myself in agreement) is an artist, and claims from his fellow-artists courteous consideration.' Robbie cut out the article and sent it to Oscar, who was by now staying in Devon. He was delighted by the expression of solidarity from such a quarter:

My dearest Bobbie, Thank you so much for the 'New Review'. Gosse's mention of me is most charming and courteous. Pray tell him from me what pleasure it gave me to receive so graceful a recognition from so accomplished a man of letters. As a rule, journalists and literary people write so horribly, and with such gross familiarity, and virulent abuse, that I am rather touched by any mention of me that is graceful and civil.

How are you? Are there beautiful people in London? Here there are none; everyone is so unfinished. When are you coming down? I am lazy and languid, doing no work. I need stirring up. With best love.[3]

Oscar spent the last two months of 1892 and much of the early part of 1893 at Babbacombe Cliff, a sizeable house in Torquay, rented from a distant cousin of Constance's, Lady Mount-Temple, ostensibly so that he could work on his next comedy, *A Woman of No Importance*, away from the distractions of London and his family. Edmund Gosse happened to be in the vicinity in mid-December and set out to call on him, before getting cold feet, as he confessed somewhat coyly to Robbie:

> I drew to the very doorstep of Babbacombe Cliff, and then had less resolution than was needed to invade his retirement. I used to know the people there, and the strange, charming house itself. I should have liked to see him there, but I was too shoy [sic] – 'such a big girl too,' – as the poet says.[4]

Robbie did not take up Oscar's suggestion that he go to stay with him in Devon, to shake him out of his lethargy. Instead, Oscar came up to London for a while. After spending Christmas at Tite Street, on New Year's Day he moved into the Albemarle Hotel for a fortnight's stay. There he could entertain his growing circle of boys, of whom Edward Shelley was only one. Another was the future priest Sidney Mavor, who was procured for Oscar by a man called Alfred Taylor, who gained particular renown in the homosexual demi-monde of London by going through a form of 'marriage' ceremony with another man. The well-connected but wayward son of a prosperous cocoa manufacturer, Taylor had become a high-class pimp, much patronized by Oscar. Now flush with money from the advantageous arrangements he had made for his plays, Oscar promiscuously indulged in his acquired taste for male prostitutes, rather as a modern pop-star might discover cocaine and have the means to feed a growing addiction. Unlike most of the other gentlemen who patronized Alfred Taylor's network of willing valets, grooms and other working-class youths, however, Oscar was a romantic. The transactions were rarely brief and merely physical; instead, he would treat the lads to dinner in the private rooms of top-class restaurants or spend the night with them at smart hotels, by his very generosity opening himself up to exploitation. John Gray was displeased by this transformation in Oscar's behaviour and his obsession with Bosie Douglas. As Oscar's ardour towards Gray had recently cooled, Gray terminated their relationship and found a more fulfilling partner in the wealthy young Russian émigré poet André Raffalovich.

Returning to Babbacombe Cliff at the end of January 1893 was an uncomfortable reminder to Oscar of the need to work to sustain his new debauched lifestyle. His mind was not fully on the task at hand. A letter from Bosie, enclosing a sonnet, made him put aside his play and write a prose-poem letter to Bosie that was to have disastrous repercussions.

> My Own Boy, Your sonnet is quite lovely, and it is a marvel that those red rose-leaf lips of yours should have been made no less for music of song than for madness of kisses. Your slim gilt soul walks between passion and poetry. I know Hyacinthus, whom Apollo loved so madly, was you in Greek days.
>
> Why are you alone in London, and when do you go to Salisbury*? Do go there to cool your hands in the grey twilight of Gothic things, and come here whenever you like. It is a lovely place – it only lacks you; but go to Salisbury first. Always, with undying love, yours
>
> OSCAR[5]

At Oxford, Bosie was neglecting his studies to concentrate on writing poetry and enjoying himself. He was a talented poet

---

*Where Bosie's mother, Lady Queensberry – who was separated from her husband – had a home.

and felt he had a mission to make a mark on the contemporary arts scene by embarking on his own literary enterprise, an undergraduate magazine called the *Spirit Lamp*. Supposedly a repository for fine new creative writing, the publication also had a hidden agenda: to provide a platform to promote what Bosie aptly dubbed 'the Love that dare not speak its name'. Had his father, the belligerent Marquess of Queensberry, realized this, he would certainly not have agreed to have one of his own poetic efforts included in an early number – an elegy to a departed friend, which began manfully 'When I am dead, cremate me'. More predictably, Alfred Douglas successfully solicited contributions from Oscar, Robbie and John Addington Symonds.

While both Bosie and Oscar's prime interests in creating or sustaining new movements in the arts were almost exclusively focused on literature, Robbie was increasingly being drawn to painting and drawing, not as a practitioner, for which he had no talent, but as someone with an expert eye. Art appreciation was an interest he shared with More Adey, and it led him into circles which Oscar Wilde – who was only superficially interested in painting, and was deaf to music – rarely, if ever, entered. Given Robbie's sociability and gentle wit, he quickly made many new friendships, one of the most important of which developed during the winter of 1892–3, with the brilliant and highly individualistic graphic artist Aubrey Beardsley. The two first met in the rooms of the art critic and disciple of William Morris's ideas about interior design, Aymer Vallance. Vallance organized a party on St Valentine's Day, 1892, to introduce his new discovery, Beardsley, to friends such as Robbie and More Adey. As Robbie recalled in his biography of Beardsley, published nearly twenty years later:

Though prepared for an extraordinary personality, I never

expected the youthful apparition which glided into the room. He was shy, nervous and self-conscious, without any of the intellectual assurances and ease so characteristic of him eighteen months later when his success was unquestioned. He brought a portfolio of his marvellous drawings, in themselves an earnest of genius; but I hardly paid any attention to them at first, so overshadowed were they by the strange and fascinating originality of their author.[6]

Aubrey Beardsley was indeed remarkable in appearance: tall, skinny and etiolated, his dark hair plastered down over his forehead. Though only nineteen when he first met Robbie, he had a mask of sickness more befitting an old man; he haemorrhaged easily and was often confined to bed, yet at times he bristled with an electric energy. His talent as a draughtsman was precocious, and if at first derivative of his mentor Edward Burne-Jones, his art soon developed its own, individual and immediately recognizable style. His first published work consisted of generally rather unmemorable caricatures of personalities for the *Pall Mall Budget*, but on the publication of Wilde's play *Salomé* in February 1893, the *Pall Mall Budget*'s editor, C. Lewis Hind, commissioned Beardsley to do an illustration based on the play. The result was an astoundingly accomplished and perverse black and white portrait of a kneeling Salomé looking deep into the eyes of the decapitated John the Baptist, from whose neck blood drips down into a lily-pond. The asymmetry of the work was shockingly original, with the focus of the scene in the extreme top right corner. The overall effect is sinister and lascivious, and when Hind saw the drawing, he nearly had a fit. There was no question of such a monstrosity appearing in his respectable publication. However, Gleeson White, the editor of a new art journal called *The Studio*, had no such qualms, and accepted it along with several other Beardsley illustrations. Robbie was much entertained by the saga of the Salomé drawing, and introduced both it and its creator to Oscar when Wilde returned to London in March for the rehearsals of *A Woman of No Importance*. The first impressions were mutually positive, and Oscar presented Beardsley with a copy of *Salomé* with the intimate inscription, 'for Aubrey, for the only artist who, besides myself, knows what the dance of the seven veils is, and can see the invisible dance. Oscar.'

Wilde had managed to finish *A Woman of No Importance* at Babbacombe Cliff despite the presence of Bosie Douglas during the latter part of his stay. In principle, Bosie was meant to study while Oscar was working; a friend and Oxford contemporary of Lionel Johnson's, Campbell Dodgson, came down to Torquay for a while, supposedly to act as Bosie's tutor. A letter Oscar sent to Dodgson soon after he left, however, suggests that the educational aspects had not been taken very seriously:

> . . . I am still conducting the establishment on the old lines and really think I have succeeded in combining the advantages of a public school with those of a private lunatic asylum, which, as you know, was my aim. Bosie is very gilt-haired and I have bound *Salomé* in purple to suit him. That tragic daughter of passion appeared on Thursday last, and is now dancing for the head of the British public. Should you come across her, tell me how you like her. I want you to like her.
> All the boys of the school send you their best love, and kindest wishes. Sincerely yours
>
> OSCAR WILDE
> Headmaster Babbacombe School[7]

Lady Queensberry, no less, had asked Oscar to keep an eye on Bosie. She was worried about her son's lackadaisical attitude to his Oxford courses, as well as by intermittent signs of the violent temper he seemed to have inherited from his Douglas ancestors. But far from being able to keep Bosie under control, Oscar was often at his loved one's mercy. He did not have the temperament to stand up to Bosie's egotistical demands, and was anyway relishing at least some of the young Lord's errant ways. For example, there was Bosie's attitude to common boys as commodities, to be enjoyed and shared. A good case in point was seventeen-year-old Alfred Wood, a lad Bosie had first met and recommended to Oscar. When Oscar returned to London, he duly fixed an appointment to meet Alfred Wood at the Café Royal. He liked what he saw, took him out to dinner and then on to Tite Street to have sex, Constance and the children being away. Over the coming weeks, young Alfred shuttled between London and Oxford, entertaining his two patrons. On one occasion, Bosie presented him with an unwanted jacket, without first checking that the pockets were empty. In fact, they contained a sheaf of letters from Oscar, including the effusive note about red rose-leaf lips. Wood showed this to some of his more unscrupulous acquaintances who advised him that this was an opportunity to make a killing. He sent a copy of one of the letters to the actor-manager Herbert Beerbohm Tree at the Haymarket Theatre, where *A Woman of No Importance* was in rehearsal, then waited for Oscar outside the theatre. Forewarned by Tree, Oscar laughed off the boy's clumsy blackmail attempt; when Wood said he could get £60 for one of the letters, Oscar declared that Wood should certainly accept the offer, as he had never been paid so much for such a short piece of prose. Nonplussed, the boy went away. But soon afterwards he called at the house in Tite Street with two accomplices, and Oscar gave him £25 to buy passage to America. In return he was given a packet of the letters, not realizing that the most incriminating one was not among them. When the omission was noted, he got Pierre Louÿs (to whom he had dedicated *Salomé*) to translate a copy into French, in the hope that if the letter were ever brought up in public then it could be passed off purely as a work of literature.

Oscar managed to make a quick trip to Paris with Sidney Mavor at around this time, but plans to return to the French capital with Aubrey Beardsley in May to attend the Salons had to be dropped because of pressures of work and Bosie's demands that he stay with him in Oxford. Instead, Beardsley travelled with his much-loved sister Mabel (who was an actress) and the American illustrator and critic Joseph Pennell and his wife. Robbie had introduced Beardsley to Pennell, at a little soirée he had organized in Beardsley's honour, in the correct belief that this would advance Aubrey's career as an artist. Although Pennell's first reaction to Beardsley's appearance had been that he looked more like a swell than an artist, and that his portfolio was the sort of thing a young lady would carry round, he changed his mind as soon as he saw the drawings inside, remarking on the strange but effective combination of Pre-Raphaelite mannerisms and modern design, the whole suffused with a certain medievalism. By 1893, Beardsley was in fact distancing himself both from the Pre-Raphaelites and medievalism, and becoming far more seduced by Japanese concepts of space and economy of line.

Robbie was also in Paris for the Salons in May 1893, which pleased Aubrey's formidable mother Ellen Beardsley, who looked on Robbie as a sort of sensible elder brother who might be able to keep Aubrey in check. Robbie's calm manner and usually conservative dress often gave this quite false impression to ladies of a certain age. Quite apart from the forbidden desires he harboured behind his respectable façade, he was incapable of restraining anyone as stubborn as Aubrey.

Beardsley, who loved to make an entrance, turned up at the

opening of the Salon Neuf on the Champs de Mars in an outfit that was a symphony of greys, apart from his brilliant gold tie. Though later derided by Wilde for allegedly being asexual ('Don't sit on the same chair as Aubrey,' the playwright once declared, 'it's not compromising'), Beardsley actually relished the sort of bohemian free relations between men and women that were possible in France to an extent that was almost inconceivable in England. On an outing to Versailles, for example, Aubrey, Mabel, the Pennells and other friends sprawled out on the lawns. When a group of American tourists appeared, Aubrey's party stripped off their clothes and flung themselves into the lake for a swim, sending the tourists' guide into a complete fluster. The English visitors' behaviour became so rowdy later in the day that the station-master at Versailles railway station locked them in the waiting room.

While in Paris, Beardsley called on the young Jewish painter William Rothenstein, who was to become another key figure in Robbie's circle. A friend of Toulouse-Lautrec and the poet Verlaine, Rothenstein had, during his three years of artistic study in Paris, integrated himself skilfully into the Montmartre scene. It was all a far cry from his origins as the son of a cloth merchant in Bradford. The same age as Aubrey Beardsley, Rothenstein was a funny-looking little fellow, affectionately christened 'The Parson' by Whistler, who was also based in Paris at this time. When that summer of 1893 Rothenstein went to Oxford to carry out a commission for John Lane at the Bodley Head, one of the most brilliant undergraduates of the day, Max Beerbohm, made a caricature of him that made him look like a demented owl. Beerbohm – who was a half-brother of Herbert Beerbohm Tree – was in fact delighted by the exotic new arrival, later recalling:

In the Summer Term of '93 a bolt from the blue flashed down

on Oxford. It drove deep, it hurtlingly embedded itself in the soil. Dons and undergraduates stood around, rather pale, discussing nothing but it. Whence came it, this meteorite? From Paris. Its name? Will Rothenstein. Its aim? To do a series of twenty-four portraits in lithograph . . . It was whispered that, so soon as he had polished off his selection of dons, he was going to include a few undergraduates. It was a proud day for me when I – I – was included.[8]

Max Beerbohm did a number of caricatures of Rothenstein over the years, as he did of Oscar Wilde, Robbie and so many other figures of the period. Max was part of Alfred Douglas's fashionable, aesthetic crowd at Oxford, so he had plenty of occasions to meet and observe Oscar – 'The Divinity', as he called Wilde – with the mixture of admiration and affectionate mockery that characterizes so many of his drawings. Though they enjoyed each other's brilliance, the two of them could be quite barbed about each other. One or two of Max's cartoons of Oscar made him look a little ridiculous, while Oscar pronounced of Max, 'The gods have bestowed on Max the gift of perpetual old age.' At the same time, Oscar was perplexed how someone so young could be so enigmatic. 'Tell me,' Oscar once asked a mutual friend, 'when you are alone with Max, does he take off his face and reveal his mask?' When Max saw Oscar at a performance of *A Woman of No Importance* at the Haymarket, in the company of Robbie and Aubrey Beardsley, he wrote to a former fellow student at Oxford, Reginald ('Reggie') Turner, a young Jewish man of letters who would prove to be one of Oscar's most faithful friends:

The last of these had forgotten to put vine-leaves in his hair, but the other two wore rich clusters – especially poor Robbie. Nor have I ever seen Oscar so fatuous: he called [the actress]

Mrs [Bernard] Beere 'Juno-like' and Mrs Kemble 'Olympian quite' and waved his cigarette round and round his head. Of course, I would rather see Oscar free than sober, but still, suddenly meeting him after my simple and lovely little ways of life since the Lady Cecilia* first looked out from her convent window, I felt quite repelled.[9]

Max might have been even more repelled had he realized the imbroglios into which Oscar, Robbie and Bosie were all getting themselves over boys. While Oscar was playing the more overtly dangerous game of consorting with rent-boys – what he called 'feasting with panthers' – Robbie's amorous attentions were channelled more towards young men from good families. And Bosie was omnivorous. Their recklessness was such that it soon became a matter of which one of the three would first be exposed to a major scandal. In the event, it was very nearly Robbie.

In July, Robbie went to stay at his mother's house in Onslow Square with a boy called Dansey, whom he had met the previous Easter at the home of Oscar Browning's brother-in-law Biscoe Wortham in Belgium. The son of a military family, Dansey was a pupil at Wortham's school in Bruges. Robbie found the boy such a satisfying partner that night at his mother's that he introduced him to Bosie Douglas. Bosie, who had a succession of infatuations with boys at this time, took this one up for a while, so long in fact that Dansey was late returning to Belgium, arriving after the new term had already begun. Wortham became suspicious, and when Dansey started receiving letters from Bosie, he intercepted them. Interrogated by Wortham, the boy revealed all that had happened between himself and Robbie, as well as with Bosie Douglas. But Wortham was faced with a

*The fifteen-year-old music-hall mimic Cissie Loftus, of whom Max had become enamoured.

78

dilemma. If he followed the matter up, it could rebound on the reputation of the school. Worse still, he suddenly realized, Robbie might have also taken advantage of his own two sons, Philip and Oswald (known as Toddy). A confrontation with Philip produced the confession referred to earlier. Beside himself with fury, Wortham did not know what to do, so he wrote to Oscar Browning for advice, little realizing that Browning would of course alert Robbie to the impending crisis. Nevertheless Wortham urged:

> Absolute secrecy in this matter is essential for all. Philip's name is not likely to come out. The events related happened some time ago & Ross has no letters of his . . . The details of the case of this boy here are too horrible. Ross is simply one of a gang of the most brutal ruffians who spend their time in seducing and prostituting boys & all the time presenting a decent appearance to the world. Two other persons* besides himself are implicated in this business. Unfortunately there are some compromising letters which it is very desirable to get at.
>
> I write to you in absolute secrecy to tell you what a scoundrel this fellow is, & he stayed with us only at Easter when he took the opportunity of our hospitality to make friends with this boy (a very nice looking gentlemanly boy of very good family of 16) whom he invited to London and seduced![10]

Anxious to avoid prosecution, Robbie and Bosie travelled to Belgium, checked into a hotel in Ostend and then went to Bruges to try to come to an agreement with the Worthams. As Mina Wortham duly reported to Oscar Browning:

*One was Bosie Douglas, the other Oscar Wilde.

16 October 1893

Biscoe was surprised last evening by a note from Mr Ross asking for an interview at the Hôtel de Flandre – with him was Lord Alfred Douglas, one of his accomplices. The fact is that there are some letters in the possession of Mr Ross & Lord Alfred Douglas which must be had – if they would give them up, nothing would be done . . . I am miserable about poor Toddy. Of course, I have no idea what his relations are with Mr Ross *now*. Up to the last few days I looked upon Mr Ross as Toddy's valued friend & I wrote to Mr Ross last summer & told him how much I valued his friendship for the 2 boys. Biscoe has written a string of questions to Toddy but there is no answer from him – he might well have written – What effect these questions may have I cannot tell – anyhow, if he has written any letters to Mr Ross, they must be had.[11]

Sitting in his rooms at King's College, Cambridge, Oscar Browning paradoxically had a clearer idea of what was going on than any of the protagonists, as he was being kept informed by both sides. Indeed, in the same post as Mina Wortham's letter came one from Robbie:

Following your advice I came out here yesterday morning and went over to Bruges in the evening & had an interview with Mr Wortham at the Hôtel de Flandre. It was very unsatisfactory. He refuses to tell me what he proposes doing. He says he possesses documentary evidence but what he intends doing with this (if it exists) he will not say. He also speaks of 'coming to terms' but does not state what those terms are beyond the fact that I have certain letters from the boy Dansey which I must hand over. He will not tell me which letters they are. I have no letters from him that could not be read in public . . . I was also confronted with Philip who repeated his story. It is an absolute fabrication. If it were true I would certainly not attempt to conceal it from *you*, as you must know perfectly well. From what you have often told me about Mr Wortham & what *you know yourself* about him it is in your power to free the whole affair of its more serious aspects without compromising yourself in any way.[12]

Biscoe Wortham was not the only person who needed to be neutralized. In London, the boy Dansey's father was threatening to take legal action against Robbie and Bosie. But the ever reliable solicitor George Lewis, acting on their behalf, pointed out to Colonel Dansey that even if Robbie and Bosie were sent to prison as the result of a successful prosecution, his son would also be at risk of punishment. More Adey also stepped in to help with negotiations on behalf of Robbie and his family. Then, thanks to Oscar Browning's good offices, there was an exchange of incriminating letters being held by the Worthams, Robbie and Bosie. On 25 October, Biscoe Wortham was thus able to write to Browning,

> At length I am thankful to say we have got to an end of this dreadful case. The letters have been returned on both sides, and now one feels relieved of a nightmare . . . It has been a *horrible case*, & the details, which I have, and am the only one who knows except the chief actors in the business are beyond anything abominable. We may be thankful that it has ended quietly, but it has been a near thing.[13]

It had indeed been a near thing for Robbie. He could easily have gone to prison, or had his reputation destroyed by a scandal. Instead, he got off extremely lightly. The affair did take a toll on his nerves, however. He went on a short visit to Cambridge, to spend time in the reassuring company of Oscar Browning. But not for the first time in Robbie's life, his family decided it would be better to get him out of temptation's way. Where better than the healthy and wholesome environment of Davos in Switzerland, where the more staid of his two brothers, Jack, was now based?

FIVE

Oscar's Downfall

THE ALPINE VALLEY OF Davos in the Swiss canton of the Grisons had recently become a fashionable destination for consumptives. Tuberculosis was no respecter of class, but in the sanitoria and hotels of the village of Davos Platz, 5,000 feet up in the mountains, affluent sufferers could get the best treatment and most comfortable facilities on offer. Dr Turban's Sanatorium, at the south-west end of the village, offered board and lodging, including medical attention, for a comparatively modest four Swiss francs a day, while the Grand Hôtel Belvedere boasted a terrace or 'solarium', where patients could sun themselves. Although the temperature fell well below zero for much of the winter, the sun was often strong and invigorating. Accompanying relatives could partake of winter sports, or gorge themselves at the fine restaurant in the Kurhaus Davos Hotel. In summer, a pleasant excursion could be made by electric tramway up the Schatz Alp. But, as a contemporary edition of *Black's Guide Book to Switzerland* noted, 'few travellers not being invalids will be tempted to make any stay at Davos, save in winter for the sake of skating on the lake and tobogganing down to Klosters'. Small wonder that Robbie felt rather as if he were being exiled to Siberia for his recent misdeeds.

His brother Jack was working in Davos as a lawyer. Perhaps like many of his co-residents, he also found the climate beneficial, as he had been seriously ill during his undergraduate days at Trinity College, Cambridge, taking six years to get his B.A. instead of the more normal three. He had been called to the Canadian Bar in 1887, and became a member of the Inner Temple in London the following year. At Davos, he and his wife Minnie settled in comfortably within the small expatriate community, which was able to support an English church, St Luke's, complete with chaplain, and an English physician. Among well-known long-term English residents during Jack Ross's time was John Addington Symonds, who went there for his health in 1877, and had several years of intense literary productivity, as well as running after local cowherds.

When Robbie arrived in Davos Platz, at the end of November 1893, Symonds was just a memory, having died suddenly while on a visit to Rome earlier in the year. But there remained a tightly knit community of expatriates with artistic and literary interests, many of whom belonged to the English Literary Society. Robbie threw himself into this circle quickly, being under the impression that he was going to have to spend two years in the area. Though his family in London knew all about the Dansey affair, More Adey had managed to conceal from them the accusations relating to Biscoe Wortham's sons, until that reverend gentleman felt it his duty to write a long letter to Aleck Ross, detailing the allegations. Robbie complained in a letter to Bosie Douglas,

> My elder brother here gets letters about the disgrace of the family, the social outcast, the son and brother unfit for society of any kind, from people at home. I am sure you will be amused to hear this.[1]

Bosie loyally dissimulated the true nature of his friend's fall from grace, informing Max Beerbohm and others that Robbie had

had to go to Switzerland because of ill-health and that he had merely quarrelled with his family. Aubrey Beardsley, for whom health and family were both important matters, was sympathetic to Robbie's supposed plight. He himself had been going through a stressful period, having been at the centre of a ferocious row over Oscar Wilde's *Salomé*. John Lane had decided that the English-language version of the play, which he and Elkin Mathews were publishing, would be enhanced by ten full-page illustrations by Beardsley. Beardsley revelled in the task, but included so many gratuitous penises and lascivious facial expressions that John Lane demanded that several be redrawn. Oscar was also displeased by some of the drawings, including a representation of his own person as a fat and effeminate moon – the moon being an image that recurs frequently during the play. He thought that Aubrey was being tiresomely childish in his wish to provoke. This was not the only aspect of the project that was trying Oscar's patience. In a fit of love's blindness, he had commissioned Alfred Douglas to translate the original French text into English, without realizing that Bosie's French was not up to the task. There were so many mistakes that a completely new version had to be prepared, for which Aubrey's help was enlisted. Beardsley claimed to find the whole affair highly amusing.

Dear Bobbie, Many thanks for your letter. I haven't found a moment to answer it sooner. How beastly dull you must be on the top of Mont Blanc or wherever you are. I do wish I could have managed to get over to see you.

I suppose you've heard all about the *Salomé* Row. I can tell you I had a warm time of it between Lane and Oscar and Co. For one week the numbers of telegraph and messenger boys who came to the door was simply scandalous. I really don't quite know how the matter really stands now. Anyhow Bozie's [sic] name is not to turn up on the Title. The Book will be out soon after Xmas. I have withdrawn 3 of the illustrations and supplied their places with 3 new ones (simply beautiful and quite irrelevant) . . . By the way Bozie is going to Egypt in what capacity I don't quite gather; something diplomatic I fancy. Have you heard from either him or Oscar? Both of them are really very dreadful people.

I long for your return.

In January I shall be over in Paris for a short time. There is a very jolly exhibition of French work at the Grafton now. Affiches, lithographs, and all that sort of thing. Let me have a line and tell me something about your vegetable life. I suppose you see papers, can I send you any books?[2]

Just as Eliza Ross had been keen to get Robbie out of England for a while, so Lady Queensberry thought a spell in Egypt would help prevent Bosie drifting into worse troubles. In Bosie's case, the idea of a sojourn in distant parts actually originated with Oscar, who was being driven to distraction by Bosie's petulance and the way the young man prevented him working. Wilde had hired rooms in St James's Place, in the hope of finishing his third comedy, *An Ideal Husband*, free from distractions. But as he later recalled sourly in his recriminatory prison letter to Bosie, *De Profundis*, Bosie would not leave him alone. At midday he would turn up, and then sit chatting and smoking cigarettes until 1.30 p.m., when Oscar would take him to lunch at the Café Royal or the Berkeley. Lunch would last a couple of hours, after which Bosie retired to White's Club, only to return at tea-time, staying until it was time to dress for dinner. That would also be taken together, at the Savoy or in the Tite Street house, with a late supper at Willis's Rooms. It was not just the time that was being taken up, when Oscar should have been writing. The meals, the champagne and all the other entertainments consumed almost all of Oscar's now considerable earnings. He later calculated that he spent about £5000 on Bosie – £300,000 in today's money. It was therefore with considerable relief that Oscar saw Bosie despatched off to Cairo, to work as an honorary attaché to the British legation, where friends of Lady Queensberry's, Lord and Lady Cromer, were in residence.

In contrast, Robbie's new life at Davos was more mundane, though he was enjoying a certain esteem among the confined expatriate society of the Swiss valley. The English-language local newssheet, the *Davos Courier*, noted with satisfaction that in London he had contributed as a literary critic to 'some of the leading London journals'. He attracted a good turn-out when he addressed the English Literary Society on 'The Didactic in Art and Literature' on 2 January 1894. The content of the paper he delivered reflected ideas he and Oscar had so often discussed in their conversations:

No achievement in Literature or Art can occur, without the English asking if it is quite moral. No picture can be painted, no novel written, without the enquiry whether it is fit and proper for their under-aged daughters, their underfed sons, and their over-aged fathers. They do not first ask if this picture is 'well' painted, if this book is 'well' written. Yet that is the only spirit in which such things should be considered at all. It is often not till years afterwards when author and artist are dead, and those who blushed are dead, that someone asked, 'Was this book well written? Was this picture well painted?'[3]

Art and literature should only be judged by artistic and literary standards, he argued. It was impossible to say what an 'immoral' book was, though one could identify a pornographic one, or one that was badly written. This was exactly the line Oscar Wilde would take when he found himself in court the following year. Robbie's talk created quite a stir, provoking an animated correspondence in the letter columns of the *Davos Courier*. In response to one particularly strident lady critic – who had not actually been present at the lecture – Robbie wrote to the Editor,

> I, Sir, have only two objects in life. The first is to amuse myself, the second is to amuse other people, and though pained in the harshness of your correspondence I am compensated by the fact that she was 'rather amused' at what I said. Had she been present no doubt she might have been 'highly amused' as more courteous critics confessed themselves to have been.[4]

Gratifying though it might have been to have made such an impact in Davos within weeks of arriving, this was all very small beer for a young man with wider literary ambitions. But at least Robbie was confident in the knowledge that friends in London were making sure he was not excluded by his absence from developments there. Indeed, Aubrey Beardsley had just commissioned him to write a piece of between 5,000 and 6,000 words for the first issue of a new venture he was involved in with his friend Henry Harland.

> If superfluous fresh air, tobogganing and snow capped mountains, have not completely killed your love of the fine arts, I am sure you will be vastly interested to hear that Harland and myself are about to start a new literary and artistic Quarterly. The title has already been registered at Stationers Hall and on the scroll of fame. It is *THE YELLOW BOOK*.
>
> In general get up it will look like the ordinary French novel. Each number will contain about 10 contributions in the way

of short stories and discursive essays from the pens say of Henry Harland, Henry James, [Hubert] Crackanthorpe, George Egerton, and Max Beerbohm. The drawings will be independent and supplied by Aubrey Beardsley, Walter Sickert, Wilson Steer, and Will Rothenstein and other past masters. The publication will be undertaken by John Lane, and the price will be 5/-.

(No. 1 appears on April 15th.)

We all want to have something charming from you for the first number. Say an essay or a short story. Now *do* send us something soon in your most brilliant style, and make up your mind to be a regular contributor . . .[5]

Harland was to be the Literary Editor and Beardsley the Art Editor. Notably absent from the list of contributors who they intended to solicit was the name of Oscar Wilde. Though relations between Oscar and Aubrey had not yet irrevocably soured – indeed, Oscar arranged for Beardsley to meet Mrs Patrick Campbell, so he could do a drawing of that actress for *The Yellow Book*'s first number – nevertheless both Beardsley and John Lane at the Bodley Head felt that Wilde was too dominant a personality to be included. Even if he agreed to write something, he would be likely to overshadow the other contributors. And although *The Yellow Book* was aiming to be 'modern' and provocative – its yellow covers reminiscent of the *risqué* novels being smuggled in from Paris – Beardsley's prescient fear was that having Wilde associated with it might bring misfortune. Ever cheeky, Beardsley asked Max Beerbohm to send in a gently satirical portrait of Wilde, 'A Peep into the Past', for the first number, but in the end, Max contributed a piece on cosmetics instead. When the publication came out, Oscar found Max's piece 'quite delightfully wrong and fascinating'. And as he gloated in a letter to Bosie Douglas, who disliked Beardsley,

'The *Yellow Book* has appeared. It is dull and loathsome, a great failure. I am so glad.'

Robbie, meanwhile, got a reprieve from Davos. It was decided that he should accompany Aleck and their brother-in-law Charles Jones on a visit to Canada, where they would join Mary Jones. Being almost entirely dependent on his mother's allowance for survival, Robbie had little choice in the matter. Besides, it would give him an opportunity to rediscover his roots, as well as spend time with the Joneses, who had been such a comfort during past periods of crisis. After a short spell in London at the beginning of 1894, Robbie duly set sail with his family party, thereby missing the next stages in the unfolding drama of Oscar and Bosie. He appears to have had little or no contact with England while he was away, being kept busy with family visits and sight-seeing. He was quite happy to play the role of dutiful relative for a few weeks, knowing that he would be freer to rejoin more stimulating companions when Aleck and he returned to London in June.

As for Bosie, when his assignment in Egypt was over, he returned to Europe, settling first in Paris. From there he bombarded Oscar, who had hoped to break with him definitively, with entreaties to come and join him. When Oscar failed to respond, Bosie went so far as to telegraph Constance Wilde, begging her to get her husband to write. Not for the first or last time, there was a reconciliation; Bosie returned to England and the fateful relationship took up where it had left off. This was despite the increasingly virulent campaign by the Marquess of Queensberry to keep his son and Oscar Wilde apart. The Marquess wrote to Bosie, informing him that he had heard 'on good authority, though this may be false' that Constance was petitioning to divorce Oscar for sodomy and other crimes. 'If I thought the actual thing was true, and it became public property,' he continued, 'I should be quite justified in shooting him at sight.' There was no basis to the rumour, and Bosie laughed off his father's threat, replying with the terse and inflammatory telegram, 'What a funny little man you are.' Oscar was dismayed, realizing that this would act like a red rag to a bull. Yet he was unable to remonstrate effectively with Bosie, who reacted to any criticism with angry defiance. The ensuing rows only served to upset Oscar, who by now made no secret of the emotional hold Bosie had over him. From Worthing, where he took rooms with his family that summer, to write his fourth and last comedy, *The Importance of Being Earnest*, he wrote to his beloved:

> . . . Dear, dear boy, you are more to me than any one of them has any idea; you are the atmosphere of beauty through which I see life; you are the incarnation of all lovely things. When we are out of tune, all colour goes from things for me, but we are never really out of tune.
> I think of you day and night . . .[6]

Inevitably Bosie came down on a visit to Worthing, though this meant that Oscar's work was once more interrupted. Oscar had made some friends among local lads on the beach, who now became Bosie's playmates as well. Constance Wilde was not best pleased. As Bosie wrote to Robbie, 'I had great fun, though the last few days the strain of being a bone of contention between Oscar and Mrs Oscar began to make itself felt.' Constance felt that Bosie had changed her husband for the worse. Oscar's obsession with Bosie meant that he often treated Constance callously; Pierre Louÿs was so disgusted by evidence of this while he was on one of his visits to London that he broke off his friendship with Oscar.

Robbie found himself in a difficult position, given his love for Oscar, his affection for Constance, and the strong bond of friendship he had developed with Bosie. The situation was made more acute by the fact that Bosie tended to divide people into two camps: those who were considered to be in favour of him, and those who were in favour of his father; Robbie had to tread very warily not to be seen to be wavering towards the enemy camp.

Because the battle Bosie was now waging was as much to spite his father as it was to keep the forbidden relationship with Oscar flourishing, even Oscar often found himself accused of letting the side down by not engaging wholeheartedly in actions calculated to enrage the increasingly deranged Marquess even further. Moreover, when Oscar fell ill with influenza in Brighton, where the two lovers had moved after Worthing, Bosie refused to look after him with the devoted attention Oscar had shown him when he had had flu a few days previously. Indeed, Bosie stormed out of the lodgings where Oscar lay prostrate, when Oscar pathetically asked him to fetch some lemonade. Bosie then checked himself into the Grand Hotel, leaving the bedridden Oscar to his own devices. On 16 October, his fortieth birthday, Oscar received a letter from Bosie, enclosing the bill from the Grand, and concluding chillingly, 'When you are not on your pedestal you are not interesting. The next time you are ill I will go away at once.'

Cut to the quick, Oscar decided there and then to break forever with Bosie. He planned to go to see his old friend Sir George Lewis – who had been engaged by Queensberry to act for him – to ask him to inform the Marquess that he would never see his son again. But as Fate would have it, as he waited at Brighton for the train to take him to London on 19 October, he read in the newspaper an account of the death of Bosie's eldest brother, Francis, Viscount Drumlanrig, while out shooting. A verdict of accidental death was recorded by the coroner, but there were strong suspicions that he had committed suicide, like several of his recent ancestors. The Marquess of Queensberry had been hounding Drumlanrig with almost as much vigour as he had been chasing Bosie, having come to the conclusion, on rather scant evidence, that Drumlanrig was having a homosexual relationship with his employer, Lord Rosebery, who had become Prime Minister in March, upon Gladstone's retirement. As he read the newspaper article about Drumlanrig's death, Oscar lost all of his resolve to end his destructive affair with Bosie, and immediately on his arrival in London sent loving condolences. As he communicated a few days later to the writer and criminologist George Ives,

> I have been so upset by the terrible tragedy of poor Drumlanrig's death . . . It is a great blow to Bosie: the first noble sorrow of his boyish life: the wings of the angel of Death have almost touched him: their purple shadow lies across his way, for the moment: I am perforce the sharer of his pain.[7]

Soon the two were inseparable again, Bosie more thrilled than disturbed by reports that Queensberry was going around London, bursting into restaurants and hotels, a riding whip in his hand, ready to thrash them both if he found them together. The Marquess's homophobia was taking on a paranoid aspect; as he informed anyone ready to listen, the 'queers' were taking over the country, and his boy had to be rescued from 'that cocksucker' Oscar Wilde.

To add fuel to the flame, a new literary magazine *The Chameleon* appeared in Oxford, edited by an undergraduate called Jack Bloxam, who rather took Oscar's fancy. *The Chameleon*'s first issue was even more overtly homosexual than Alfred Douglas's *Spirit Lamp* had been, including poems by Douglas and a short story by Bloxam himself, 'The Priest and the Acolyte', about a priest who serves a poisoned chalice of wine to a boy communicant and himself after their sexual affair has been discovered. The offending publication was added to the evidence that the Marquess of Queensberry was collecting about Wilde and his circle, along with statements from rent-boys, that Oscar and his kind were corrupters of youth.

Dismayed by the way Bosie was monopolizing Oscar's affections once more, Constance appealed to Robbie to use his influence to make Oscar understand the responsibilities he had towards her and the children. At Christmas 1894, Robbie sent her flowers and presents for the boys. And when Oscar and Bosie suddenly went off to Algiers in February, to enjoy some winter sunshine and the compliant Arab boys, it was to Robbie that Constance turned to ask him to contact Oscar to see if he would send her some money to help with household expenses. Robbie telegraphed back that he could send her £5 himself, if she needed it. Now installed at Babbacombe Cliff with Lady Mount-Temple, Constance replied, 'you are a real friend, such as I knew you always to be! If I do want anything I will let you know, and you shall let me have the £5, but at this moment I have no expenses and can well wait until Oscar returns.'

Oscar's trip to Algeria was yet another act of folly instigated by Bosie, who decided that the two of them needed an adventure between the opening night of *An Ideal Husband* at the Haymarket, on 3 January 1895, and that of *The Importance of Being Earnest*, at the St James's, on 14 February. As Oscar wrote ambiguously to his great friend Ada Leverson, on the eve of his departure, 'Yes: I fly to Algiers with Bosie tomorrow. I begged him to let me stay to rehearse, but so beautiful is his nature that he declined at once.' Algeria was popular as a destination for Europeans with a taste for sex tourism. The French-run hotels and the food were good. A clan of young local girls known as the

Oulad Nail traditionally prostituted themselves to earn money for their dowries, while numerous Arab boys were more than willing to obtain quick release with generous foreign gentlemen. As Oscar wrote to Robbie,

> There is a great deal of beauty here. The Kabyle boys are quite lovely. At first we had some difficulty in procuring a proper civilized guide. But now it is all right, and Bosie and I have taken to haschish: it is quite exquisite: three puffs of smoke and then peace and love. Bosie wakes up at night and cries like a child for the best haschish.
>
> We have been on excursion into the mountains of Kabylia – full of village people with fauns. Several shepherds fluted on reeds for us. We were followed by lovely brown things from forest to forest. The beggars here have profiles, so the problem of poverty is easily solved.
>
> . . . Bosie sends his love, so do I.[8]

In fact, Bosie became so enamoured of one of the 'little brown things' that he set off in pursuit, abandoning Oscar, who spent his last few days in Algeria in the company of André Gide, who was there coincidentally. When the time came to leave for London, Oscar declared prophetically, 'I have been as far as I can in my own direction. I can't go any further. Now *something* must happen.'

The 'something' would clearly be instigated by the Marquess of Queensberry. The question was when and how he would strike. The management of the St James's Theatre, where *The Importance of Being Earnest* was in its final rehearsals, got wind of a plan by the Marquess to disrupt the play's opening night, as he had done with a play by Tennyson many years before. Accordingly, his ticket was cancelled, and he was refused entry; instead, accompanied by one of the prize-fighters he liked to have along as a menacing presence, he prowled around in the snow outside the theatre before leaving a bouquet of what one wit described as phallic vegetables at the stage door. Inside, the mood was electric. Robbie had already seen the play with Ada Leverson at its dress rehearsal, so he knew what the likely reaction would be to what has subsequently become known as the most perfect comedy of manners in the English theatre. With very few exceptions, such as Bernard Shaw, the critics were as ecstatic as the paying members of the glittering audience. Bosie, by now making his way back from Algiers, was not present to share Oscar's St Valentine Day's triumph, unlike Robbie. The success of the play resonated across the Atlantic, with the *New York Times* declaring, 'Oscar Wilde may be said to have at last, and by a single stroke, put his enemies under his feet.'

The Marquess of Queensberry, on the other hand, was incensed by Wilde's moment of glory. On the afternoon of 18 February he called in at Oscar's Club, the Albemarle, where he left a visiting card with the hall porter. On it was scrawled the almost illegible message, 'To Oscar Wilde posing Somdomite [sic]'. The Marquess's spelling and grammar tended to go haywire when he was really upset. As Oscar was not in the club at the time, the porter put the card in an envelope where it awaited its addressee for the next ten days.

Oscar meanwhile was staying at the Avondale Hotel in Piccadilly; even Constance, who was still in Torquay, did not know he was there, and had to ask Robbie for his address. Since the autumn of 1894, Robbie had effectively become Oscar's part-time secretary, fetching letters from Tite Street, and answering some of the more urgent correspondence. Bosie moved into the Avondale when he arrived back in London, but Oscar put his foot down when he insisted on bringing a young man to stay with him, at Oscar's expense. Petulantly, Bosie then moved out, subjecting Oscar to a stream of recriminatory notes over the next few days.

Oscar was thus in a tense mood when he eventually called at the Albemarle Club and was handed the Marquess of Queensberry's card. The missive had exactly the effect its originator intended. For Oscar, it was the final straw, causing him to write despairingly to Robbie, in a note that was sent round by messenger to Robbie's rooms in Hornton Street:

Dearest Bobbie, Since I saw you something has happened. Bosie's father has left a card at my club with hideous words on it. I don't see anything now but a criminal prosecution. My whole life seems ruined by this man. The tower of ivory is assailed by the foul thing. On the sand is my life spilt. I don't know what to do. If you could come here at 11.30 please do so tonight. I mar your life by trespassing ever on your love and kindness. I have asked Bosie to come tomorrow.[9]

It was significant that it was Robbie to whom Oscar instinctively turned, as a source of advice as well as of support. For all Oscar's philandering, and his wide network of professional and social contacts, Robbie still occupied a key place in his life. It was equally significant that Oscar wanted to hear Robbie's calm appraisal of the situation before being subjected to Bosie's inevitably emotional response. But in that he was thwarted, for when Robbie arrived at the Avondale Hotel that night, as requested, Bosie was already there. Robbie urged that Oscar should take no action, but Bosie saw this as an opportunity to put his father not just in the dock but in prison.

Legal advice was of course needed. Oscar sent a note to Sir George Lewis, who had to decline his services, as he was still acting for the Marquess of Queensberry (though later he reportedly said privately that had he been free to advise, then he would have told Oscar to tear up Queensberry's card and forget about it). As second-best, Oscar then turned to a solicitor recommended by Robbie, Charles Humphreys, who specialized in criminal cases. Oscar and Bosie went round to see Humphreys the following morning. Ignoring Robbie's suggestion that they should be open with Humphreys about their relationship, they insisted repeatedly that there were no grounds to Queensberry's accusations. In that case, Humphreys declared, the Marquess could be successfully prosecuted. Any qualms that Oscar had on financial grounds were quashed when Bosie said that his mother Lady Queensberry and his surviving brother Percy – who also hated their father – would cover the costs of the action. Accordingly, Oscar, Bosie and Humphreys went round to Marlborough Street Police Station where they asked for Queensberry's arrest. The Marquess was brought to Marlborough police court and was committed for trial.

For most of March 1895, Oscar and Bosie tried to live life as normally as possible. They took Constance to see a performance of *The Importance of Being Earnest*, and later went for a week's holiday to Monte Carlo. While Bosie played the tables, Oscar sat around pensively; after a few days, the hotel management asked them to leave, as other guests were scandalized by their presence. Back in London, true friends such as Ada Leverson and her husband Ernest rallied round, but many others distanced themselves. Constance stopped going out of the house so as to avoid any embarrassing snubs.

While Queensberry's investigators were busy assembling damning evidence about Oscar's lifestyle over the past three or four years – including a list of the boys he had patronized through Alfred Taylor – Oscar started rounding up supporters who would be prepared to appear in court. In his capacity as a well-known Literary Editor, Frank Harris agreed to testify that *The Picture of Dorian Gray* was not an immoral book. As

Queensberry was planning to enter a plea of justification for his alleged libel, Oscar was anxious to prove that neither in word nor deed had he attempted to corrupt youth. But when Oscar informed Harris that indiscreet letters to boys might be introduced as evidence by the defence, Harris realized that the affair was far more serious than Oscar had been letting on. Given the climate of the day, and the fact that a jury would tend to sympathize with the Marquess of Queensberry's desire to protect his son from undesirable influences, however extreme his measures, Harris believed that Oscar would lose his libel action. Over lunch at the Café Royal, at which Bernard Shaw was also present, Harris advised that Oscar should drop the case and leave for Paris immediately, taking Constance with him. On the Continent he would be safe from prosecution, and could attempt to defend his name and reputation by letters to British newspapers from a distance. Shaw concurred. At that point, Bosie Douglas arrived. He flew into a temper when he heard what Harris was suggesting and stormed out, Oscar sheepishly following in his wake.

When Queensberry's lawyers submitted his Plea of Justification, prior to the trial, it listed fifteen separate counts involving a dozen boys with whom Oscar was alleged to have committed sodomy. These included the young blackmailer Alfred Wood, the clerk at the Bodley Head, Edward Shelley, and one of the Worthing beach-boys, Alfonso Conway. As expected, the alleged immorality of *Dorian Gray*, as well as maxims Wilde had published in *The Chameleon*, also figured.

The court in the Old Bailey where the case opened on 3 April 1895 was packed. In the gallery were many of Oscar's friends and supporters, including Robbie. They laughed out loud when Oscar made witty remarks in defence of his work – including some of his gushing letters and flamboyant remarks to boys – prompting the judge to threaten to clear the court. But the defence could scent blood almost from the first moment when Oscar stupidly, vainly, lied about his age. He adopted a manner of almost supercilious aesthetic superiority, arguing that philistines could hardly be expected to appreciate the finer sensibilities of the artist. His cross-examination by Queensberry's barrister, Edward Carson (coincidentally a former fellow student of Oscar's at Trinity College, Dublin), was relentless. Wilde had been consorting with 'some of the most immoral characters in London', Carson declared; people like Alfred Taylor and some of the rent-boys cited in the defence's evidence. Oscar maintained that dealing with valets and grooms and others of lowly station enabled him to appreciate better the diverse nature of the human condition, as well as providing him with opportunities to lend a helping hand to those less fortunate than himself. However, any lingering doubts anyone might have had about his true motivation were dissipated when Carson suddenly asked him if he had kissed a lad called Walter Grainger, who for a while had worked as Bosie's servant. 'Oh, dear no!' Oscar retorted. 'He was a peculiarly plain boy. He was, unfortunately, extremely ugly. I pitied him for it.'

Next, Carson announced that he was going to call various boys who would testify to 'shocking acts' committed with Oscar. Aware that the case was going irrevocably against his client, Wilde's barrister, Sir Edward Clarke, realized that the prosecution had to be abandoned before things got worse. He tried to negotiate an agreement with the defence, but Edward Carson insisted that the entire Plea of Justification be allowed. That is what the judge directed the jury to rule. There was applause and cheering from Queensberry's supporters in court as the Marquess left, not only a free man, but vindicated in his belief that it was in the public interest that Oscar Wilde's sins be publicly acknowledged. Aware that a criminal prosecution of Wilde was now inevitable, he declared, 'I will not prevent your flight, but if you take my son with you, I will shoot you like a dog.'

After consultations with his lawyers, Oscar repaired to the Holborn Viaduct Hotel, along with Robbie, Bosie and Percy Douglas. There he wrote a short letter to the *Evening News*, stating that it would have been impossible for him to prove his case without putting Alfred Douglas in the witness-box against his father, something he was not prepared to do, though Bosie had been keen. 'Rather than put him in so painful a position I determined to retire from the case, and to bear on my own shoulders whatever ignominy and shame might result from my prosecuting Lord Queensberry,' Oscar concluded.

He then sent Robbie off to cash a cheque, and moved to the Cadogan Hotel in Sloane Street, where he was joined by Reggie Turner, who was sufficiently worldly wise to understand the viciousness with which Oscar would be treated from now on. Robbie soon arrived with the money, and both he and Reggie tried in vain to persuade Oscar to catch the afternoon boat-train for Dover, to escape to France. Oscar refused, mumbling repeatedly that it was too late. He sent Robbie to Tite Street, to tell Constance what had happened; she burst into tears and said she, too, hoped Oscar would get away. Back at the hotel, Robbie had to deal with a new visitor, the MP George Wyndham, a cousin of Bosie's, whom Bosie had gone to fetch at the House of Commons. Oscar refused to see him, knowing that he would only add to the pressure to get him to flee. At five o'clock, a newspaper reporter arrived, to inform Oscar that a warrant for his arrest had been issued; the authorities had deliberately delayed matters, to give him a chance to slip away. Firmly planted in his armchair, glass in hand, Oscar declared, 'I shall stay and do my sentence whatever it is.'

Shortly after six, two detectives arrived. 'We have a warrant here, Mr Wilde,' one intoned, 'for your arrest on a charge of committing indecent acts.' Oscar staggered slightly as he rose, as if drunk, then gathered up his overcoat. As the policemen took him down to a waiting cab, he turned to Robbie and asked him to go back to Tite Street, to fetch a change of clothes. Robbie duly set off on his errand, knowing that the tasks ahead would be infinitely greater and more painful.

SIX

Standing by Oscar

WHEN ROBBIE GOT back to Tite Street, he found that Constance had already left with the children, to stay with relatives, away from prying eyes. She had locked the doors of the bedroom and library, which meant that Robbie and Oscar's loyal house-servant Arthur had to break open the bedroom door so that a bag could be packed with Oscar's clothes. Robbie then hurried over to Bow Street police station, where Oscar was being temporarily held before being transferred to Holloway Prison. Robbie was not allowed to see Oscar, nor to leave the clothes. Later, he returned to Tite Street, where Arthur helped him break into the library, in order to remove some of Oscar's personal papers and manuscripts, fearing, correctly, that some of these would prove compromising if they fell into the prosecution's hands. Emotionally drained by the events of the day, and rather than go back to the rooms he shared with More Adey in Hornton Street, he went to his mother's house and broke down in tears.

Three days later, Oscar wrote to More and Robbie jointly from Holloway:

Dear More and Bobbie, Will you tell the Sphinx*, Ernest
*Oscar's pet name for Ada Leverson.

103

Leverson, Mrs Bernard Beere (Church Cottage, Marylebone Road) how deeply touched I am by their affection and kindness.

Inform the committee of the New Travellers Club, and also of the Albemarle, that I resign my membership (Piccadilly and Dover Street).

Bosie is so wonderful. I think of nothing else. I saw him yesterday.

They are kind in their way here, but I have no books, nothing to smoke, and sleep very badly.[1]

Several newspapers mentioned that Robbie had been with Oscar when Wilde was arrested. His own reputation was therefore compromised and his family were worried he might be arrested. Rumours were rife of a forthcoming witch-hunt against known homosexuals, prompting hundreds of gentlemen to leave quietly for the Continent, where some of them would stay for years. Eliza Ross urged her son to do the same but, like Bosie, he wanted to stay to support Oscar in the run-up to his trial. Mrs Ross was only able to change her son's mind when she said she would pay £500 towards Oscar's defence costs if Robbie left. With heavy heart, he crossed the Channel with Reggie Turner and settled into the Hôtel Terminus at the Gare Maritime in Calais, which was as near to England as it was possible to be while still being safe on foreign soil. There they were able to get daily English newspapers brought over on the Dover ferries, the editorials filled with invective against homosexuals in general and Oscar in particular. The French press, in contrast, was mystified why the English apparently considered sodomy a crime second only to murder.

Mindless of any personal risk, Bosie went to visit Oscar daily at Holloway. As Douglas recalled in his *Autobiography*:

The visitor goes into a box rather like the box in a pawnshop. There is a whole row of these boxes, each occupied by a visitor, and opposite, facing each visitor, is the prisoner whom he is visiting. The two sides of visitors and prisoners are separated by a corridor about a yard in width, and a warder paces up and down the corridor. The 'visit' lasts, as far as I can remember, a quarter of an hour. The visitor and the prisoner have to shout to make their voices heard above the voices of the other prisoners and visitors. Nothing more revolting and cruel and deliberately malignant could be devised by human ingenuity. Poor Oscar was rather deaf. He could hardly hear what I said in the babel. He looked at me with tears running down his cheeks and I looked at him.[2]

Despite the distressing conditions, Oscar drew strength from these visits, and the clear evidence of Bosie's current devotion, as he informed the Leversons: 'A slim thing, gold-haired like an angel, stands always by my side. His presence overshadows me. He moves in the gloom like a white flower.' As the days went by, however, Oscar's barrister, Sir Edward Clarke – who had offered to represent him without a fee – became convinced that the 'angel's' continued presence could prejudice the case, so he persuaded Oscar to ask Bosie to go abroad. Bosie explained his sudden departure to newspaper reporters by saying that he had to visit his sick mother in Italy, but in fact, when he left on the morning of 24 April, he only went as far as Calais. There he discovered that Robbie had gone to Rouen, so he telegraphed him to come back, which he did. That same day, in London, there was an unruly creditors' sale of the Wildes' possessions at the Tite Street house, which took place at Queensberry's instigation. Pictures, furniture, china and signed first editions of books by Wilde's friends went for knock-down prices; other things were quite possibly stolen by souvenir-hunters, as they simply disappeared. The losses would have been even greater had Robbie not had the foresight to remove some manuscripts and documents on the day of Oscar's arrest.

In Calais, Robbie, Bosie and Reggie were able to follow day by day the trial that opened at the Old Bailey on the 26th, thanks to the extensive coverage in the newspapers. Oscar was tried alongside Alfred Taylor, the procurer, which could hardly help his case, though Taylor carried himself with great dignity throughout. On the fifth day, when the defence was presenting its case, Oscar responded to hostile cross-examination from the prosecuting counsel by putting forward an eloquent argument for the 'love that dare not speak its name':

> . . . It is beautiful, it is fine, it is the noblest form of affection. There is nothing unnatural about it. It is intellectual, and it repeatedly exists between an elder and a younger man, when the elder man has intellect, and the younger man has all the joy, hope and glamour of life before him. That it should be so the world does not understand. The world mocks at it and sometimes puts one in the pillory for it.[3]

There was spontaneous applause from many of the spectators in the gallery when he finished. Max Beerbohm, who was among them, was deeply impressed and wrote to Reggie Turner that, 'He never had so great a triumph, I am sure.' Several of the jurors were obviously nonplussed by the case, as they failed to reach a verdict on various counts. They were dismissed and a retrial was ordered, for the next session. Perhaps partly because Lord Rosebery's name had been raised with relation to the Wilde affair, and some senior Liberals feared they would lose the forthcoming election if there appeared to be a conspiracy to keep Oscar out of jail, there was a clear direction from on high that nothing should be done to enable the Tories to claim that the case was not being prosecuted vigorously enough. After a few days' delay, Oscar was granted bail, which was put up by Percy Douglas and a sympathetic Anglican clergyman, the Reverend Stewart Headlam. Oscar found sanctuary with the Leversons, having earlier been turned away from a couple of hotels before spending an excruciatingly awkward night at his brother Willie's. Again, he came under pressure from friends to flee. Frank Harris later claimed that he arranged for a yacht to be on standby at Erith in Kent, to smuggle Oscar out of the country. But Oscar refused to go, not just because of the losses this would cause the guarantors of his bail, but also because of a sense of family honour. 'If you stay,' Lady Wilde told him, 'even if you go to prison, you will always be my son. It will make no difference to my affection. But if you go, I will never speak to you again.'

Oscar was heartened by letters from France. Robbie, Bosie and Reggie had left Calais, settling in the more congenial surroundings of Rouen, where both the architecture and the food were better. They were able to make excursions to Dieppe, though Bosie soon became bored, mainly because the casino in Dieppe was closed. He therefore moved on to Paris, taking a young man with him as a companion. He found a hotel where the proprietor asked solicitously after Oscar, and told Bosie he could stay as long as he liked, without worrying about paying the bill. Bosie assured Oscar of his devotion, and urged him to keep up his spirits. In return, Oscar wrote:

> Every great love has its tragedy, and now ours has too, but to have known and loved you with such profound devotion, to have had you for a part of my life, the only part I now consider beautiful, is enough for me. My passion is at a loss for words, but you can understand me, you alone. Our souls were made for one another, and by knowing yours through

love, mine has transcended many evils, understood perfection, and entered into the divine essence of things.[4]

It was just as well that Constance never read this letter, with its implied devaluation of Oscar's relationship with her and the children, let alone of that with Robbie. She called to see her husband at the Leversons and spent two hours vainly trying to persuade him to go abroad, before leaving the house in tears. In the event, it was she who quit the country, to stay with her brother Otho Holland in Switzerland, having sent the boys on ahead with their governess. To protect them from opprobrium, she changed their name to Holland after Oscar's conviction. She never lived in England again.

On all sides, relatives were trying to influence the main players in the Wilde drama, to try to limit the damage. Lady Queensberry, who learned that Bosie was writing self-justifying letters to newspapers in both England and France, as well as telegraphing unwanted advice to Oscar's lawyers, asked Percy Douglas to go over to France to try to calm him down. More Adey was approached to see if he would be prepared to go to stay with Bosie for a while, as a paid companion, to act as a restraining influence. Initially he refused, saying his first loyalty was to Robbie, but later he relented and joined Bosie – an interesting foretaste of the future situation in which mutual friends would have to choose between the two. Eliza Ross was horrified to hear that Robbie and Bosie had been staying together, and insisted that they stay well apart.

It was fortunate for Robbie, in his highly strung state, that he had the calming influence of Reggie Turner to fall back on. Although the two young men had seen quite a bit of each other in London, as members of Oscar's coterie, it was their enforced stay together in France which really forged their friendship. An exact contemporary of Robbie's, Reggie was a literary Jew of uncertain parentage – possibly the illegitimate child of the first Lord Burnham, by an unknown woman. He was physically unprepossessing, but more than made up for this by his brilliant wit, talent for mimicry, spontaneous parody and flights of comic improvization. As Lord David Cecil noted in his biography of Max Beerbohm (who was probably Reggie's greatest friend), Reggie's ability to win admirers while he was up at Merton College, Oxford, was 'not due to his looks; fantastically ugly, with a nut-shaped head, blubbery lips and a huge snout-like nose, he was continually winking and blinking. But he had intelligence and sensibility, a warm, delicate, generous nature, and an extraordinary gift of humour.' Beerbohm considered him the most amusing man he had met in his entire life, and Wilde 'borrowed' several of Reggie's witticisms, with his permission.

Day after day, Robbie and Reggie would chew over the latest developments in the Wilde case, as well as discussing the sometimes contradictory advice they were receiving from their friends in London. Max Beerbohm was urging Reggie's return:

> I am sure it would be much better for you, as I suppose you have been more or less talked about as you were in the Garden of Gethsemane at the supreme moment – Why not show yourself on English territory – I must say I think it rather bad luck that you – a comparatively new friend of Oscar – should have been with him at that unpleasant crisis – Do come back . . .[5]

Wiser counsel came from the more established figure of Edmund Gosse, who intimated to Robbie that he should not even think about trying to come home yet, as it would take a while for the scandal to die down.

> I am very glad indeed to hear from you, because I wanted to write to you and hate sending off letters to vague addresses.

The recent intolerable events have vexed my soul – mainly (I confess) on your account, my regard for you turning what would else (perhaps) have been comedy, or satiric drama, into pure tragedy.

Now the great thing is to forget. Your action throughout, so far as I understand it, has been Quixotic and silly but honourable. In this dark world no one can do more than walk by the light of his conscience. If it is any pleasure for you to know it, you preserve all our regard (my wife's and mine), and in future, calmer times we shall both rejoice to see you and give you any support we can, if ever you want support. I miss your charming company, in which I have always delighted, and we all miss it, for you are a favourite with every member of this family. I would say to you – be calm, be reasonable, turn for consolation to the infinite resources of literature, which, to your great good fortune, are open to you more than to most men. Write to me when you feel inclined, and however busy I am I will write in reply, and in a more happy season you must come back, to be truly welcomed in this house.

My wife unites with me in joy that you have written to us, and in the expression of true and warm sympathy.[6]

The one thing Robbie could not do, however, was forget; neither his love for Oscar, nor the anguish he now felt at Oscar's suffering. The second trial opened on 20 May, in front of Mr Justice Sir Alfred Wills. For five days, much of the same evidence and arguments from the first trial were rehearsed again, though this time the outcome was different. The jury – whose foreman interrupted the judge's summing-up to ask whether a warrant had ever been put out for Alfred Douglas's arrest (which it had not) – took only a few minutes to find Oscar guilty on all counts except the one relating to the publishers' clerk Edward Shelley.

The judge then passed sentence on Oscar and Alfred Taylor, to whom he declared:

> It is no use for me to address you. People who can do these things must be dead to all sense of shame, and one cannot hope to produce any effect upon them. It is the worst case I have ever tried. That you, Taylor, kept a kind of male brothel it is impossible to doubt. And that you, Wilde, have been the centre of a circle of extensive corruption of the most hideous kind among young men, it is equally impossible to doubt.
>
> I shall, under the circumstances, be expected to pass the severest sentence that the law allows. In my judgement it is totally inadequate for such a case as this. The sentence of the Court is that each of you be imprisoned and kept to hard labour for two years.[7]

There was an isolated cry of 'Shame!' from the gallery, but as Oscar was bundled out of the court, mumbling 'My God! My God!', cheering and dancing broke out in the street outside, where a gaggle of female whores had gathered. Queensberry held a celebratory dinner, and the *Daily Telegraph* trumpeted, in keeping with the spirit of the time, 'Open the windows! Let in the fresh air.' Equally triumphantly, the *News of the World* pronounced that 'The aesthetic cult, in its nasty form, is over.'

By bitter coincidence, Oscar's sentencing fell on Robbie's twenty-sixth birthday. To make matters worse, news had arrived that his brother Jack's wife Minnie had died in Davos. Her body was shipped over to England for burial near Shrewsbury on 28 May. Robbie was summoned home by the family, to share in Jack's bereavement, and as it now seemed that he was in no further danger, with Oscar in jail, they decided he might as well stay for the time being, though keeping a low profile. Thus began a period of his life when he shuttled to and fro between England and the Continent.

Before Wilde's downfall, Robbie had started receiving a number of commissions to write the sort of whimsical, light-hearted pieces he was rather good at. Aubrey Beardsley had asked him to do some occasional verse for a publication called *Pick-me-up*, and the publisher William Heinemann asked for a limerick – 'having heard so much of your amazing capacity for making these' – to appear in an 1896 Almanac that he was preparing, adding cautiously that 'it must be strictly remembered that the book is to be allowed in the drawing-room'. Now, however, Robbie was in no mood to compose comic verse, nor is it likely that anything with his name under it would have been published in any mainstream English publication at this time. Even Aubrey Beardsley, who was not gay, and had certainly not been involved in corrupting young men (other than through his art, perhaps) found himself expelled from *The Yellow Book*'s team. He never really forgave Oscar Wilde for the way his own brief career was set back merely through guilt by association.

Devoid of literary outlets, and unable to settle down to months of serious reading, as Edmund Gosse had suggested, Robbie instead identified a cause that would not only keep him occupied, but would also, if it succeeded, be of immense practical assistance to Oscar and his family, namely to sort out Oscar's finances before he came out of prison. That way, in principle, Oscar would be able to start with a clean slate and deal with the rights of his plays and other literary works in a way that an undischarged bankrupt could not do. The threat of bankruptcy was indeed looming, as on 21 June the Marquess of Queensberry, not satisfied with having sent Oscar to purgatory for two years, destroyed his household and ensured that no play by Wilde could be staged in England for years, filed a petition in the Bankruptcy Court, requesting a Receiving Order for the costs awarded against Oscar at the time of the libel action. The Order was duly issued the following month. The first public hearing was scheduled for 24 September, which gave Robbie time to start trying to assemble funds from those friends who still harboured generous feelings towards the disgraced play- wright. Several had already contributed to Oscar's legal costs; others were simply not in a financial position to help out. Robbie reckoned he needed to obtain pledges of around £2,000 (about £120,000 in today's money) to cover the most pressing debts, although Oscar's total outstanding liabilities were over £3,500. Among those people who Robbie now approached was Oscar Browning, to whom he explained:

> No names of subscribers will be *made public* so none of the charitably disposed need fear lest the appearance of their names might give the impression that they were in any way connected with Oscar Wilde or sympathized with him except as one who has suffered or will suffer for the next two years the most terrible and cruel torture known to English justice and Anglo-Saxon hypocrisy. Several of those who have con- tributed most generously were his severest critics and outspoken opponents prior to his trial.[8]

At the 24 September hearing, Robbie put in an appearance in the corridor of the Bankruptcy Court, raising his hat in a gesture of respect and loving support as Oscar was brought in from Wandsworth Prison (to which he had been moved after spells in Holloway and Pentonville). Seeing Robbie was a boost to Oscar's shattered morale. He had had a distressing visit from Constance only three days previously. She had travelled over specially from Switzerland, largely to inform him that she had decided to ignore her lawyers' advice that she should divorce him. As she told William Wordworth's great-grandson, the journalist Robert Sherard, a heterosexual admirer of Oscar's who had been in Paris when the Wildes honeymooned there, but now lived near Wandsworth, 'It was indeed awful, more so than I had any conception it could be. I could not see him and I could not touch him . . . He has been mad for the last three years, and he says that if he saw Lord A. he would kill him.'

In the right circumstances, love can quickly turn to hate. And over the five months since he had last seen his 'golden boy', Oscar had had much time for reflection. It was not just that prison was so much worse than he had imagined, with the hideous punishment of the treadmill, the inadequate food, the plank bed on which it was impossible to sleep properly and the prohibition on speaking to other prisoners. Or even his realization that it was largely because of Bosie's vendetta against his father that he, Oscar, had to undergo such torment. In addition there were the reports Oscar had been getting of Bosie's behaviour in France. He had caused a scandal in Le Havre, where he had been staying with More Adey, by engaging a couple of pretty young boat-boys to serve on a boat he had hired. And he insisted on writing articles and poems for the French press which he considered to be in Oscar's defence, but were rather exercises in self-justification. He had agreed to write an article for the *Mercure de France*, giving his version of the events leading to Oscar's downfall, in which he wanted to quote some of Oscar's love-letters. Incredibly, he wrote to the prison governor asking him to approach Oscar for permission to use them, which Oscar angrily refused. Even a petition Bosie sent to Queen Victoria in June, begging clemency for his lover, probably did more harm than good. A request he sent to be allowed to visit Oscar in prison was turned down flat by the authorities, which Bosie chose to interpret as a personal insult. He could not understand why people seemed to be turning against him.

Even Robbie, who tried to see the best in Bosie at this stage, felt he could have done more to help Oscar out financially. Though Bosie did not have substantial funds himself – and quickly spent whatever he received – his mother and his brother Percy did. Bosie was well aware of the bankruptcy proceedings and managed to get a message to Oscar through a solicitor's clerk who took Oscar's depositions. The clerk startled Oscar by suddenly saying, 'Prince Fleur de Lys wishes to be remembered to you.' When Oscar stared blankly for a moment, the man went on, 'The gentleman is abroad at present.' Oscar laughed sardonically at the grotesque inappropriateness of the message, contrasting it most unfavourably with Robbie's noble gesture in the corridor.

The hearing was adjourned until 12 November. Even though Robbie had indeed managed to raise enough money to cover the main debts, suddenly last-minute creditors arrived with a further £400 in demands. There was no way the money could be found at short notice, so regretfully Robbie agreed that the bankruptcy must go ahead, meaning that Oscar's affairs were put into the hands of the official receiver. Oscar was in a poor state when the news was broken to him, as he had spent some of the intervening weeks in the prison infirmary with dysentery. Robbie was able to spend a little time with him in a private room at the court, sadly noting his dishevelled appearance. In a touch that would have amused Oscar in better days, a journalist for the *Labour Leader* who was present at the court wrote that the prison authorities had cut his hair 'in a shocking way'.

Oscar's humiliation was still not yet complete. Just over a week after his bankruptcy was declared, he was moved from Wandsworth to Reading Gaol. This involved a change of trains at Clapham Junction, but the connection was not immediate. For half an hour, early on a rainy afternoon, he had to stand on the platform, in his shabby prison uniform, handcuffed to a guard. As suburban trains came and went, he was widely recognized, and a crowd gathered, laughing and jeering at him and spitting in his face. As he wrote later in *De Profundis*, 'For a year after that was done to me, I wept every day at the same hour and for the same space of time.'

By now, Bosie was living in Italy. After a month in Sorrento, he moved to Capri, where he took out a year's lease on the Villa Caso in the Strada Postano. He invited Robbie to come out to stay with him, not just to sample the local boys, for whom his namesake, the Scots novelist Norman Douglas, developed such a taste at almost exactly the same time, but also to discuss Oscar. The visit, which lasted over two months, was not a great success. After Christmas, the weather turned terrible, so much so that they decamped to Naples in mid-January. Worse, though, was what Robbie found to be Bosie's completely self-centred perception of Oscar's predicament. Underlining this, Bosie wrote to More Adey, from Capri, on 25 November:

Of course, I *know everything* and I know from what I have heard from Bobbie that my instinct was right and that Oscar has changed about me. I am writing to you now, dear More, unknown to Bobbie, to beg you to do what you can for me with Oscar. If only you could make him understand that though he is in prison he is still the court, the jury, the judge of my life and that I am waiting hoping for some sign that I have to go on living. There is nobody to play my cards in England, nobody to say anything for me, and Oscar depends *entirely* on what is said to him, and they all seem to be my enemies . . .

I am not in prison but I think I suffer as much as Oscar, in fact more, just as I am sure he would have suffered more if he had been free and I in prison. Please tell him that . . .[9]

Robbie had to leave Naples in late January to be back in London in time for his sister Lizzie's wedding to a young doctor, Morgan Blake. On 23 February. he was able to accompany Ernest Leverson on a visit to Reading Gaol, to see Oscar. It was a difficult occasion for all concerned. Just four days previously, Constance had again come over from Switzerland personally to break the news to him of his mother's death two weeks before. This time, she had been allowed to kiss him and comfort him and they had talked of the children. It was agreed that she would grant him an income of £200 a year upon his release, and that he would get a third of his life interest in her marriage settlement were she to predecease him. By the time Robbie and Ernest Leverson came to see him, however, Oscar was worrying about the practicalities of the arrangements. Robbie tried to reassure him that, together with More Adey, he and Ernest would ensure that the best possible conditions would await his release from prison.

Death then struck Robbie's family on 7 March; his brother-in-law Charles Jones passed away, at the age of fifty-five, leaving Mary a widow with eight children. Robbie suddenly found his responsibilities as uncle greatly increased. Having so often enjoyed the Joneses' hospitality in the past, there was no way he could shirk his duty, even though he had other pressing things on his mind. Mary did not approve of the amount of attention he was giving to Oscar's affairs, or indeed of many of his acquaintances, but Robbie was by now a past master at keeping different compartments of his life separate and of fulfilling conflicting roles as best he could.

He had a second chance to visit Oscar, in May 1896, in the company of Robert Sherard. Oscar complained that in cold weather, his ear ached and bled a little, following a fall in the prison chapel at Wandsworth. He was also suffering from anaemia and gout, though he said he was sleeping better at

Reading than he had been at Wandsworth. His main fear, he told Robbie, was that he was going mad, and he wanted to know what Robbie thought. Robbie recounted the visit at great length in a letter to More Adey, giving the clearest picture that exists of Oscar halfway through his sentence. Even a short extract gives a harrowing impression of just how deep Oscar had sunk:

> He is much thinner, is now clean shaven so that his emaciated condition is more apparent. His face is dull brick colour. (I fancy from working in the garden). His eyes were horribly vacant, and I noticed that he had lost a great deal of hair (this when he turned to go and stood in the light). He always had great quantities of thick hair, but there is now a bald patch on the crown. It is also streaked with white and grey . . . The remarkable part of the interview was that Oscar hardly talked at all except to ask if there were any chance of his being let out, what the attitude of the press and public would be, as to whether any of the present Government* would be favourably disposed to him. He cried the whole time and when we asked *him* to talk more he said he had nothing to say and wanted to hear *us* talk. That as you know is very unlike Oscar.[10]

Oscar complained several times that the prison authorities treated him cruelly; the doctor was particularly unkind. He was forbidden pencil and paper, except for writing a strict quota of letters, though he was allowed to read; the problem was that he had already exhausted the meagre stock of the prison library. He made several requests to Robbie for books – including Chaucer, Dante and Pater – if permission to receive them could be obtained. When Robbie mentioned that Alfred Douglas was planning to bring out a volume of poems in France, and hoped

*The Conservatives had won the 1895 election.

to dedicate it to Oscar, Oscar growled, 'I would rather not hear about that *just now*.' The following day, he used up one of his quota of letters to write to Robbie unequivocally:

> You said that Douglas was going to dedicate a volume of poems to me. Will you write at once to him and say he must not do anything of the kind. I could not accept or allow such a dedication. The proposal is revolting and grotesque. Also, he has unfortunately in his possession a number of letters of mine. I wish him to at once hand over all these without exception to you; I will ask you to seal them up. In case I die here you will destroy them. In case I survive I will destroy them myself . . .
>
> Also, Douglas has some things I gave him: books and jewellery. I wish them to be handed over to you – for me . . .
>
> In writing to Douglas you had better quote my letter fully and frankly, so that he should have no loophole of escape. Indeed he cannot possibly refuse. He has ruined my life – that should content him.[11]

Robbie can have evinced little pleasure at passing on this message exactly as requested. Nor would he have been surprised by the tone of hurt from the flabbergasted Bosie when he received it. Bosie said he would withdraw his book, even at this late stage, as he would not wish to publish it without the dedication to Oscar. But he had no intention of surrendering Oscar's letters. 'Possession of these letters and the recollections they may give me, even if they can give me no hope, will perhaps prevent me from putting an end to a life which has now no *raison d'être*.' In fact, he did publish his book of poems, after a few months' delay, without the dedication.

Trying to stay on the right side of both Oscar and Bosie was more than even Robbie's talent for friendship and diplomacy could manage. He ended up upsetting both, at least for a while. By faithfully conveying Oscar's feelings to Bosie, he was increasingly seen by Bosie as hostile to him. But Robbie also began to alienate Oscar in the way that he defended the interests of Constance and the children. Paranoia is not meant to be infectious. But it is as if Bosie had transmitted it to Oscar, who over the coming months became convinced that Robbie, More Adey and Ernest Leverson, in varying degrees, were siding with Constance and trying to deprive him of what he was entitled to. The reasons for Oscar's mental degeneration are not hard to find, and Robbie tried to be understanding. At times, though, it must have felt as though the weight of the world was being thrust on his shoulders. It was not just Oscar and Bosie and his own sister Mary who needed support. Out of the blue, Ellen Beardsley suddenly called on Robbie to rescue her son Aubrey.

Beardsley had been on the Continent since February, first in Paris, where he had seen the première of Wilde's *Salomé*, produced by Aurelien Lugné-Poë at the Théâtre de l'Oeuvre. Putting on the play was a slap in the face for British hypocrisy, and news of its production was one of the few cheerful things Oscar had to mull over. Beardsley found Paris conducive for work, his main project at present being a series of drawings on the theme 'The Rape of the Lock'. But when the publisher Leonard Smithers arrived, en route for Brussels, Aubrey decided on the spur of the moment to accompany him. At first things went well in the Belgian capital, and Aubrey became involved with a girl called Rayon, but then his health gave way. He suffered a number of haemorrhages and had to be confined to bed. He still managed to do some work and his spirits rose when his sister Mabel came over briefly to nurse him. When his tubercular lungs were showing signs of improvement, the two of them were even able to go out for meals nearby. A Belgian doctor subjected him to an unpleasant but seemingly effective treatment of 'blisters'. He was forbidden to eat fish or drink wine – the latter a particularly trying prohibition – and by early May, he felt he was probably well enough to travel back to England, if someone could come over to fetch him. Mabel had long since returned home, however, and was by now tied up with a theatrical engagement. So Ellen Beardsley turned to Robbie. She had great faith in Robbie's practical skills and told him that Aubrey listened to him in a way that he never listened to her. Much as he wished to help, Robbie had to decline, because of his obligations to Oscar and to his family, which meant that Mrs Beardsley had to go to Brussels herself. When she had got Aubrey safely back, and installed him at Crowborough, Sussex, Robbie went to stay with him for a few days.

It is perhaps not surprising that under all the accumulated stress, Robbie's own health should suffer. The accident he had had with a cricket ball at his preparatory school had caused permanent damage to one of his kidneys. He was increasingly in pain and suffered intermittent fevers. After much consultation it was decided that only an operation to remove the damaged organ would bring him relief. It was not a decision to take lightly, as the operation itself could have proved fatal. One of London's top surgeons, Sir Frederick Treves, founder of the British Red Cross Society and an acknowledged pioneer in improved ways of dealing with cases of appendicitis, was chosen to operate. In preparation, Robbie wrote his will, put his affairs in order, and mentally prepared himself for the possibility of death.

SEVEN

An Uncomfortable Triangle

FOR SEVERAL WEEKS following the removal of his kidney, Robbie's life hung in the balance. Sir Frederick Treves was not at all sure he would pull through. The crisis drew Robbie and his mother even closer together than they had been in the past. It was therefore taken for granted that once the worst danger was over, in mid-July 1896, he would go to recuperate at the house she now occupied at 11 Upper Phillimore Gardens in Kensington. The combination of Eliza Ross's care and Robbie's religious faith undoubtedly enabled him to recover. Even in his weakest moments, Robbie could gain strength from prayer. His Catholic convictions had solidified since his boyhood continental travels with his mother. In 1894, he had formally converted. Interestingly, he found it considerably easier to reconcile his religion with his sexuality than did several of the other future Catholic converts in his circle, including Alfred Douglas, as Robbie never really thought of homosexuality as a sin, in the way that the Church unambiguously taught.

Oscar Wilde considered the devout side to Robbie's nature amusing as well as admirable. In happier days, he dubbed him 'St Robert of Phillimore, Lover and Martyr', describing him, with tongue in cheek, as 'a saint known in *Hagiographia* for his extraordinary power, not in resisting, but in supplying temptations to others. This he did in the solitude of great cities, to

123

which he retired at the comparatively early age of eight.' To Ada Leverson, Oscar recounted an associated fairy-tale:

> There was a certain saint, who was called Saint Robert of Phillimore. Every night, while the sky was yet black, he would rise from his bed and, falling on his knees, pray to God that He, of His great bounty, would cause the sun to rise and make bright the earth. And always, when the sun rose, Saint Robert knelt again and thanked God that this miracle had been vouchsafed. Now, one night, Saint Robert, wearied by the vast number of more than usually good deeds he had done that day, slept so soundly that when he awoke the sun had already risen, and the earth was already bright. For a few moments Saint Robert looked grave and troubled, but presently he fell down on his knees and thanked God that, despite his neglectfulness of His servant, He had yet caused the sun to rise and make bright the earth.[1]

Towards the end of August 1896, Eliza and Aleck Ross took Robbie to stay at Margate, in the hope that sea air would assist his recuperation. Yet a full month later, he was still looking very much under the weather, as More Adey reported in a letter to Oscar in Reading Gaol, dated 23 September:

> Robbie is still at the sea, with his brother and mother, who has taken a house there for him. She sends you kind messages saying she often thinks of you and prays for your welfare. Robbie is going on well, the doctors say, but he suffers a great deal of dyspepsia which affects his spirits very much. You know how much he thinks and feels for you. He looks very ill still. He had his hair cut very short when he was at his worst and, owing to his continued weakness, it has not yet grown again and is very thin.[2]

Oscar's own situation had improved considerably over the summer. Although the authorities remained deaf to pleas from Bosie Douglas and others to grant him an early release, the appointment of a new governor at Reading, Major J. O. Nelson, transformed his prison conditions. Major Nelson was a far more humane man than his predecessor and evinced real sympathy for Oscar's plight. One of the first things he did following his appointment was to go to Oscar and say, 'The Home Office has allowed you some books. Perhaps you would like to read this one; I have just been reading it myself.' Oscar burst into tears of gratitude. Over the next few months, More Adey was able to send dozens of books into the prison for Oscar, with Major Nelson's approval.

It was also with Major Nelson's encouragement that Oscar was able to manipulate the prison rules, which allowed him to write a limited number of letters, so that he could compose a long epistle nominally addressed to Bosie. This would review and analyse all that had happened to him over the previous five years, culminating in the renunciation of his past follies as a result of the reflection forced upon him by his stay in prison. Oscar spent much of the period January to March 1897 writing what he originally called *In Carcere et Vinculis* – which Robbie renamed *De Profundis* – in his cell. Every evening, the pages he had completed would be taken away and kept in the Governor's office. Composing *De Profundis* was a cathartic experience, which enabled Oscar to come to terms with his downfall and present suffering, as well as to pour out onto paper all the bitterness and resentment against Bosie that had been boiling up inside him over the previous eighteen months.

Since Oscar's angry refusal to allow Bosie to dedicate his volume of poems to him, Bosie had made no attempt to communicate with him directly, instead cajoling Robbie and More

Adey to intercede on his behalf. This Robbie tried to do, at the risk of alienating both sides. When he wrote to Oscar in November 1896, expressing concern that Oscar's virulent denunciations of Bosie in recent letters to friends, including himself, could lower people's estimation of Oscar's character, Oscar replied in terms that foreshadowed the condemnation of his lover in *De Profundis*:

> Do not think that I would blame *him* for my vices. He had as little to do with them as I had with his. Nature was in this matter a stepmother to each of us. I blame him for not appreciating the man he ruined. An illiterate millionaire would really have suited him better. As long as my table was red with wine and roses, what did he care? My genius, my life as an artist, my work, and the quiet I needed for it, were nothing to him when matched with his unrestrained and coarse appetites for common profligate life: his greed for money: his incessant and violent scenes: his unimaginative selfishness. Time after time I tried, during those two wasted weary years, to escape, but he always brought me back, by threats of harm to himself chiefly.[3]

Bosie responded to such reproaches, passed on by Robbie, not with remorse but with rage. Unable to shout his frustration directly at Oscar, instead he berated Robbie. Unwilling to accept that what Robbie was telling him about Oscar's feelings was the objective truth, Bosie began to see what he thought were hidden motives:

> You still seem to cling to the idea that Oscar does not want to see me. The wish is father to the thought. You probably overlook the fact that I am passionately devoted to him, and that my longing to see him eats at my heart day and night . . . You make no allowance for jealousy, the most terrible of all

sufferings. You have seen Oscar yourself, and can see him again as often as you like, and that is all you care.[4]

The jealousy was entirely one-sided, though Bosie – who was increasingly displaying symptoms of paranoid schizophrenia – became convinced that Robbie was also jealous of him, because Bosie had been able to rouse degrees of passion in Oscar in a way that Robbie never had. To make matters even more stressful for the invalid Robbie, Oscar, too, was becoming critical of him, mainly, as Oscar erroneously believed, because of the way he was allegedly conspiring with Constance to deprive him of his entitlement on his release from prison. As Constance was also chiding Robbie about advice he was giving her, which conflicted with views she had been getting from her lawyers, notably regarding her marriage settlement, Robbie was in a no-win situation.

Frustrated by the way that his friends, including Robbie, were trying to organize his affairs for the period after he was released, Oscar wrote to More Adey:

Everything that you do is wrong and done in the wrong manner. Robbie is better as a guide, for if he is quite irrational he has the advantage of being always illogical, so he occasionally comes to a right conclusion. But you are not merely equally irrational, but are absolutely logical: you always start from the wrong premises, and arrive logically at the wrong conclusion.[5]

Such letters upset Robbie so much that Reggie Turner had to write to Oscar, on the eve of his release, begging him to stop criticizing Robbie.

The most beautiful thing I have ever known is Bobbie's devotion to you. He has never had any other thought than of you; he has only looked forward to one thing, the time when he would be able to talk to you freely and affectionately again. It is very rare to find such complete devotion, and I fear, dear Oscar, that you have gone very near to breaking his heart.[6]

It was the tradition that prisoners were freed from the first prison they served time in, which in Oscar's case was Pentonville. Accordingly, on 18 May 1897, he was transferred from Reading to London. As he left Reading Gaol, Major Nelson handed him the completed manuscript of *De Profundis*. The following morning, he was collected from Pentonville by More Adey and the Reverend Stewart Headlam, and taken to Headlam's house in Bloomsbury to rest. There was no serious question of his staying in England; the self-righteous British public would not put up with it. Robbie was already over in France with Reggie Turner, preparing Oscar's welcome in his chosen adoptive home. However, Oscar lingered so long at Stewart Headlam's, chatting away to Ada and Ernest Leverson, who came to visit him, and making an abortive request to go into a Roman Catholic retreat for six months, that he missed the morning boat-train to Newhaven. More Adey, who had undertaken to get him safely to France, accompanied him to the port late in the afternoon, to catch the night ferry to Dieppe. From Newhaven, Oscar telegraphed to Robbie:

Arriving by night boat. Am so delighted at prospect of seeing you and Reggie. You must not mind the foolish unkind letters. More has been such a good friend to me and I am so grateful to you all I cannot find words to express my feelings. You must not dream of waiting up for us. In the morning we will meet. Please engage rooms at your hotel. When I see you I shall be quite happy, indeed I am happy now to think I have such wonderful friendship shown to me.[7]

The telegram was signed 'Sebastian Melmoth', the pseudonym he and Robbie had devised to provide him with the veneer of a new identity. St Sebastian was one of Oscar's favourite martyrs, while Melmoth was the hero of Charles Maturin's novel – a nice and typical mixture of the sacred and the profane.

As Robbie later recalled in the preface to a volume of his correspondence with Oscar that he had been busy compiling when he died:

> We met them at half past four in the morning, a magnificent spring morning such as Wilde anticipated in the closing words of De Profundis. As the steamer glided into the harbour Wilde's tall figure, dominating the other passengers, was easily recognisable from the great crucifix on the jetty where we stood. That striking beacon was full of significance for us. Then we began running to the landing stage and Wilde recognised us and waved his hand and his lips curled into a smile. His face had lost all its coarseness and he looked as he must have looked at Oxford in the early days before I knew him and as he only looked again after death . . . There was the usual irritating delay and then Wilde with that odd elephantine gait which I have never seen in anyone else stalked off the boat. He was holding in his hand a large sealed envelope. 'This, my dear Bobbie, is the great manuscript about which you know.'[8]

Oscar's instructions were that Robbie should have two copies of the manuscript of De Profundis made, and then send the original to Bosie Douglas. First, though, Oscar had to be settled in to the Hôtel Sandwich. Reggie Turner had arranged for him to have a set of matching luggage, and a dressing-case containing fine hairbrushes and other gentlemanly accoutrements, embossed with the initials S.M.; Oscar took a childish delight in this symbolic new beginning, impishly writing immediately to Ada Leverson, 'I am staying here as Sebastian Melmoth – not Esquire but Monsieur Sebastien [sic] Melmoth – I have thought it better that Robbie should stay here under the name of Reginald Turner, and Reggie under the name of R. B. Ross . . .'

Oscar's friends had managed to raise £800 for him, to see him comfortably through the first few months of exile. But to Robbie's dismay, imprisonment had not curbed Oscar's flair for extravagance. If anything, two years of deprivation had made him even hungrier for luxury. As he confessed in exaggerated terms to Reggie, after Robbie and Oscar moved on 26 May to the Hôtel de la Plage in the little village of Berneval-sur-Mer, just a few miles along the coast from Dieppe:

> The population came at dawn to look at my dressing-case. I showed it to them, piece of silver by piece of silver. Some of the old men wept for joy. Robbie detected me at Dieppe in the market place of the sellers of perfumes, spending all my money on orris-root and the tears of the narcissus and the dust of red roses. He was very stern and led me away. I have already spent my entire income for two years. I see now that this lovely dressing-case with its silver vials thirsty for distilled odours will gradually lead me to the perfection of poverty.[9]

The choice of Berneval was accidental. They had hired a horse and trap to look for a quiet spot where Oscar could work, not too far from town, and the horse had led them there, as it was its own home. In summer, the village was delightful, with its pebble beach and dramatic cliffs, and at first Oscar was enthusiastic. What is more, few English tourists strayed there. Already in Dieppe Oscar had had several unpleasant encounters with English visitors who recognized him and made a point of publicly snubbing him. The French were in general far more forgiving and considerate. Several younger writers, in particular, made the pilgrimage from Paris to Dieppe or to Berneval, to pay homage to the author of *Salomé*. Oscar took great delight in these visits, usually inviting his guests for lunch or dinner, at his expense.

It was not just Oscar's financial irresponsibility which worried Robbie, as he prepared to return to England. Though Bosie Douglas had been expressly forbidden by Oscar from coming to see him, he deluged him with letters and telegrams almost from the first moment Oscar set foot on French soil. At first these were reproachful, as Bosie berated Oscar for turning against him. But then Bosie changed tack, telling Oscar that the thing he most wanted in life was to live with him and to make amends for the catastrophe that had occurred. Robbie argued that Oscar must resist such blandishments strongly. Not only did he believe that Bosie would ruin any chance Oscar had of rehabilitation, but also a reunion with Bosie would jeopardize the allowance Oscar was due to receive from Constance under an agreement that had been reached between Robbie, More Adey and her lawyers. She was now living in Italy, suffering greatly from complications to a spinal injury she had received when she fell badly at the house in Tite Street. Initially, Oscar tried to persuade her to come to Dieppe to live with him, but she was not convinced of his commitment to restarting married life, suspecting, probably correctly, that he was not so much interested in being with her again, but rather saw her as the means of getting back into contact with their two sons.

Robbie offered to stay on at Berneval with Oscar, even at the risk of antagonzing his own family. He was worried that Oscar would soon find the loneliness of existence there too great. But Oscar was buoyant during the first few weeks in the village, not least because he was writing fluently. One of the first things he did was to write a long appeal to the *Daily Chronicle*, describing the plight of children in prison, many of whom were incarcerated for very minor offences, such as stealing a rabbit. Robbie advised against sending the piece to the newspaper, as he was afraid it would invite gratuitous attacks on Wilde. But in the event, it was favourably received, and Robbie admitted that he had been wrong. Encouraged by the reaction, Oscar started working on various ideas for plays, not comedies like his pre-trial successes, but dramas on biblical themes. And he began to compose a lengthy poem, that would become *The Ballad of Reading Gaol*. Robbie promised to ensure that it would be published.

Robbie liked to feel needed. Indeed, Ada Leverson once astutely remarked that he slightly resented any friend who did *not* need him. But he realized that it would probably be more helpful to leave Oscar alone to find his own feet again, while he went back to London, initially for a period of six weeks. He could easily return to Berneval sooner if Oscar wanted him, though in many ways he could be just as useful being in England. Oscar had appointed him his literary executor, which would involve more arduous work than either of them realized. As it was, Oscar feared some people might think he was exploiting Robbie's good nature. He wrote to Robbie on 28 May, the day after Robbie left:

This is my first day alone, and of course a very unhappy one. I begin to realise my terrible position of isolation, and I have been rebellious and bitter of heart all day . . .

For yourself, dear sweet Robbie, I am haunted by the idea that many of those who love you will and do think it selfish of me to allow you and wish you to be with me from time to time. But still they might see the difference between your going about with me in my days of gilded infamy – my Neronian hours, rich, profligate, cynical, materialistic – and your coming to comfort me, a lonely dishonoured man, in disgrace and obscurity and poverty. How lacking in imagination they are! If I were rich again and sought to repeat my former life I don't think you would care very much to be with me. I think you would regret what I was doing, but now, dear boy, you come with the heart of Christ, and you help me intellectually as no one else can or ever could do. You are helping me to save my soul alive, not in the theological sense, but in the plain meaning of the words, for my soul was really dead in the slough of coarse pleasures, my life was unworthy of an artist: you can heal me and help me. No other friend have I now in this beautiful world. I want no other. Yet I am distressed to think that I will be looked on as careless of your own welfare, and indifferent of your good. You are made to help me. I weep with sorrow when I think how much I need help, but I weep with joy when I think I have you to give it to me.[10]

In fact, Oscar was not entirely friendless. Apart from Robbie, he had Reggie Turner and More Adey, the Leversons, Stewart Headlam and generous benefactors such as the heiress Adela Schuster and the socialite and philanthropist Mrs Bernard Beere. What he lacked in France, however, was a band of acolytes, amongst whom his conversation could fizz and sparkle. Even when he encountered past friends, he could not be sure of their reaction. He spotted Aubrey Beardsley in Dieppe one day, walking in the company of the painters Charles Conder and Jacques-Émile Blanche. Beardsley steered his two companions into a side street, to avoid a public encounter. But Oscar had seen him, and felt slighted. On another occasion, the two did meet, and Oscar invited Aubrey over to Berneval for lunch – an appointment the artist did not keep. He was frightened news of contact with Wilde would get back to André Raffalovich, who was providing him with an allowance; Raffalovich had specifically forbidden him to see the man he considered to have wronged John Gray. Nonetheless, in August, when Robbie was over on a three-week visit to Berneval, and Aubrey was installed at the Hôtel Sandwich in Dieppe, the three of them went out on a shopping trip together. Beardsley agreed to design the frontispiece for *The Ballad of Reading Gaol*, though he never managed to fulfil the commission.

Another visitor to Dieppe that summer was Robert Sherard the young Paris-based littérateur and Wilde's future biographer. He was startled to spy through an open window Oscar and Robbie in a passionate embrace in the villa Oscar had now taken at Berneval. Oscar was in a boisterous mood for several weeks. He had a little wooden bathing hut built for himself on the beach, and Sherard was surprised and pleased to see how fit he was. Nevertheless, Oscar complained to Sherard that he was weary of having to pay carriage from Dieppe on telegrams that Bosie was sending him, begging for a reunion. Robbie became increasingly convinced that Oscar would succumb to Bosie's blandishments. However critical of Bosie Oscar was when he was speaking or writing to Robbie, since June he had been writing the sort of effusive letters to Bosie, full of endearments, that he had sent prior to his imprisonment. It was becoming a matter not of whether the two would meet again, but when and how.

Neither Berneval nor Dieppe would be a good place, as Oscar was aware that he was being watched by a private detective hired by the Marquess of Queensberry, who was ready to create more trouble if the two lovers were reunited. Lady Queensberry, however, had taken a lease on a suite of rooms in Paris for Bosie, in the avenue Kléber, and Bosie invited Oscar to stay there, in the hope that the prospect of life in Paris would be a temptation impossible to resist. Oscar replied that he could not face Paris

Robbie's maternal grandfather, Hon. Robert Baldwin,
Joint Premier of Canada

Robbie's father, Hon. John Ross,
Attorney General of Canada

Robbie's mother,
Augusta Elizabeth ('Eliza') Ross

Robbie aged about 13   Aleck and Robbie, c. 1888

Robbie's brothers Jack and Aleck

Oscar Wilde, c. 1885

Oscar Wilde in 1894

Constance Wilde, c. 1894

Lord Alfred ('Bosie') Douglas, 1893

The Marquess of Queensbury,
1896

Will Rothenstein and Max Beerbohm

Aubrey Beardsley (self-portrait)

Robbie with Reggie Turner

Robbie, c. 1916

Seigfried Sassoon, 1916

Oscar and Robbie's last resting place, Père Lachaise, Paris

yet, suggesting instead that they meet up in Rouen. Bosie replied that he could not afford the journey; on several occasions during the summer, he had bemoaned his supposedly penurious state in letters to Oscar, and had even asked him for money. The uncertainty about a reunion, which Oscar both craved and dreaded, added to the sense of emptiness Oscar felt once Robbie had gone back to England and *The Ballad of Reading Gaol* was nearing completion. Oscar wrote to Robbie on 24 August:

Thanks for the cheque. I have sent it to the Dieppe bank.
My poem is still unfinished, but I have made up my mind to finish it this afternoon, and send it to be type-written. Once I see it, even type-written, I shall be able to correct it: *now* I am tired of the manuscript.

Do you think this verse good? I fear it is out of harmony, but wish you were here to talk about it. I miss you dreadfully, dear boy.

> The Governor was strong upon
>   The Regulation Act:
> The Doctor said that Death was but
>   A scientific fact;
> And twice a day the Chaplain called
>   And left a little Tract.

It is, of course, about the condemned man's life before his execution. I have got in 'latrine:' it looks beautiful.

Since Bosie wrote that he could not afford forty francs to come to Rouen to see me, he has never written. Nor have I. I am greatly hurt by his meanness and lack of imagination.[11]

Oscar did indeed get his manuscript despatched to the publisher Leonard Smithers later that day, with a request that it be typed up. Completing the poem left him not elated but dejected and, as he complained in a letter to Will Rothenstein, he felt he had no creative energy left in him to get on with the sort of work he ought to be doing: writing plays. He decided to go to Dieppe for a few days, as Berneval bored him, but then a telegram arrived from Bosie agreeing to a meeting in Rouen after all. They spent a day and a night together at the Hôtel de la Poste there, on 28–9 August. Douglas later wrote in his *Autobiography*: 'I have often thought that if he or I had died directly after that, our friendship would have ended in a beautiful way. Poor Oscar cried when I met him at the station. We walked about all day, arm in arm or hand in hand, and were perfectly happy.'

Oscar was once more totally smitten, as if all the past pain had been forgotten. Back in Dieppe, two days later, he wrote to Bosie:

My own Darling Boy, I got your telegram half an hour ago, and just send you a line to say that I feel my only hope of again doing beautiful work in art is being with you. It was not so in old days, but now it is different, and you can really recreate in me that energy and sense of joyous power on which art depends. Everyone is furious with me for going back to you, but they don't understand us. I feel that it is only with you that I can do anything at all. Do remake my ruined life for me, and then our friendship and love will have a different meaning to the world.

I wish that when we met at Rouen we had not parted at all. There are such wide abysses now of space and land between us. But we love each other. Goodnight, dear.[12]

Everyone was indeed furious. Oscar had to explain his decision to Robbie face-to-face, as Robbie returned to France the following week to find out what was going on. As Oscar had now decided that Berneval was suicidally tedious, and even Dieppe left him restless, he perversely asked Robbie to meet up with him in Rouen, though at least he chose a different hotel from the one he had stayed in with Bosie. Reggie Turner was also in Rouen at the time, but there was little sense of jollity in the air. Robbie felt that so much of the work he had been doing on Oscar's behalf would now prove to have been in vain. The fact that Oscar was aware of this hardly made things better. 'I love him as I always did,' Oscar told Robbie apropos of Bosie, 'with a sense of tragedy and ruin.'

The atmosphere was made worse by appalling weather, which convinced Oscar that he could not stay in northern France. He had to have sun. And as Bosie had suggested they live together in Italy, that was where he headed – to Naples, with a brief stop in Paris en route. For Constance, who was living further up the coast, this was adding insult to injury. She wrote to Oscar, angrily forbidding him to take up with Bosie again, but her efforts were in vain, even though this would mean she might cut off Oscar's allowance. Robbie, too, received a metaphorical slap in the face when he questioned the wisdom of Oscar's action. Oscar wrote from the Hôtel Royal des Étrangers in Naples, on 21 September:

My going back to Bosie was psychologically inevitable: and, setting aside the interior life of the soul with its passion for self-realisation at all costs, the world forced it on me.

I cannot live without the atmosphere of Love: I must have love and be loved, whatever price I pay for it. I could have lived all my life with you, but you have other claims on you* – claims you are too sweet a fellow to disregard – and all you could give me was a week of companionship. Reggie gave me three days, and Rowland [Fothergill]† a sextette of suns, but for the last month at Berneval I was so lonely that I was on the

---

*i.e., Robbie's mother.
†Architect and antiquarian, who later preferred to be known as 'John'.

brink of killing myself. The world shuts its gateway against me, and the door of Love lies open.[13]

The reproach to Robbie was unfair and cruel, and upset him greatly. He felt that his love and friendship had been betrayed and that Oscar was acting like a madman, careless of the effects his resumed relationship with Bosie would have on so many people, not least Oscar himself. For once, Robbie lost his natural reserve and sent a series of blistering letters to Naples, highlighting Oscar's irresponsibility and accusing him of ingratitude. On 1 October 1897, Oscar replied, from the Villa Giudice at Posillipo, on the outskirts of the city:

> I have not answered your letters because they distressed me and angered me, and I did not wish to write to *you* of all people in the world in an angry mood. You have been such a good friend to me. Your love, your generosity, your care of me in prison and out of prison are the most lovely things in my life. Without you what would I have done? As you remade my life for me you have a perfect right to say what you choose to me, but I have no right to say anything to you except to tell you how grateful I am to you, and what a pleasure it is to feel gratitude and love at the same time for the same person.[14]

Under the circumstances, Robbie would have been quite entitled to break with Oscar, but his twin senses of love and duty were too strong. What is more, Oscar knew he could continue to count on that devotion. Robbie was essentially acting as his literary agent in London and, even at this emotionally strained time, was assiduously carrying out the task of chasing Leonard Smithers about the arrangements for the publication of *The Ballad of Reading Gaol*. Once Oscar realized that the modest but crucial sum of £3 a week he was getting from Constance was now in jeopardy, and Bosie had no money, it was important to him that an advantageous deal be struck. This Robbie saw to, even though he did not think particularly highly of the poem itself, feeling that there was an unevenness of mood and style and a surfeit of melodramatic adjectives. At times, he felt, the poem verged on propaganda, but when he made that point to Oscar, he was told that this was part of its intent. Oscar did make various alterations to the text, in accordance with Robbie's criticisms, but by the end of October, he felt that he had done as much as he could. 'All your suggestions were very interesting,' he wrote to Robbie, 'but, of course, I have not taken them all: "black dock's dreadful pen" for instance is my own impression of the place in which I stood: it is burned into my memory.'

Robbie's challenge of obtaining the best terms for Oscar was complicated by the fact that Oscar was regularly corresponding with Leonard Smithers directly, often in quite an aggressive manner. Robbie was furious when he heard that Oscar had also been trying to interest an English newspaper in publishing an extract from the poem, as a means of getting some ready cash. Robbie feared that far from boosting prospective sales of the poem in book form, it would pre-empt it. Robbie became so exasperated by the way Oscar kept interfering in the publication arrangements, often without keeping him fully informed, that towards the end of November he wrote to Leonard Smithers saying that he no longer wished to be connected with Wilde's affairs, as he found he no longer enjoyed his confidence. When Smithers passed on this information, Oscar retorted that Robbie was under a complete misapprehension.

> Robbie has done everything for me in business that anyone on earth could do, and his own generosity and unwearying kindness are beyond any expression of praise on my part, though, I am glad to say, not beyond my powers of

gratitude . . . It would be fairer of him to say that it is too much worry to go on, than that he finds he has not my confidence. Such a statement is childish.[15]

In a further letter to Smithers, Oscar was even more reproving of Robbie. 'After all it is on me that the whole tragedy has fallen: and it is mere sentimentality for the spectators to claim the crown of thorns as theirs, on the grounds that their feelings have been harrowed.' To Robbie himself, Oscar complained, 'you stab me with a thousand phrases: if one particular phrase of mine shrills through the air near you, you cry out that you are wounded to death'.

This was more than Robbie could bear. He decided he must break with Oscar, except for professional dealings, and even considered getting away completely by going to Canada. He wrote to Bosie Douglas, outlining his reasons for wanting to terminate the relationship. Indeed, for the next couple of months, Oscar and Robbie, like an estranged married couple, communicated not directly but through letters to mutual friends. These were full of accusations, counter-accusations and remorse. Leonard Smithers was the recipient of most of Oscar's laments, which became ever more extravagant as the weeks went by. On 6 December, he wrote: 'I am quite broken-hearted about Bobbie's attitude towards me . . . But nothing can ever spoil the memory of his wonderful devotion to me.' On 10 December, 'I would gladly go on my knees from here to Naples if Robbie would be nice to me.' And on 11 December, '. . . if he will kindly send me a pair of his oldest boots I will blacken them with pleasure, and send them back to him with a sonnet. I have loved Robbie all my life, and have not the slightest intention of giving up loving him.'

There was deep hurt on both sides. Oscar was particularly bitter that Robbie and More Adey had agreed with Constance's lawyers that Bosie was 'a disreputable person'. The significance of this was that a clause in the agreement that had been reached regarding Oscar's allowance from Constance enabled her to suspend it if Oscar associated with any 'disreputable person'. As Robbie had himself spent two months with Bosie in Naples only the previous year, there was more than a hint of hypocrisy in his condemnation of Oscar for sharing Bosie's roof. However, it became clear that the only way that Oscar could continue to receive money from Constance – without which he risked becoming destitute – was if he ceased living with Bosie. Once that decision had been firmly taken, Bosie left the villa for Paris. Early in February 1898, Oscar also headed for the French capital, to begin a phase of solitary living in cheap hotels, the first being the Hôtel de Nice, in the rue des Beaux-Arts, on the Left Bank.

In a sense, this formal separation of Oscar and Bosie was a victory for Robbie, though that was not how he saw it. He continued to work for Oscar's interests, including sending out complimentary copies of *The Ballad of Reading Gaol* (whose author was named only as 'C.3.3', Oscar's cell number in Reading) to people such as Major Nelson and Edmund Gosse, when it was published in January. But he needed some time for his emotional wounds to heal. And he realized that for his own good, he must look to the future and concentrate on developing a life quite separate from that of Oscar Wilde.

EIGHT

Competing Demands

THE SUCCESS OF *The Ballad of Reading Gaol* took everyone by surprise, including Robbie. Some of Wilde's enemies attacked it, predictably, including W. E. Henley, who declared acidly that 'the trail of the Minor Poet is over it all'. But most reviewers were generous and genuine in their praise. *The Pall Mall Gazette* judged it the most remarkable poem that has appeared that year; even if it was still only early March, the pronouncement was gratifying. Robbie dutifully cut out all the reviews and sent them to Oscar in Paris. More significantly, people were buying the little book, which ran into six impressions in the first five months. This would guarantee some income, though the pleasure of that for Oscar was overshadowed by frustration that Constance was behind with his allowance.

Meanwhile it was Aubrey Beardsley who was currently giving Robbie far more cause for concern than Oscar. Beardsley's health had deteriorated steadily, prompting his mother to take him down to Menton on the French Riviera, in the hope of delaying the inevitable. When her son suffered a massive haemorrhage at the beginning of March, Ellen Beardsley summoned her daughter Mabel to join them. On 16 March, it was Mabel who wrote to Robbie to inform him that Aubrey had passed away that morning. 'He looked beautiful. He died as a saint. Pray for him and for us.' The funeral was held the following day, attended by staff from the Hôtel Cosmopolitan, where he had died, and various members of Menton's little expatriate English colony. Mabel had placed Aubrey's copy of *La Dame aux Camélias*, by Alexandre Dumas *fils*, in the coffin.

The obituaries in the British press were hardly flattering. However brilliant Beardsley's technique may have been, too much of his subject matter was still deemed unwholesome. Nevertheless, friends such as Aymer Vallance, Henry Harland and John Gray rallied round and produced more glowing personal tributes. Robbie was commissioned to write a eulogy, which would appear later in the year in a Leonard Smithers edition of *Ben Jonson His Volpone: or, the Foxe*, for which Aubrey had managed to complete seven out of twenty-four illustrations before he died. Early in May, Robbie helped Ellen and Mabel to organize a memorial mass at the fashionable Jesuit chapel in Farm Street, Mayfair. As well as making practical arrangements, such as hiring carriages, Robbie picked up half of the bill. Ellen followed her late son and Robbie by converting to Catholicism, which bound her even more closely to both of them.

In the meantime, Constance Wilde died in Genoa, at the age of forty, after an unsuccessful operation on her spine. Bosie Douglas, who happened to be in Paris, went to Oscar's hotel to console him, and was rather taken aback when Oscar said that the night before he had heard about her death, he had dreamt that she had visited him and that he had said to her, 'Go away, go away, leave me in peace.' Though Oscar telegraphed Constance's brother Otho on 12 April that he was 'overwhelmed with grief', that was not how he struck those who saw him in the flesh. He telegraphed Robbie as well, asking him to come over to Paris immediately, which he did, though he rejected Oscar's suggestion that he stay in the same hotel. Robbie wrote to Leonard Smithers a few days later:

I ought to have written to you ages ago, but it is quite impossible with Oscar to get anything done . . .

You will have heard of Mrs Wilde's death. Oscar of course did not feel it at all. It is rather appalling for him as his allowance ceases and I do not expect his wife's trustees will continue it. He is in very good spirits and does not consume too many . . .

Oscar has only seen Douglas once. I went to see his lordship. He is less interested in other people than ever before, especially Oscar, so I really think that alliance will die a natural death.

Oscar is very amusing as usual but is very abstracted at times. He says that *The Ballad of Reading Gaol* doesn't describe his prison life, but his life at Naples with Bosie . . .[1]

In fact, Constance's trustees did not revoke Oscar's allowance. He now received, in quarterly instalments, paid through Robbie, £150 a year, which is more than many workmen of the time earned. But he still found it impossible to put a brake on his expenses. He had discovered that it was easy to pick up male prostitutes and drifters on the boulevards, and he was generous to some of his new acquaintances, including a charming young Anglo-French sailor called Maurice Gilbert, in whom Bosie, Robbie and Reggie Turner also all took an active interest. In fact, Gilbert went to stay with Reggie for a while in May, in his rooms in London, where Reggie now had a sinecure writing a frivolous column for the *Daily Telegraph*. As Oscar observed tartly to Leonard Smithers (whose own taste was more for adolescent girls) towards the end of the month, Gilbert arrived back in Paris 'looking tired and beautiful'. He seems to have been a great success in London, and is full of pleasant reminiscences of the inhabitants. My friend Robbie Ross especially seems to have taken quite an interest in him. He is so fond of children, and of people, like myself, who have childlike simple natures.' When one scandalized Frenchman spotted Oscar kissing Gilbert in a Paris street one evening, exceeding even the local bohemian levels of tolerance, the news quickly spread around the French literary and artistic worlds that the disgraced playwright had clearly sunk back into his wicked old ways.

A new and unattractive facet of Oscar's character now was his constant whining about how poor he was. He moved out of the Hôtel de Nice into another establishment in the same street, the Hôtel d'Alsace, which was actually cleaner and friendlier, as well as cheaper. Throughout May and much of June, Oscar sent Robbie almost daily letters moaning about the non-appearance of cheques, or the inadequacy of his living arrangements. Yet he could not resist at the same time passing on details of his latest assignations with boys, including Maurice Gilbert, who was now dividing his time between Oscar and Bosie, just as the black-mailer Alfred Wood had done before the trials. Gilbert, like Bosie, was addicted to racing, though with less of a knack for backing dud horses. He also, so Oscar rhapsodized to Robbie, had the most wonderful mouth: 'It has the curves of Greek art and English flowers.' Both Oscar and Bosie had ample chance to appreciate it, as the three of them spent quite a lot of time at Nogent, outside Paris, together.

Robbie was dismayed that his prediction to Smithers about the petering out of the Wilde–Douglas relationship had been proved wrong, and that Oscar was now seeing so much of Bosie again. He was convinced Oscar would write nothing while he was in Nogent. In response to Oscar's merry accounts of his and Bosie's escapades – almost invariably accompanied by pleas of poverty – Robbie's letters became increasingly censorious again, provoking Oscar to write in July:

It is a curious thing, dear little absurd Robbie, that you now always think that I am in the wrong. It is a morbid reaction against your former, and more rational estimate of me.

The only thing that consoles me is that your moral attitude towards yourself is even more severe than your moral attitude towards others. Yours is the pathological tragedy of the hybrid, the Pagan-Catholic. You exemplify the beauty and uselessness of Conscience.[2]

Perhaps Oscar felt a little guilty afterwards, as he wrote the following month, asking if he could dedicate the forthcoming published text of *The Importance of Being Earnest* to him. Robbie accepted, but when he left in late September with Reggie Turner for a two-month tour of Italy, breaking the journey at Dieppe on the way, the two of them deliberately avoided Paris. Their itinerary took them to Florence, Rome and Naples, all of which Robbie knew well. Robbie was able to share his love of Giotto and Botticelli with his friend, who had never been to Florence before. But when they got to Rome, Reggie rather punctured Robbie's knowledgeable discourse on a Burne-Jones mosaic in the American Church by asserting that one of the virgins looked just like the 'fast' actress Mrs Patrick Campbell. Nonetheless, Reggie was deeply impressed with what he saw in Italy, and would later choose Florence as his home. For his part, Robbie had his interest in fine art rekindled, and determined to spend more of his time and energy in study and writing when he got back to London. Despite a plea from Oscar to be sure to call on him on their return journey, Robbie and Reggie carefully circumvented Paris again.

Oscar's letters could not be so easily avoided. One in late November begged Robbie to advance him his December allowance, as the innkeeper in Nogent was threatening to sell some of his clothes and Bosie's dressing-case which they had had to leave behind when they were unable to settle the bill. Robbie curtly pointed out that he had already used that pretext once before when trying to get an advance. This elicited an apology from Oscar by return of post, as well as a playful threat. As he had not yet written the dedication to Robbie that would appear at the front of *The Importance of Being Earnest*, Oscar hinted he might make it cold and terrible if Robbie kept lecturing him – something along the lines of 'To R. B. Ross, in recognition of his good advice'. For good measure, Oscar sent the same warning to Reggie, adding, 'At present [Robbie] is a combination of the University Extension Scheme and the Reformation, but he is always a dear: and when he knocks me down with the Decalogue, I introduce Narcissus to him, as the only repartee.' Reminding Robbie of his own sexual predilections was, Oscar realized, quite an effective way of parrying unwelcome censure for his own behaviour. 'It is quite true,' he wrote to Robbie, 'that when you talk morals to me, which you do quite beautifully, I always pipe on a reed and a faun comes running out of the thicket. You at once say "What a lovely faun!" The rest is silence.' In the end, the dedication Oscar settled on was

'To Robert Baldwin Ross:
in appreciation
in affection.'

Oscar was by now shamelessly soliciting money from past acquaintances who wrote to him or ran into him. Many, like André Gide and Vincent Sullivan, obliged. But Frank Harris decided that rather than hand over money to Oscar, much of which would soon disappear into the pockets of boys from the boulevards, he would invite him down to spend Christmas on the Riviera instead, where in principle the conditions would be ideal for writing. Though Oscar later complained that Harris neglected him badly during his stay at Napoule, postcards he sent to Robbie at the time were testimony that he was having a wonderful time. He had an emotional reunion with Sarah Bernhardt, who was starring in *Tosca* in Nice. At least as good for his morale was the discovery that 'the fishing population of the Riviera have the same freedom from morals as the Neapolitans have'. When Harris chided him for not getting on with any writing, Oscar announced that he was thinking of composing a sort of counter-statement to *The Ballad of Reading Gaol*, which would be a celebration of freedom rather than imprisonment, joy instead of sorrow, and kissing instead of hanging. He intended to entitle it 'The Ballad of the Fisher-Boy'.

Happy in the knowledge that Oscar would be well-fed and provided with champagne over Christmas, Robbie, in London, sent as presents to close friends and useful literary contacts copies of the *Volpone* that contained his Beardsley eulogy. A perfectionist by nature, he fretted that the production was marred by several misprints, but Max Beerbohm wisely advised him to ignore them:

I have read your essay with much admiration, and with much irritation that you don't write more often. Why don't you? . . .

I don't really think that the misprints in the essay matter much. When one has written a thing it is horrible to find a misprint – but my experience is that no one else ever finds them at all. On page 24 of my *Works* there is a misplaced comma, which has darkened much of my life and has often made me appear more bitter than I really am. It and the death of Lucien de Rubempré* are the only things I have never been quite able to dismiss. And yet no one has ever called my attention to it. So be comforted. I admit that I am still, even with the grave between us, a little jealous of Aubrey – but I

*The hero of Balzac's *Illusions perdues*.

feel for your admiration for him, and I love your essay because it is so charmingly written and erudite and full of Bobbyisms which only Bobbyists like myself will understand and revel in.[3]

The fact that Robbie was not writing more was a sore point. Though he never had any pretension to becoming a great writer like Oscar Wilde, he must have realized that to chide Oscar for not writing when he himself was producing so little was inconsistent, to say the least. Yet apart from his Beardsley eulogy, and a rather insignificant short story published in the *Canadian* magazine, he had penned almost nothing for about two years. It was not just a lack of time, for although his work on Oscar's behalf and being a dutiful son to Eliza Ross were time-consuming, he did not have a full-time job to eat up precious hours of the day when he could have been writing. Rather, he was still unsure exactly what was his forte. Max Beerbohm was not alone in appreciating 'Bobbyisms', Robbie's wry turn of phrase and mischievous yet not malevolent sense of humour that made him such a delightful conversationalist. But Robbie did not have the ability of an Oscar Wilde, to make aphorisms into works of art, or the talent of a Reggie Turner for popular journalism. Instead, the field in which he now set out to make a mark was one neither of those friends and mentors could have excelled in: art criticism.

The recent trip to Italy had provided one stimulus. William Rothenstein offered another. Now based in England, Rothenstein was being pestered by a fellow painter, Charles Conder, who was still in Paris, to help him sell his work. Conder had spent much of the 1880s in Australia. The Art Gallery of New South Wales bought an oil painting of his in 1888, when he was aged only twenty but a decade later, he had still failed to win the recognition in England that he craved. At first, there was little that Will

Rothenstein could do to help, as he was struggling to make his own mark in London, but then an opening appeared thanks to the adventurous and idiosyncratic John Rowland Fothergill.

Fothergill was both an archaeologist and an architect; Oscar Wilde had commissioned him the previous year to build him a sort of 'French villa beautiful' at Berneval, though this proved to be a pipe-dream. Fothergill lived with the eminent classical scholar Edward Warren at Lewes House, described by Rothenstein in his *Memoirs* as 'a monkish establishment where women were not welcome'. The house and garden were full of splendid Greek and Roman treasures, several of distinctly dubious provenance. Pre-Christian art was Fothergill's speciality, but he followed contemporary artistic trends and was keen to assist young painters and sculptors. Though not a wealthy man himself, he decided the best way to do that was to start a small gallery, where Conder and Rothenstein, Max Beerbohm, Walter Sickert, William Orpen and Augustus John could all exhibit. The plan was that Rothenstein would be responsible for choosing the artists, and Walter Sickert's younger brother Robert would be manager, while the business side would be run by a man called Arthur Clifton. Suitable premises were located in Ryder Street in St James's, and the gallery was given the name 'Carfax'. The gallery did indeed launch Charles Conder in England, where he settled and found his feet. Moreover, it proved a magnet for Robbie; he was able to get to know many contemporary artists more intimately and deepen his appreciation of current trends.

To both Robbie's and Oscar's frustration, the published text of *The Importance of Being Earnest* was coldly ignored by British reviewers when it came out. Though the later impressions of the briskly selling *The Ballad of Reading Gaol* now bore Wilde's name alongside 'C.3.3', it was still far too soon for London's literary establishment to rehabilitate the playwright. To add to

Oscar's discontent, the three months Frank Harris had kindly sponsored on the Riviera had come to an end, without his producing any new work. Unwilling to return to Paris, he seized the offer of hospitality extended by a wealthy young American homosexual called Harold Mellor, who lived in Gland in Switzerland.

En route to Gland, Oscar made a detour to Genoa, to visit Constance's grave. He reported to Robbie that it was very pretty; a marble cross with dark ivy-leaves inlaid. 'It was very tragic seeing her name carved on a tomb – her surname, my name, not mentioned of course – just "Constance Mary, Daughter of Horace Lloyd, Q.C." and a verse from *Revelations*.' He left flowers and pondered on the uselessness of regrets. His homage to his late wife complete, he then picked up a young Florentine actor called Didaco, who had 'a face chiselled for romance', and spent the next three days seeing the sights of Genoa with him.

Oscar hoped to find happiness, or at least tranquillity, in Switzerland. Mellor's house, half an hour away by train from Geneva, was attractive and comfortable. There were attentive Italian servants, including Mellor's young lover Eolo, whose father, Oscar wickedly suggested to Robbie, had sold the boy to Mellor for 200 lire. Board and lodging were of course free, but the host proved not to be as generous with champagne as Oscar had been anticipating, instead providing Swiss *vin ordinaire*, which Oscar considered disgusting. Even worse was the lack of 'fauns' to admire in the neighbourhood. As Oscar bemoaned in a letter to More Adey after he had been at Gland for a few days, 'Swiss people are carved out of wood with a rough knife, most of them; the others are carved out of turnips.' On 15 March after he had only been there a fortnight, he informed Robbie ominously, 'I don't like Mellor very much, and would like to get away, but, at present, it is impossible.' By the end of the month,

Oscar had convinced himself that Mellor was mad. There was insanity in his family, Oscar reported to Robbie, which in Harold Mellor's case manifested itself in misanthropy and meanness. Having completed a revised version of the text of *An Ideal Husband*, on which he had been working, and which he dedicated to Frank Harris, Oscar declared he could stand Gland no longer. In a letter to Leonard Smithers, headed 'At the House of the Enemy, Among the Cities of the Plain', Oscar revealed that he was going to head for Genoa, 'where I can live for ten francs a day (boy *compris*)'.

In vain, Oscar tried to persuade Robbie to join him in Italy, where he had found an agreeable room over a restaurant at Santa Margherita in Ligure. 'I never see you. You would do me no end of good . . . I believe at the holy season of Easter one is supposed to forgive all one's friends,' he wrote plaintively. Robbie had earlier offered to meet him in Paris, but Oscar protested that Paris was too expensive. Robbie countered that he was not well enough himself at present to make the long journey to Italy, to which Oscar replied:

> I am so sorry you are ill. I am wretched, which makes me sympathetic.
>
> Whatever I do is wrong: because my life is not on a right basis. In Paris I am bad: here I am bored: the last state is the worse.
>
> I wish I could see you. A few days with you would be a tonic.[4]

As April went by, Oscar became more and more dejected. He was drinking heavily and running up bills he had no means of paying. Eventually he made his state sound so pathetic that Robbie felt there was no alternative but to go to Santa Margherita himself to lift Oscar out of his depression, settle his debts and accompany him back to Paris. Robbie warned him that if he did not stop drinking, he would soon be dead, which did at least curb Oscar's alcoholic intake for a few months.

Robbie was back in London in June to be a witness, alongside Max Beerbohm, Charles Conder and Will Rothenstein's brother Albert, to the Kensington Registry Office wedding of Rothenstein and the actress Alice Kingsley. The bride's father, Walter Knewstub, had been assistant to the late Dante Gabriel Rossetti, and through Alice, Rothenstein became friendly with Rossetti's younger brother William, who was a distinguished art critic and one of the seven Pre-Raphaelite 'brothers'. The Rossettis were a very close-knit family, as well as enjoying a wide circle of friends, into which not just the Rothensteins but also Robbie was drawn.

Robbie continued to be dogged by ill-health during the summer of 1899; even a short stay with More Adey at Wotton-under-Edge during August did little to restore his vitality. When he returned to his mother's house in Upper Phillimore Gardens, however, it became a question of who was looking after whom, as Eliza Ross was far from well herself. The family therefore decided it would be best for both of them if they went to Italy for the winter. Will Rothenstein, who had rented a house at Vattetot-sur-Mer, near Dieppe, for the summer, conveyed his dismay at the news:

> From an entirely selfish point of view I am most distressed to hear that you are to winter in Rome – entirely selfish I know, because one should winter anywhere rather than in Town. Rome is a beautiful city, containing many interesting antiquities, and also on account of the immense benefit to your Mother's health which I hope it will bring; and probably you yourself require a rest which a number of friends make so imperative. But you are a person, who whatever qualities or faults you may have, are above all *missed*; and of few indeed

can this be said. Kensington without Robbie – one might as well migrate to Hampstead! . . .

I hope to see Oscar if I go to Paris – the one thing I am afraid of is his wanting to borrow money. Will you write me a word of this matter?[5]

Will and Alice Rothenstein did indeed visit Oscar in Paris, where he was installed once more in the Hôtel d'Alsace. They went out to dinner together several times during the first week of October; Oscar's allowance was now being paid monthly, usually arriving on the first of the month, which meant that he was relatively happy for the first few days of every month. Moreover, Rothenstein was elated at having secured some exquisite drawings and casts from Auguste Rodin for the Carfax Gallery, so the mood was decidedly jolly. Robbie and Eliza Ross, accompanied by Robbie's young niece Lilian (usually called Lily), later passed through Paris on their way south. Mrs Ross seems to have had no qualms about meeting Oscar again, though it must have been an odd encounter for both of them, given their conflicting claims on Robbie's devotion, and all that had happened to Oscar over the past four years. Jealousy put aside, Oscar later remarked to Robbie how delighted he was that Mrs Ross looked so well, despite her ill-health.

Robbie's sojourn in Rome was like that of a character in an E. M. Forster novel. Every morning he would accompany his niece Lily to the ruins or churches or museums, then in the afternoon, they would take Mrs Ross out for a drive in a carriage. As he complained to Will Rothenstein, 'in the ancient capital of the world, or the capital of the ancient world, nothing ever happens so I cannot write you a letter with any news'. Yet he was not without friends. Both John Fothergill and Edward Warren were in town, and Fothergill was in entertaining form, as Robbie recounted:

He really has a 'Phlair' (American spelling) for antics at all events. He got a beautiful Greek head which is going to Boston. He works most fearfully hard every day in the new museum where recent finds are placed and is becoming quite learned about forgeries. Now that he has got over his exaltation at being elected to the august brotherhood of archaeologists and is no longer mysterious he is as charming as he used to be.[6]

In February 1900, Robbie succumbed to influenza, which made him feel 'like a washed-out cat'. But if he hoped for sympathy from Oscar in Paris, he was to be disappointed. In response to a petulant query from Robbie as to why Oscar had not answered an invitation to join the Rosses in Rome for a short holiday, Oscar replied that he had not received it, and was anyway far sicker than Robbie, as he was suffering from food-poisoning. Robbie's brother Aleck had been in Paris, so Oscar informed him:

Aleck lunched with Bosie and me one day and I lunched alone with him on another. He was most friendly and pleasant and gave me a depressing account of you. I see that you, like myself, have become a *neurasthenic*. I have been so for four months, quite unable to get out of bed till the afternoon, quite unable to write letters of any kind. My doctor has been trying to cure me with arsenic and strychnine but without much success, as I became poisoned through eating mussels, so you see what an exacting and tragic life I have been leading.[7]

This letter was actually in Maurice Gilbert's handwriting; Oscar had presumably dictated it in bed. Gilbert had become a most attentive companion, providing exactly the sort of solicitous nursing that Oscar liked when he was ill, and which Bosie had so singularly failed to provide at Brighton years before.

Even Bosie had become less dismissive of the sick, however, visiting Oscar quite regularly when he was in Paris, having moved his own base back to England. He helped out financially from time to time, though nothing like as much as he could have done. The Marquess of Queensberry had died on 31 January 1900, summoning up just enough energy to spit in his second son Percy's face when Percy came to see him on his death-bed. A fierce agnostic for most of his life, Queensberry then had a last-minute conversion to Catholicism and received conditional absolution by a priest. In his will, he left £20,000 to Bosie, as well as a greater fortune to Percy. Robbie urged Oscar to ask Bosie to settle some money on him, to supplement the allowance from Constance's trustees. But when Oscar raised the idea with Bosie, Bosie said he needed the money for himself, and accused Oscar of 'wheedling like an old whore'. Oscar confided to Frank Harris, 'He has left me bleeding.' But like a spaniel who licks the hand of the temperamental owner who kicks him hard from time to time, Oscar kept coming back for more.

Just as Bosie, in true schizophrenic form, could veer from being an absolute charmer to become a vicious monster, so Oscar was displaying dramatic mood-swings. This could happen not just from day to day, but from hour to hour. One moment savouring the absurdities of life, the next on the verge of despair, he left many of his friends, including Robbie, confused. To aggravate matters, Oscar had also become an unashamed liar. He had always seen Truth in subjective terms, as something that could and maybe should be embellished in the interest of Art. But now he often dissimulated his real state and feelings, not for Art's sake, but for pecuniary gain. As a man of the theatre, he was very good in this new role. Robbie had soon rumbled what he was doing, responding with a mixture of exasperation and amused affection as stories about Oscar's mendacity filtered back to him. On one occasion, Oscar gave such a good performance of abjection when he ran into the Australian operatic soprano Nellie Melba in a Paris street that she opened her purse and poured everything in it into his hands. His afternoons were often spent sitting on the terrace of fashionable cafés such as the Grand in the boulevard des Capuccines, waiting for someone to pass by who would buy him a drink.

Some friends and acquaintances, including André Gide, tried to avoid catching his eye when they happened to walk past a café where he was installed, especially when he was in disreputable company. Sometimes Oscar was hurt by this, at other times merely entertained. In a letter in late March informing Robbie that he had decided to accept an offer from Harold Mellor to pay for him to go to Italy, Oscar gleefully reported,

> Only an hour after I, with 'waving hands' like Tennyson's Vivien,* had evolved a new evangel of morals, dear Aleck passed before the little *café* behind the Madeleine, and saw me with a beautiful boy in grey velvet – half rough, all Hylas. Alas, the eye he turned to me was not the sightless one.† His smile was terrible. It was like one of [Walter] Besant's novels.
>
> I really felt it very much. At luncheon I had been singularly ethical. I am always ethical at the Café de la Paix.
>
> Wire, or write at once to me, chez Mellor, Gland, Vaud, and tell me a good hotel. Also bed out some Narcissi. It is their season.
>
> With best love, dear horrid irritating Robbie.[8]

Oscar also told Robbie, only half-teasingly, that he was thinking

---

*From Tennyson's *Idylls of the King*.
†Aleck had been blinded in one eye by a childhood accident. Normally he did turn a blind eye to Robbie and Oscar's homosexual escapades.

of becoming a Catholic during his forthcoming visit to Rome, as he would rather like to have done when he was first there as a student, 'though I fear that if I went before the Holy Father with a blossoming rod it would turn at once into an umbrella or something dreadful of that kind'.

Oscar and Robbie only coincided very briefly in Rome, as the Rosses had decided to move on to Venice. Oscar remarked peevishly that there was nothing worse than 'renters in gondolas', but in fact Harold Mellor and he wanted to tour the south anyway. They spent a notable week at Palermo in Sicily, which Oscar considered the most beautifully situated town in the world. He raved about the mosaics there, and in Palermo Cathedral struck up a friendship with a fifteen-year-old seminarist called Giuseppe, whom Oscar kissed every day behind the high altar in exchange for a few coins – or so he claimed. At Naples, the object of his attentions was a blue-uniformed 'sea-god' from the Regia Marina School.

Back in Rome for Easter, Oscar managed to get a ticket to a general papal audience with Leo XIII, who was carried past, resplendent in white, seated on a golden throne. Oscar wrote to Robbie, 'I have seen nothing like the extraordinary grace of his gesture, as he rose, from moment to moment, to bless – possibly the pilgrims, but certainly me.' Oscar attributed to this blessing his sudden cure from the after-effects of the mussel poisoning, which had been plaguing him for nearly five months. The fact that Harold Mellor had suddenly returned to Switzerland, leaving him to his own devices, only heightened the joy of the stay in Rome. Needless to say, Oscar had acquired a young companion, named Armando, though he dropped him when the boy's demands for clothes became incessant; 'he really bayed for boots, as a dog moonwards'. Far more satisfactory was a youth called Omero – 'slim, dandy-like, elegant, and without a single great curve' – whom Robbie had passed on to him before leaving for Venice. Oscar teased, 'Omero has never received your letter. I need not say I have not given him your London address – at least not your real one: he now believes that your real name is Edmondo Gosse, and that your address is the Savile.'

Oscar succeeded in getting a second, more private audience with the Pope. As he informed More Adey, 'My position is curious: I am not a Catholic: I am simply a violent Papist. No one could be more "black" than I am.' The combination of the Pope, olive-skinned boys and brilliant blue skies made Rome the ideal city, and he determined to return to spend the winter there. In the meantime, he toured the monuments with Omero, who never seemed to have noticed any of them before, and indulged a new enthusiasm: photography.

Robbie was continuing to send Oscar his allowance from Venice, but the extra funds from Harold Mellor were running out. So in mid-May, Oscar left Rome for Naples and Genoa, then on to Gland, where Mellor was waiting with his automobile to drive Oscar to Paris. 'I suppose one of us will arrive safe,' Oscar wrote to Robbie. 'I hope it will be me.' The car broke down, but by early June, Oscar was ensconced once more in the Hôtel d'Alsace, making frequent sorties with Maurice Gilbert to visit the Paris Exhibition, which had opened while he was in Rome. Frank Harris was in town, working hard on Bosie, to try and get him to be more generous with his handouts to Oscar, instead of frittering away his inheritance on racehorses. Harris and Wilde collaborated on an idea Oscar had had for a play, though it was actually Harris who eventually wrote what would become *Mr and Mrs Daventry*. It later transpired that Oscar had sold options on the play to various people, each of whom thought he or she had an exclusive deal.

Around the same time, summer 1900, Robbie arrived back in London with his mother, both of them refreshed by their eight-month continental stay. He immediately set about writing what would be one of his most successful short stories, 'A Case at the Museum' – a Gothic black comedy, full of Bobbyisms. The anti-hero is a distinguished foreign archaeologist and palaeographer, Professor Lachsyrma, who lives in London and sometimes works for the British Museum. He has a workroom in Bloomsbury, stuffed full of artefacts, including an Egyptian mummy. The Professor has just scored a great *coup* by discovering in a Cairo antiquarian's shop a papyrus manuscript of lost poems by Sappho. But one afternoon, he is visited by a stranger, who reveals himself to be both a forger and a blackmailer. The visitor is able to prove that he forged the manuscript that the Professor has authenticated. Exposure would mean the ruin of his reputation. The blackmailer asks for so much money, however, that the Professor picks up a knife and stabs him fatally. 'For the first time he found himself an actor in modern life . . . The entire absence of horror appalled him. Even the dignity of tragedy was not there.' He wonders frantically if there is anyone with whom he can share his dreadful secret.

> There was young Fairleigh, who was always so modern, and actually read modern books. *He* might have coped with the blackmailer alive, but hardly with his corpse. You cannot run round and ask neighbours for coffins, false beards, and rope in the delightful convention of the *Arabian Nights*, because you have grazed modern life at a sharp angle, without exciting suspicion or running the risk of positive refusal.[9]

Then the Professor has the inspired idea of hiding the corpse inside the Egyptian mummy. He carefully opens the cartonnage case and extracts the mummified body, so he can replace it with that of the blackmailer. He then laboriously unwinds the hundreds of yards of material from the embalmed corpse, and discovers that, along with various other small funerary treasures, there is a little wooden cylinder grasped in one skeletal hand. On examination, this proves to contain a papyrus, on which are written the genuine, lost poems of Sappho. Evil has triumphed, and the Professor's reputation is safe. Over the next few weeks, he embalms the body of the blackmailer, according to the ancient methods, then presents the reconstituted mummy to the British Museum, which makes it one of their prize exhibits.

As with much of Robbie's writing, the story was especially geared to appeal to a limited number of *cognoscenti*, in this case John Fothergill in particular, and their mutual friends. The story was published in the *Cornhill* magazine in October 1900, and provoked enthusiastic comment from Max Beerbohm and others. However, it is not certain that Oscar ever had the chance to read it. The previous month, he had chided Robbie for not keeping him abreast of what he was up to:

Your letter is very maddening: nothing about yourself: no details, and yet you know I love middle-class tragedies, and the little squabbles that build up family-life in England. I have had delightful letters from you quite in the style of Jane Austen. You, I know, are the Cinderella of your family, and lead them all a dreadful life, like your *Märchen* prototype. You turned your dear mother's carriage into a pumpkin, and won't let your sisters wear your slippers, and always have the comfortable ingle-nook by the fire, except in summer, when you make poor Aleck sit there.[10]

Such camp high spirits were illusory, as Oscar's morale was sinking fast. He was worn down by new arguments over money with both Bosie and Frank Harris. Then, on 10 October, he had to have an operation on his ear, which had been giving him increasing pain. He telegraphed to Robbie to come over as soon as he could. Robbie arrived on Oscar's birthday, 16 October, and found his friend in remarkably fine fettle for someone who had suggested he was about to expire. Reggie Turner was there, as well as Robbie's brother Aleck. Oscar joked from his bed that when the trumpet of the Last Judgement was sounded, he would turn and whisper, 'Robbie, Robbie, let us pretend we do not hear it!'

On 29 October, Oscar got out of bed for the first time since his operation. He was served dinner in his room, but then insisted on going out for a walk with Robbie. They went to a café, where Oscar ordered an absinthe. Robbie said concernedly, 'You'll kill yourself, Oscar. You know the doctor said absinthe was poison for you.' But Oscar replied, 'And what do I have to live for?' The following day, they went out for a drive in the Bois de Boulogne, but Oscar started to feel giddy and had to be taken back to the hotel. An abscess developed in his ear, and the pain got worse. Morphine, which the devoted hotel-keeper, Jean Dupoirier, was administering on the doctor's prescription, ceased to bring sufficient relief, and was supplemented by chloral and opium. It was not surprising that Oscar was groggy for much of the time, especially as he spent many of his waking hours sipping champagne. There were odd moments of levity, such as when Oscar told Robbie and Reggie that he had dreamt that he was supping with the dead, to which Reggie quipped, 'My dear Oscar, I'm sure you were the life and soul of the party.' Oscar found that hysterically funny. But in general he was morose and convinced that death was near. He begged Robbie to get *De Profundis* published after his death, and to try to clear off his debts.

Still, Robbie was not convinced Oscar was dying, or that his own presence was really necessary. He was under great pressure to join his mother, who had gone down to stay in the South of France, but only with the greatest reluctance did Oscar let him leave, on 12 November, asking him to look out for a nice spot in the hills behind Nice where he could go when he had recovered. For the next two weeks, Reggie faithfully stayed by Oscar's bedside for much of the day, as he became increasingly delirious, often speaking nonsense, in a mixture of English and French. Yet at times he could converse almost normally, and once even asked for a newspaper. By the 28th, however, the doctors saw little hope of recovery, and Reggie telegraphed Robbie, 'Almost hopeless'. Robbie quickly packed a bag and boarded the night train from the Riviera.

NINE

Life after Oscar

OSCAR WAS UNABLE to speak when Robbie reached his bedside on the morning of 29 November, but he held his hand firmly. It was clear that he was dying, and Reggie said he had been drifting in and out of consciousness for some time. As a Catholic, who dearly loved Oscar, Robbie was in a dilemma. Oscar had given such conflicting indications over the years about his attitude to the Church of Rome. How seriously could one take statements he had made such as 'Catholicism is the only religion to die in'? Like most aspects of life, religion was something he had never been able to resist undermining with his anarchic wit; his comments about his last trip to the Eternal City, including the audiences he had with the Pope, were hardly pious. Yet he had told a correspondent of the *Daily Chronicle* who had visited him at the Hôtel d'Alsace earlier in the month that 'much of my moral obliquity is due to the fact that my father would not allow me to become a Catholic. The artistic side of the Church and the fragrance of its teaching would have cured my degeneracies. I intend to be received before long.'

After much soul-searching, Robbie decided to fetch a Catholic priest to bring solace to his dying friend. The Passionist Fathers were able to provide an English-speaking Father, Cuthbert Dunne. Back at the hotel, Robbie asked Oscar if he wished to see the priest, and Oscar held up his hand in what seemed to be assent. Father Dunne then asked him if he wished to be received into the Catholic faith, and Oscar again held up his hand. The priest thereupon delivered conditional baptism, absolved him and anointed him. As Robbie wrote to Oscar's benefactress Adela Schuster, he regretted that he had not facilitated Oscar's conversion earlier, in Rome, where Oscar had asked him to introduce him to a priest who could instruct him. At the time, Robbie had not been sure Oscar was entirely committed to becoming a Catholic, and feared that he might regret it afterwards. The fact that Oscar had subsequently called him 'the cherub with the flaming sword, forbidding my entrance into Eden' only served to strengthen Robbie's doubts about Oscar's seriousness of intent. But now the act was done, and Robbie was happier in his own soul.

Before dawn the following morning, as Robbie and Reggie Turner held vigil by the bedside, a death rattle began in Oscar's throat. But it was not until after two in the afternoon that he expired. Jean Dupoirier cleaned away the blood and other fluids he had emitted in his final hours and dressed him in a fresh white night-shirt. Then Father Dunne put a rosary in his hand and spread palm fronds on the bed. Maurice Gilbert, using Oscar's camera, took a photograph of him laid out, stark against the hideous patterned wallpaper that had been the subject of his last recorded *bon mot*: 'My wallpaper and I are fighting a duel to the death. One or the other of us has to go.'

Because Oscar was registered at the hotel under the assumed name Sebastian Melmoth, in contravention of French law, the authorities wanted to take his body away to the morgue, but Robbie managed to enlist powerful support to prevent that happening. He then telegraphed Bosie, who came over to Paris in time for the funeral on 3 December, having ignored earlier messages suggesting he visit Oscar while he was dying.

Cuthbert Dunne said requiem mass at St Germain-des-Prés, then a small cortège followed Oscar's hearse to the cemetery at Bagneux. In the first carriage were Robbie, Bosie, Reggie and Jean Dupoirier. Bosie claimed the place of principal mourner and reportedly nearly slipped into the grave as Oscar's coffin was lowered into the eleventh plot in the seventh row of the seventeenth section of the undistinguished graveyard. Harsh words were exchanged by the graveside, though no one ever revealed what they were. Perhaps Robbie reproached Bosie for staying away during Oscar's last illness. Or maybe Bosie found the funeral arrangements shoddy and expressed his displeasure; certainly they were modest, in no way reflecting the glory of Wilde at the zenith of his success. Whatever the cause, the altercation on this emotive occasion did nothing to improve relations between the two most important young men in Oscar's life.

There were wreaths from several people unable to be present, including More Adey, Harold Mellor and Adela Schuster, as well as flowers that Robbie had arranged in the names of Oscar's sons Cyril and Vyvyan. A simple stone was erected, with a quotation in Latin from the Book of Job: 'To my words they durst add nothing, and my speech dropped upon them.' The grave was only a temporary concession that Robbie had arranged; later he would be able to decide whether to purchase it outright, or move the body to a more permanent resting-place.

Robbie's grief was profound, yet as he told a young admirer of Wilde's, Louis Wilkinson, Oscar's death was actually a welcome release as he had become deeply unhappy and would have become more so as time went by. Moreover, Robbie was anxious that friends did not over-dramatize the tragedy of Oscar's end, nor exaggerate his poverty. One of the first things Robbie did when he rejoined his mother at Menton, after the funeral, was to write at length to Adela Schuster, setting down the facts, in the

futile hope that this would help prevent a myth developing. As
he pointed out, since January, Oscar had been given £400 over
and above the £150 allowance he received via Robbie from
Constance's trustees; £300 had come from the Queensberry
family, and £100 from George Alexander, who had bought the
rights to *An Ideal Husband* and *The Importance of Being Earnest*
from the official receiver. Harold Mellor had paid all of Oscar's
expenses in Italy, and other friends had provided help in France.
In fact, for most of the time since his release from prison he had
been able to enjoy life's pleasures:

> Two things were absolutely necessary for him, contact with
> comely things as Pater says and social position. Comely things
> meant for him a certain standard of living and this since his
> release *he was able to have* except for a few weeks at a time or
> perhaps months. Social position, he realized after 5 months
> he could not have. Many people were kind to him but he was
> too proud or too vain to be forgiven by those whom he
> regarded as social and intellectual inferiors. It galled him to
> have to appear grateful to those whom he did not, or would
> not have regarded, before his downfall . . . He chose therefore
> a Bohemian existence entirely out of note with his genius and
> temperament. There was no use arguing or exhorting him.
> The temporary deprivation of his annuity produced no result.
> You cannot ask a man who started on the top rung of the
> ladder to suddenly start again from the lowest rung of all.
> Among his many fine qualities he showed in his later years
> was that he never blamed anyone but himself for his own
> disasters. He never bore any ill will to anybody and in a char-
> acteristic way was really surprised that anyone should bear any
> resentment against him. For example, he really did not under-
> stand how cruel he was to his wife, but I never expect anyone
> to believe that.[1]

Robbie was probably the only person – other than Oscar himself, Major Nelson and a lady typist who had taken dictation at Robbie's Hornton Street rooms – to have read the whole text of *De Profundis* at this stage. He was aware that Oscar had poured out all of his bile against Bosie in that document, after which he was largely purged of resentment, even if Bosie's periodic rages and limited financial generosity caused him pain. Bosie himself seems not to have read the copy of the document that Robbie had sent him in the summer of 1897, in accordance with Oscar's wishes. Much later, Bosie half-remembered throwing it on the fire after perusing only a few lines. Fortunately Robbie had only sent him one of the typed copies, not the original, as Oscar had originally requested. Mindful of the damaging nature of Oscar's recriminations in *De Profundis*, Robbie had no intention of releasing the complete text publicly while Bosie was still alive, or of making the gist of its damning contents known for the time being.

At Menton, replying to letters of condolence was one way Robbie could come to terms with his own sense of loss. As he confessed to Will Rothenstein:

> I feel poor Oscar's death more than I should and far more than I expected. I had grown to feel, rather foolishly, a sort of responsibility for Oscar, for everything connected with him except his genius and he had become for me a sort of adopted prodigal baby. I began to love the very faults which I would never have forgiven in anyone else.[2]

The 'prodigal baby' now laid to rest, Robbie determined to transfer his paternal concern – at first inevitably from a distance – to Oscar's two boys, both of whom had been sent to public schools in England. The elder, Cyril, then a fifteen-year-old at Radley, actually learned of his father's death from an announcement in the newspaper. But soon after a letter from Robbie arrived, forwarded by the Hollands' solicitors, who were the only means of contact he had with the boys, Cyril replied:

> I am glad you say that he loved us. I hope that at his death he was truly penitent; I think he must have been if he joined the Catholic Church and my reverence for the Roman Church is heightened more than ever . . .
>
> It is of course a long time since I saw my father but all I do remember was when we lived happily together in London and how he would come and build brick houses for us in the nursery.
>
> I only hope it will be a lesson for me and prevent me from falling into the snares and pitfalls of this world.[3]

Robbie was in little mood to celebrate Christmas, or the new century, which was correctly marked at midnight on the night of 31 December 1900. He remembered Oscar's remark that the great British public would never tolerate his seeing in the new era. Queen Victoria herself only managed it by three weeks, expiring at Osborne on the Isle of Wight and unleashing a wave of almost hysterical mourning, whose diminished force inevitably reached the little colony of expatriates in Menton, including the Rosses. Menton, or Mentone, as most of the British residents called it, was particularly well-endowed with invalids, who were attracted by the mild climate of its sheltered location. They clustered in the hotels along the seashore, while above them, like the banks of an amphitheatre, rose the old town, with its steep, narrow, dark, traffic-free streets, inhabited by the native Mentonese. The town had enjoyed independence from 1848 to 1860, under the protection of Sardinia, before being ceded to France, and it still had an Italianate air, with its lemon groves and olive trees, and pines on the upper slopes. It was an ideal place to recuperate, as Robbie and his mother did for several months, while he fended off repeated suggestions that he should write a memoir of Oscar. Arthur Humphreys, the manager of Hatchard's bookshop in Piccadilly, and sometime admirer of Constance Wilde, even suggested a collaborative effort by Robbie, Bosie and Frank Harris. As Robbie pointed out, it would be hard to reconcile their perspectives on the subject. Besides, Robbie felt it was too soon to try to convey an accurate impression of Wilde, as the only sort of readers likely to buy the book would be people with a prurient interest in his demise.

Robbie returned to London in the late spring, fortified and ready for a new challenge. This came from an unexpected direction, when William Rothenstein decided to leave the Carfax Gallery following an argument with Charles Conder. Rothenstein learned that Conder had told someone that Rothenstein had persuaded him while he was drunk to sign a disadvantageous agreement for the sale of his fashionable fans and silk panels in the gallery. Incensed by this groundless accusation, Rothenstein stormed round to Conder's home and hit him. Farcically, when Conder complained about being assaulted in his own house, Rothenstein retorted that he could hardly have invited him round to his own, to strike him there. The incident made Rothenstein realize that his artistic temperament was not suited to the diplomacy and finesse needed for running a gallery successfully. When he withdrew, John Fothergill also decided to pull out of the project, and Robbie stepped in, in partnership with More Adey. Arthur Clifton, the business manager, would remain, to give a degree of continuity. Robert Sickert had already left. Eliza Ross, who presumably subsidized Robbie's takeover of the Carfax, must have been relieved that her youngest son at last had something wholesome yet stimulating to occupy his mind.

He might well have had second thoughts had he realized just how amateurish his predecessors had been, and how much disorder they had left behind. He soon discovered that many items in the stock-book could not be accounted for, mainly drawings which appeared neither to have been sold nor returned to their owners, including some important works by Rodin. The mess took most of August and September to sort out. By November, however, Robbie was ready to oversee the first major exhibition under the new management, which featured works by Max Beerbohm, bringing together one hundred caricatures of political and artistic figures and a satirical series of drawings entitled 'The Second Childhood of John Bull'. The Boer War was then entering its final stages, which meant that some critics were not in a mood to appreciate Beerbohm's irreverent treatment of public figures. But here Robbie was able to exercise some influence through his many well-placed contacts. Edmund Gosse, notably, managed to get a planned savage review in *The Times* toned down by button-holing the critic. Gosse was particularly amused by Beerbohm's drawing of R. L. Stevenson and W. E. Henley, and chivvied all his friends and acquaintances to go to see the show. Sales were brisk, and it was a very satisfying début for the new team.

Despite the demands of his new responsibilities, Robbie was not neglecting his duties as Wilde's literary executor. He applied to the Court of Bankruptcy to have his own position – accorded him informally in a letter Oscar had sent from prison – officially confirmed. An officer at the Court smiled indulgently at Robbie, telling him unequivocally that Wilde's works would never command any interest whatsoever. He was soon proved wrong. In December 1901, *The Importance of Being Earnest* was revived at the Coronet Theatre, before moving to the St James's the following year. As George Alexander had acquired the rights to the play, no income would go to Wilde's estate, though Alexander tried to get Robbie to accept a token payment for himself, in recognition of the work he had been doing on Oscar's behalf.

Even if it took years, Robbie was determined that he would eventually ensure that all Wilde's output would be performed and read again, and that the benefits would go to Oscar's sons. This was despite the fact that the boys' guardian, Adrian Hope, a relative of Constance's, took the view that Cyril and Vyvyan should have nothing to link them with their father at all. Earlier, Robbie had suggested to Bosie Douglas that he clear off Oscar's debts, thereby discharging his bankruptcy. Under this plan, Robbie would administer the Wilde estate on Bosie's behalf, and when it became solvent, would repay Bosie his outlay. But Bosie turned the scheme down. It is hard to reconcile his seemingly hard-hearted attitude with the love and respect for Oscar that suffuses the remarkable sonnet he wrote after Oscar's death, originally entitled 'To Oscar Wilde', but known to the world as 'The Dead Poet':

> I dreamed of him last night, I saw his face
> All radiant and unshadowed of distress,
> And as of old, in music measureless,
> I heard his golden voice and marked him trace
> Under the common thing the hidden grace,
> And conjure wonder out of emptiness,
> Till mean things put on beauty like a dress
> And all the world was an enchanted place.
>
> And then methought outside a fast locked gate
> I mourned the loss of unrecorded words,
> Forgotten tales and mysteries half said,
> Wonders that might have been articulate,
> And voiceless thoughts like murdered singing birds.
> And so I woke and knew that he was dead.

173

As Robbie was well aware, Bosie's nature was full of contradic-
tions, which were exacerbated as Bosie now developed a sexual
interest in young women. Just because Bosie had often been
unkind to Oscar, and neglected him, did not mean that he did
not love him. As Oscar himself had said, in the refrain in *The
Ballad of Reading Gaol*, all men kill the thing they love.
Moreover, Oscar had inadvertently encouraged Bosie's self-
centred nature by almost worshipping him and making his
adulation plain. Of course, Bosie's selfishness was real. He could
have done so much to ease Oscar's situation during his final
months in Paris. Instead he chose to use the money he had
inherited from his father to run a racing stables at Chantilly,
which had long been an unrealizable dream. The enterprise
seems to have swallowed up most of his inheritance within a
period of about eighteen months. Nevertheless Douglas later
described the period at Chantilly as the happiest of his life.

By mid-1901, however, Bosie was back in London and
receiving increasingly amorous letters from a young lady poet
and admirer by the name of Olive Custance. She had contributed regularly to *The Yellow Book*, and was a great favourite
of its editor Henry Harland. She had also produced a volume of
verse entitled *Opals*, a copy of which she sent to Bosie in
homage. Olive came from a well-established Norfolk family; her
father, Colonel Frederic Custance, had been in the Grenadier
Guards and regularly attended Edward VII's shooting parties at
Sandringham. The Colonel would certainly not have approved
of her making the acquaintance of the key player in the Oscar
Wilde scandal, so when Olive and Bosie decided to meet, they
arranged to do so in the anonymity of what is now the Victoria
and Albert Museum in South Kensington. Unfortunately,
because they used separate entrances, they managed to miss each
other, but Olive, accompanied by her maid, then boldly went
round to Bosie's rooms in Duke Street. The attraction was

immediate and mutual, but it was dangerous for her reputation to visit him at home. What they needed was a discreet meeting-place, put at their disposal by a compliant host – a role willingly fulfilled by Robbie at the Carfax Gallery. In the gallery, the self-styled 'Page' (Olive) could encounter her 'Prince' as if by chance, or out of opening hours, and their relationship could develop.

At first marriage seemed impossible, but there was a keen desire on both sides to find some solution to their predicament. When Bosie visited America in the autumn, largely in the hope of finding a wealthy heiress as a bride, he somewhat preposter-ously mused why Olive could not dress up as a boy and travel with him. Olive's *gamine* nature undoubtedly attracted him, just as his superficially feminine beauty attracted her. Aware of each other's bisexuality, they were able to be remarkably honest with each other. Bosie wrote to Olive from America, admitting that at first he used to wish that she had been a boy, but adding that he was now glad she was not; in return, she sent him love letters she had received from a lesbian admirer.

Bosie returned to England in the New Year 1902 without having managed to capture an heiress; even in America, he was considered too much of a risk, despite his title. Olive must have hoped that now he would court her with more assiduity, whereas he, characteristically, went up to Scotland for some shooting with his brother Percy instead. He was shaken out of his apparent indifference when Olive suddenly announced that she was going to marry his former schoolfriend George Montagu. Montagu was a brilliant 'catch', who had been elected to Parliament two years before, and was due to inherit both an earldom and a very substantial income. Edward VII personally sent a message of congratulations to Olive's mother. However, Bosie had no intention of losing Olive in this way and arranged to meet her over dinner in a private room at Kettner's – the scene of so many intimate meals he had enjoyed with Oscar Wilde –

where he assured her of his total devotion and suggested that they elope. The idea was that she would carry on as if nothing had happened, even attending a weekend house-party where she would meet some of Montagu's family, while Bosie arranged a special marriage licence. The details were further elaborated at another clandestine meeting at the Carfax Gallery a few days later. Robbie was fully appraised of the scheme and, as a fellow conspirator, sat at the back of St George's Church, Hanover Square, on 4 March, while the pair were secretly married. There were just two official witnesses, Bosie's sister Lady Edith Fox-Pitt and a young lawyer friend, Cecil Hayes, who was at the time Private Secretary to Lord Denbigh. Straight after the ceremony, the bride and groom drove to Victoria Station and boarded a train for Paris, where they would spend their honeymoon. Colonel Custance was furious when he learned what had happened, and the King expressed his deep displeasure. But before long, the Custances accepted the *fait accompli*, and when the Colonel discovered that he and Bosie shared a keen interest in hunting, he decided that the young man was not such a scoundrel after all.

Robbie always professed great devotion to Olive, or Lady Alfred Douglas, as she was now styled. Yet the marriage created a new barrier between Robbie and Bosie. Robbie was worried that Olive would inevitably be hurt by Bosie. Moreover, it was almost as if Bosie were renouncing, even denying, his past life. The fact of marriage did not bother Robbie. Though exclusively homosexual himself, he had no difficulty in accepting other people's bisexuality. After all, despite being claimed posthumously by the gay movement, Oscar had been essentially bisexual, even if the main focus of his erotic interest from the time of meeting Robbie was young men. And it was common practice for many youths who were available to please gentlemen for a small financial consideration, whether in London or on the

Continent, at the same time to have girlfriends, make women pregnant, marry and settle down. Yet somehow Bosie's quest for normality and respectability through marriage – albeit initially in a typically scandalous fashion – grated with Robbie. It felt like a betrayal.

Not that Robbie himself intended to remain exclusively emotionally bound to the late playwright. He had had plenty of sexual adventures, both during Oscar's lifetime and since. And early in 1903, he met a young man with whom he entered into a relationship quite unlike his other brief encounters with boys. Frederick (Freddie) Smith was an attractive, unpretentious, eighteen-year-old clerk; not someone of Robbie's class or intellectual capacity, but nonetheless keen to learn and improve himself. The fact that Robbie was almost twice his age does not seem to have particularly bothered either of them; indeed, theirs was almost a mirror-image of the generational gap between Oscar and Robbie when they had first known each other. But as the relationship with Freddie developed – soon cloaked by the superficial respectability of Freddie's employment as Robbie's secretary – it became a matter for gossip and for family concern.

Robbie certainly needed a secretary. Organizing exhibitions, and dealing with the difficult temperaments of exhibitors, including Will Rothenstein, produced a great deal of correspondence. On top of that, there was a growing amount of work in his role as Wilde's literary executor. The Germans were particularly precocious in staging and acclaiming the disgraced playwright's works. The first Berlin production of *Salomé* took place in 1901 and ran for over two hundred performances. Sir Claude Philipps, art critic and Keeper of the Wallace Collection, saw the play in Munich two years later, and reported back to Robbie that the 'dear, stolid, unprejudiced Germans' looked on placidly as the action moved to its terrible and revolting climax. So long as Wilde's bankruptcy lasted, however, the royalties from such productions were swallowed up by the receiver; in July 1903, Wilde's creditors, including the Queensberry family, received their first dividend.

Robbie spent a great deal of time and energy trying to keep track of Wilde's literary legacy, and challenging pirate editions of his work. In this, he was fortunate to find some willing collaborators, not least a strange bibliophile and amateur sailor by the name of Walter Ledger, who collected Wildeana and wrote to Robbie asking for assistance in compiling a Wilde bibliography. Seven years Robbie's senior, Ledger was a confirmed bachelor with a penchant for walking around in nautical dress. He was a member of the Royal Yacht Club, but had actually qualified as an architect. He was also a manic-depressive. At times he would turn positively violent, while at others he would shun all human contact. Robbie learned to handle these different moods sensitively, and added Ledger to his growing stable of the sick, the unstable and lame ducks who gravitated towards him for friendly support and advice, the provision of which seems to have been almost a necessity for Robbie's own sense of well-being. At Walter Ledger's urging, Robbie arranged a meeting for him with Bosie Douglas. Conscious of how scornful Bosie would be of an undistinguished forty-year-old man kitted out in bell-bottoms and an open-necked sailor's shirt, Robbie insisted that Ledger wear morning dress for the occasion.

Meanwhile, the Carfax Gallery's fortunes were mixed. Robbie discovered that the public's taste was fickle and had to be gauged carefully if the business was to stay afloat. People might spend several minutes standing before an Augustus John admiringly, for example, but then they would buy a 'safer' William Orpen instead. Works by Rothenstein and others, for whose promotion the gallery had of course been founded, often sold poorly, and inevitably Robbie received flak from artists whose egos had been bruised. Rothenstein accused Robbie of being unsympathetic, prompting Robbie to retort in exasperation that, 'You always see me when I am dead beat and that is why I seem unsympathetic . . . When you have doubts about me and my lack of sympathy if you will consult with Alice without reference to me I can leave my views and my character with her in trust.' Like many gay men, Robbie often found it easier to relate to wives than to their heterosexual husbands, and Alice Rothenstein was a particularly striking example.

In April 1903, the Carfax's fortunes improved considerably with an exhibition of paintings by the art critic Roger Fry, whom Robbie had known slightly when he was at Cambridge. At this stage, Fry, like Robbie, was unimpressed by much modern art and the output of many of his colleagues in the New English Art Club, instead seeking inspiration in the work of seventeenth-century landscape artists such as Claude Lorrain. Fry's paintings of this period struck a chord with the Edwardian public, enabling Robbie to inform him excitedly that:

> The whole exhibition has really been a *terrific* success from our point of view and I hope from yours. It has far exceeded our expectations, especially in view of the fact that so few people have responded to the invitations. I suppose a good many have been away, but those who came have bought and that is more important. Of course those who turn up now complain that all the best things have gone and this is inevitable. We rehung the gallery a few days ago bringing unsold watercolours into the light and this was a success in that four sold from the newly hung wall.[4]

Commercially the Fry exhibition was the best the gallery had had since Max Beerbohm's show, and it marked an important watershed in the gallery's fortunes. Henceforth it was seen as a place where connoisseurs would meet and where fine pictures could be found – a reputation that was subsequently enhanced with successful exhibitions of the eminently fashionable portrait artist John Singer Sargent (none of whose pictures was actually for sale), William Blake and Edward Calvert. Among the serious buyers Robbie was able to woo was Edward Marsh, a civil servant and art lover who was very well-connected among the hierarchy of the Liberal Party, in particular being a friend of Herbert Asquith, who had been Home Secretary at the time of Oscar Wilde's trials and imprisonment. Robbie persuaded Eddie Marsh to buy an important private collection of English paintings belonging to Herbert Horne, a friend of his who wanted to realize some capital so he could go and live in Florence. This *coup* did wonders for Robbie's reputation in the London art market, so that he would often be approached to assist with deals that were not strictly part of the Carfax Gallery's work. Similarly, he found himself being asked to sit on committees of various kinds, including that of a new body called the Arundel Club, which arranged for works of art to be photographed, so they could be appreciated by a wider public. Though always over-worked and often in a state of near exhaustion, he was rarely able to say no to such requests, even when he was asked to take the minutes of meetings.

Of even greater satisfaction was the November opening at the Carfax of the biggest-ever exhibition of Aubrey Beardsley's work, much of which was on loan from private collections, including Robbie's own. Holding the exhibition was an act of personal tribute to his dead friend. Although some enlightened critics shared Robbie's view that Beardsley was a genius, more were hostile, and several still found his drawings obscene. It would be a long time before his work would achieve general approval. As far as Robbie was concerned, the fault lay with the critics, not with the artist, as made clear in his study of Beardsley, published in 1909:

Aubrey Beardsley did not shirk a difficulty by leaving lines to the imagination of critics, who might enlarge on the reticence of his medium. Art cant and studio jargon do not explain his work. It is really only the presence or absence of beauty in his drawing, and his wonderful powers of technique which need trouble his admirers or detractors. Nor are we confronted with any conjecture as to what Aubrey Beardsley might have done – he has left a series of achievements. While his early death caused deep sorrow among his personal friends, there need be no sorrow for an 'inheritor of unfulfilled renown'. Old age is no more a necessary complement to the realization of genius than premature death. Within six years, after passing through all the imitative stages of probation, he produced masterpieces he might have repeated but never surpassed. His style would have changed. He was too receptive and too restless to acquiesce in a single convention.[5]

That other receptive and restless personality of Robbie's recent past, Oscar Wilde, was also once again at the forefront of his mind during the autumn of 1904. Robbie had been coming under increasing pressure from a German admirer of Wilde's, Dr Max Meyerfeld, to allow him to translate and publish extracts from *De Profundis*. At first Robbie was reluctant, not just because of the considerable amount of expurgation that would be necessary to produce a text that would remove all recognizable references to Alfred Douglas, but also because he still felt it would be premature. However, Meyerfeld persisted on the grounds that Wilde had become one of Germany's favourite foreign authors. The composer Richard Strauss was at work on an opera based on *Salomé* which would be staged the following year. Largely in acknowledgement of the Germans' recognition of Wilde's literary standing, irrespective of his personal disgrace, Robbie eventually acquiesced. Yet Meyerfeld still had to badger

Robbie, by mail and in person, during visits to England, before Robbie finally produced a heavily edited text, which was translated and published in the literary periodical, *Die Neue Rundschau* in 1904.

It then occurred to Robbie that he might test the water in England by getting an edited version of *De Profundis* published there as well, if any reputable publisher were willing to undertake the task, given that Oscar's name 'did not bring very agreeable memories to English ears', as Robbie wrote in the introduction he contributed to the 1908 British edition. Methuen seized the chance, and one of the firm's readers, E. V. Lucas – a near neighbour of Robbie's in Kensington – worked with him on preparing the text for publication. As far as Lucas was concerned, it was a labour of respect, even atonement:

> . . . please don't suggest payment. I really like to think it possible to do something for your friend. I hope if I had known him personally I should have been able to muster some of your fidelity; and I have always felt a little guilty in making no effort – for strangers can do these things if they like – to let him know that he had a few friends after he left prison even among those whose names he had never known. When I was quite young I was a pretty good shot with a stone. I believe I have not willingly, or in my right mind, thrown one for some years, – I mean at human weakness. Plenty at the Pretentious Ross I hope; but I doubt often if that is much of a pastime for gentlemen.[6]

Robbie was encouraged by Lucas's charitable attitude to think that at least some of the British reading public would respond positively to *De Profundis*, and that it would enable them to see through the fog of prejudice and glimpse the true nature of the man, as he made clear in his introduction: 'I venture to hope that *De Profundis*, which renders so vividly, and so painfully, the effect of a social *débâcle* and imprisonment on a highly intellectual and artificial nature, will give many readers a different impression of the witty and delightful writer.' Robbie pointed out that for some time, curiosity had been expressed about the manuscript, as Oscar had mentioned its existence to many other friends. In sending Robbie instructions regarding its eventual publication, Oscar had written:

> I don't defend my conduct. I explain it. Also there are in my letter certain passages which deal with my mental development in prison, and the inevitable evolution of my character and intellectual attitude towards life that has taken place; and I want you and others who still stand by me and have affection for me to know exactly and in what mood and manner I hope to face the world. Of course, from one point of view, I know that on the day of my release I shall be merely passing from one prison into another, and there are times when the whole world seems to me no larger than my cell, and as full of terror for me.[7]

Robbie was understandably nervous about the reaction to the book's publication. Keen above all to restore Oscar's reputation, he prayed his action would not have the opposite effect. In thinking so much about Oscar, however, Robbie seems to have failed completely to take into account the effect of publication on himself. Having carefully expunged all direct reference to Bosie Douglas, it seems never to have crossed Robbie's mind that many people would jump to the conclusion that this great, passionate epistle had actually been addressed to himself.

TEN

New-Found Stability

The expurgated version of *De Profundis* was published on 23 February 1905, having been authenticated by Max Meyerfeld. Such a guarantee of provenance was common in the art and museum worlds, but very rare in the literary field except, paradoxically, as a device used in fiction, when an author would claim a putative origin for a work which in fact he had invented himself. In this case, the publisher Algernon Methuen and Robbie were anxious to stress the work's authenticity, to avert any claims of forgery. Even so, at least one critic in France accused Robbie of either having written the manuscript himself or melded letters that Oscar had written to him. This prompted Robbie to comment wryly, 'Were I capable either of the requisite art, or the requisite fraud, I should have made a name in literature ere now.'

Robbie sent out advance copies to a large number of friends, influential literary figures, clergy and acquaintances of Oscar's, in the hope of ensuring that the book would be widely noticed. Major J. O. Nelson, who had been transferred from Reading Gaol to Knutsford in Cheshire, replied, 'I think it is one of the grandest and saddest efforts of a truly penitent man. One has to read but little to recognize what literature has lost in the death of a man like poor Oscar Wilde.' Edmund Gosse confessed that, 'there were many conflicting impressions in my mind when I laid it down, but a book would hardly contain them. I should like – and shall soon hope – to discuss them with you. The publication of so extraordinary a document is an event in English literature, an event which I welcome cordially.' George Alexander said simply, 'I shed many tears.'

Several of Robbie's friends paid tribute to his own role in looking after Oscar's interests, both before and after his death. Will Rothenstein noted that, 'the production of *De Profundis* is clearly your own labour of love. No one who knew it will easily forget your loyalty and constant kindness to Oscar. Reading the book brought it vividly before me. You who now sacrifice yourself for so many once did it for the few.' Yet Rothenstein remained highly ambivalent about Oscar himself, even after reading the book. 'Poor Oscar, how shallow was your artistic imagination – you could not realize sorrow until you were shut up in a stone cage,' he addressed the dead playwright through Robbie. 'Had you done so before you would never have been content to encourage evil instead of goodness. Therein lay the only sin which can be laid to your charge.'

George Bernard Shaw relished the text, finding it quite as 'exhilarating and amusing' as he had Oscar himself. For him, *De Profundis* was as much comedy as tragedy. As he informed Robbie, 'the unquenchable spirit of the man is magnificent: he maintains his position and puts society squalidly in the wrong – rubs into them every insult and humiliation he endured – comes out the same man he went in – with stupendous success . . . The British Press is as completely beaten by him *de profundis* as it was *in excelsis*.'

Algernon Methuen was delighted to report that advance sales had gone so well that he had already ordered a second impression. The first reviews were also highly encouraging, though not all the critics were favourably impressed. Both *The Times* and the *Daily Telegraph* predictably made some unpleasant remarks, but it was Alfred Douglas's review in the *Motorist and Traveller* which

Robbie read with the keenest interest. Clearly unaware of what was in the unexpurgated version, or indeed of the fact that *De Profundis* was the same long epistle to him that he had discarded eight years previously, Bosie opined that it was an 'interesting but rather pathetically ineffective book' which could not rank within measurable distance of Wilde's best work. However, he conceded that 'the trace of the master hand is still visible, and the book contains much that is profound and subtle on the philosophy of Christ as conceived by this modern evangelist of the gospel of Life and Literature'.

Bosie and Olive were then living with their two-year-old son Raymond in a lovely old farm house at Lake Farm about six miles outside Salisbury, though they also rented a town house in Chelsea. In the country, Bosie was able to shoot and fish, both on his own property and at Wilsford Manor where his cousin Pamela, née Wyndham, and her husband Edward Tennant – the future Lord Glenconner – lived. In London, Bosie still kept in touch with Robbie. The young Compton Mackenzie, at this period studying law at Oscar's and Bosie's alma mater Magdalen College, Oxford, happened to be visiting Robbie when Bosie paid a call one day in May 1905. More Adey and Reggie Turner, who had discovered a new vocation as a novelist, were also present. As Mackenzie recalled in the third volume of his autobiography:

> Douglas came in and stood on the fender fidgeting and scratching himself as usual and kept sliding off it. Then Robbie read a letter from G. B. Shaw pointing out that *De Profundis* was Wilde's final score off the British public, and that it was a gigantic *blague*, the final pose even in prison. Douglas said Shaw was probably right and Robbie got angry. Douglas criticized Wilde's life in Paris and Robbie said the one most to blame for that was Douglas himself.

Douglas lost his temper, kicked the fender and marched out of the room. He came back for a moment and told Robbie he did not know what he was talking about. Then he slammed the door, and presently downstairs we heard the front door slam. More Adey was walking about looking more vague than ever and Reggie Turner said Bosie was so impossible that he should have to put him in his next novel, when all the reviewers would say that Mr Turner's characters were far from true to life.[1]

Robbie's tetchiness was probably partly attributable to the strain he was feeling from a recent double bereavement, which had severely dampened the pleasure he felt at the success of *De Profundis*. On 14 March 1905, his mother Eliza died suddenly. A cremation was arranged at Golders Green cemetery just two days later, so soon after her death, in fact, that some friends, such as Max Beerbohm, didn't have time to send any flowers. His mother's death left a huge gap in Robbie's life, predictably. He had spent so much of the past thirty-five years in her company, each of them looking after the other. It was from her that he had inherited his great sense of compassion. Much of Eliza's own youth had been spent soothing her troubled father, Robert Baldwin, and half of her life had been spent in widowhood, at times weighed down with cares relating to her wayward youngest son. Yet she was far from self-pitying, being sensitive always to the problems and suffering of others. At the same time, she could be exasperating. As Robbie had complained to his eldest brother Jack in a letter the previous year, she often displayed a desire 'to live in the land of make-believe'. It was not only concern about her health that made her a restless traveller; her nature rebelled against putting down strong roots anywhere, or forming close attachments beyond her immediate family. But she had stood by Robbie, even when he did things of which she strongly disapproved, and which had brought a degree of shame upon the family. There were moments of iciness between her and Robbie, but these never led to a serious rupture. Before Robbie could properly come to terms with the loss of his mother, however, Jack died as well, just a fortnight later, at the age of forty-six. Though he had never been as close to Jack as he was to his other brother Aleck, Robbie was nonetheless shaken by this second reminder of mortality.

In a macabre development, in early summer rumours originating in the United States began circulating that Oscar Wilde was still alive and living incognito. They were only effectively quashed when *The Sphere* published a picture of Oscar's humble grave at Bagneux. In writing to thank the editor, Clement Shorter, Robbie seized the opportunity to put the record straight on a few other related matters:

At the time of his death Mr Wilde owed a considerable sum of money to Paris tradespeople who out of regard for a fallen and distinguished man, (*contrary to all French instincts*) had given him considerable credit. When nursing him during his last illness he asked me, as one of his most intimate friends that in the event of his death, I would endeavour to see that those who had been kind to him were paid . . . This illness had been a great expense to his friends, and there was really no money to buy a suitable plot of ground for his grave. It also occurred to me and the other friend* who was with him at the last that it would be in bad taste to spend a large sum of money on his grave and funeral expenses until the French creditors who had shown more than human charity were fully compensated. I therefore hired a plot of ground at Bagneux and placed a simple stone over the place, and I pay a rent to the French

*Reggie Turner.

Government for the use of the 'concession temporaire'. It shocks a great many visitors to Bagneux to learn that the grave is only a temporary one. But *two thirds* of the French creditors have been satisfied, and by next year Wilde's last wishes will have been carried out. I shall then remove the remains to a permanent resting place at Père Lachaise – and a suitable monument will be erected over them.[2]

Bernard Shaw had already put Robbie in touch with the young American sculptor who would design that monument, Jacob Epstein. Epstein had settled in London, bringing with him what Shaw described as 'amazing drawings of human creatures like withered trees embracing'. Epstein was keen to exhibit at the Carfax, which he considered to be the centre of real art in London. As Shaw informed Robbie, 'it is a bad case of helpless genius in the first blaze of youth; and the drawings are queer and Rodinesque enough to be presentable at this particular moment'.

The Carfax was enjoying great success with works considerably less revolutionary than Epstein's, which meant that its needs were outgrowing the cramped premises in Ryder Street. The point was driven home to Robbie when Claude Monet visited the gallery, to see if it would be suitable for exhibiting some of his works in London, only to declare that the rooms were too small. Robbie, More Adey and Arthur Clifton accordingly started searching for more spacious accommodation, which they found nearby at 24 Bury Street. This enabled them to diversify and to experiment with new artists, although Bernard Sickert, the art critic of the upmarket literary weekly, the *Academy*, to which Bosie Douglas regularly contributed articles, accused the Carfax of establishing a school of maiden-aunt water-colourists, who made 'an idol of insipidity and a *culte* of incompetence'. His hackles raised, Robbie made a quick riposte:

While your critic B.S. has paid us a high compliment in speaking of the *Carfax School*, we fear the distinguished artists of whom he disapproves will hardly care for the kettle which he had tied to their tails, to indulge in retort. But we do not profess to act as their spokesmen. None of them requires any defence; if that was necessary they would find more eloquent and learned champions than we can pretend to be . . . Certain pictures do not belong to any time or movement, and illustrate no particular theory; they are never old-fashioned because they have never been fashionable. That certain critics do not like them or become ribald about them is an interesting circumstance in the life of the *critic* but it has nothing to do with art.[3]

Just before Christmas, Robbie travelled to Dresden, to see the first performance of Strauss's *Salomé*. He did not enjoy the production very much, but it was a fitting end to a year of great achievement in his campaign to rehabilitate Oscar Wilde. *De Profundis* was continuing to sell well, and although no benefits could yet accrue to Cyril and Vyvyan, it was now clear that before long that situation would change. Their guardian Adrian Hope had died in 1904, removing the last obstacle to their becoming the official beneficiaries of Wilde's estate, once the bankruptcy was discharged. As Robbie had been assiduously working at acquiring Wilde's copyrights, including prolonged negotiations with George Alexander over *The Importance of Being Earnest* and *An Ideal Husband*, the revenues from Wilde's works would soon allow the debts to be cleared off.

The annulment of the bankruptcy was formalized on 2 February 1906, enabling Robbie to press ahead with the preparation of a Collected Works of Oscar Wilde, which Methuen would publish, in both a de luxe and a uniform edition. Methuen was keen that a bibliographical volume should form part of the set; Walter Ledger was working on that, in partnership with 'Stuart Mason', the pseudonym used by the young bibliophile and Oxford graduate Christopher Millard. The son of a former master at Magdalen College School, and a cousin of Lord Basing, Millard was a tall, handsome young man, with a slightly clerical air, perhaps inherited from his father, who was an Anglican canon, although Millard himself was yet another Catholic convert. Behind his façade of respectability, he was a highly sensuous individual, with a ribald sense of humour and an irrepressible spirit. Robbie hardly knew him at the time when he was working with Ledger on the Wilde bibliography, yet Millard thought highly enough of Robbie to send him a bunch of meadow flowers from Oxford early in April. Exactly three weeks later, a less welcome communication arrived from Millard: a telegram informing Robbie that he had been arrested, on charges of gross indecency with a nineteen-year-old youth the previous year. Just as Oscar had responded to Bosie's plea for help fifteen years previously, now Robbie travelled to Oxford to visit Millard in prison, where he found him self-confident and amusing. But when Robbie sat in on Millard's case at Bullingdon Petty Sessions, he found the evidence so distressing that he had to leave the courtroom after an hour. Millard was found guilty and later was sentenced by an Assize Court to three months' imprisonment.

Astonishingly, Robbie reacted to this latest example of Edwardian England's homophobia by defiantly inviting his young secretary-companion Freddie Smith to move in with him in a charming house, on which he had taken a short lease, at 15 Vicarage Gardens, Kensington, just a few minutes walk from his previous rooms in Hornton Street. Robbie's remaining family were horrified by news of this arrangement, and deputed his nephew Edward Jones, who was only seven years his junior, to remonstrate with him. Far from bowing to this pressure, Robbie was furious about this interference in his personal affairs, and sent Edward packing.

Though he never flaunted his homosexuality in public, Robbie saw no reason to be ashamed of his relationship with Freddie, who had not yet turned twenty. Moreover, he was becoming increasingly proud of his young protégé, who had developed into a talented amateur actor. He used his second name Stanley on stage. Shamelessly, Robbie took advantage of his journalistic outlets to promote his lover's acting career, writing a glowing review in the *Academy* of a Bijou Theatre production of the Welsh poet Arthur Symons's morality play *The Fool of the World*. The part of Old Age was, in Robbie's view,

. . . rendered with marvellous skill by Mr F. Stanley Smith, who by a paradox very common on the stage was the youngest of the performers. I have heard him compared, not ineptly, with the child actor, Salathiel Pavy, immortalized by Ben Jonson. Elizabethan experts will remember the pretty conceit by which Ben Jonson has explained his early loss. I hope that Mr Stanley Smith may be seen and heard, not only in Elizabethan drama, in which he has already distinguished himself, but again in modern plays such as *The Fool of the World*, where the adequate rendering of small parts counts for so much.[4]

The editor of the *Academy*, Harold Child, had a particularly high regard for Robbie's journalistic abilities and commissioned articles from him almost weekly during 1906, allowing his critical eye to wander from art to drama and literature. 'Such brilliant work as yours could find a home in any paper in London,' Child once informed him. 'You chose me, and are content with our wretchedly inadequate pay, when you could get double the amount and (alas!) many more readers, anywhere else.' In the event, it was Child himself who was lured away by the prospect of higher remuneration, early in 1907, to become Literary Editor of *The Times*. It was suggested that Robbie might take over from Child at the *Academy*, but he turned down the offer. When he learned that the publication was going to be put on the market, however, he travelled down to see the Tennants at Wilsford, to try to persuade Sir Edward, as he now was, to buy the title, and then install Alfred Douglas as editor. Pamela Tennant was particularly enthusiastic about the idea, and Robbie had discussions with the Tennants' solicitors to finalize the arrangements. It was an exciting new prospect for Bosie, who moved with Olive to live in Hampstead, to be within easy reach of the journal's office. For the time being, Robbie continued to write for the *Academy* under Bosie's editorship, as did Reggie Turner, Ada Leverson and Bernard Shaw.

Another recipient for Robbie's increasing literary output occurred when Edmund Gosse was made Literary Editor of a new Books supplement to the *Daily Mail*. Robbie became a regular contributor, alongside such prominent figures as Thomas Hardy and the young G. K. Chesterton, who had received acclaim for his landmark studies of Browning and Dickens. What's more Robbie got considerably more satisfaction out of writing his pieces for the *Daily Mail* than Edmund Gosse did in being Literary Editor. As Gosse complained to Maurice Baring, 'The labour of bringing out *Books* every week has been a very trying one, largely because I am an old dog to be set a new trick. I don't know how long I will be able to keep it up.' Initially, it was amusing to be able to commission his friends to write on subjects he chose – and to be paid handsomely for it. But the novelty quickly wore off and he came under pressure from the newspaper's proprietor Lord Northcliffe to make the supplement 'a little lighter'. Obviously, Gosse did not heed his master's words attentively enough as after six months he was dismissed. Robbie wrote in commiseration and with affection:

> More than any other of your contributors I am indebted to you because you were the first editor (of a serious publication) who appreciated my work and you are the first distinguished man of letters to have expressed any appreciation of it by word or deed. It is in no spirit of egoism that I claim to reciprocate in a special way that emotion to which you refer but I cannot alas evince it in your inimitable manner, while to express what must be the general feeling of your contributors requires the art of the poets who were among us – an art not mine. The knowledge that you were a fastidious editor was to me stimulating and the labour in giving the best that was in me became a pleasure, a delightful anxiety which I shall miss more than I can tell you.[5]

Robbie was happy to acknowledge his admiration for Gosse publicly, even when Gosse was the butt of other people's jokes. Once at a dinner party, when a fellow guest asked Robbie if he could 'stand' Gosse, Robbie replied, 'Yes. I try to put up with him, for, *like you*, I am deeply indebted to him.' Nor was Gosse the only person who was rewarded with Robbie's loyalty. When Christopher Millard was released from prison, for example, Robbie rallied round to find him a job at the *Burlington* magazine, while other friends and collaborators of Millard's, including Walter Ledger, distanced themselves from him. Millard went abroad for a while, convinced that he would find a more tolerant environment on the other side of the Channel. Robbie endorsed the move, but equally warmly welcomed him back when he changed his mind after a few months. Shunned by many people because of his conviction, Millard was always a welcome guest at Vicarage Gardens.

In the summer of 1907, by an extraordinary coincidence, Oscar Wilde's younger son, Vyvyan Holland, started to attend W. D. Scoones' crammers in Garrick Street, Covent Garden, where Robbie himself had been a student twenty years before. Not yet twenty-one, Vyvyan had spent a couple of years studying law at Trinity Hall, Cambridge, but as his closest relations wanted him to go into the Far Eastern Service of the diplomatic service, it was felt that spending the summer vacation attending Scoones' classes in such subjects as political economy and German composition would help his prospects. After only a few days at Scoones', Vyvyan struck up an acquaintance with a fellow student, Sir Coleridge Kennard, who was also destined to enter the diplomatic service. As their friendship developed, Kennard revealed that he knew exactly who Vyvyan was, as his mother, Helen Carew, had been a friend of Oscar's, and would very much like to meet him. That evening, Kennard took Vyvyan home with him. Mrs Carew spoke warmly of Oscar – the first time for a dozen years that Vyvyan had heard his father talked about with respect. She then raised the subject of Robbie and all that he had done for Oscar, and was astounded when Vyvyan indicated he had no idea who she was talking about. Vyvyan said he would be happy to meet Robbie, so Mrs Carew hosted a dinner for them the following week, at which Reggie Turner and Max Beerbohm were also present. Vyvyan recounted this event in his autobiography, *Son of Oscar Wilde*:

It was a highly emotional meeting, and from the moment I met Robbie Ross, I knew that I had found a true friend of my own, one who would be loyal and true and never betray me. And the impression I had at that moment remained with me until Robbie's untimely death almost exactly eleven years later.

Robert Ross's appearance was very different from what I

had anticipated. I had pictured him in my mind as a tall, melancholy, clean-shaven man, with a shock of greying hair and a flowing tie; something like W. B. Yeats, in fact. He turned out to be small and neat, with a tidy moustache. The worries of his life had deprived him of a great deal of his hair, but he had a roguish, almost boyish look that attracted me at once. He had an infectious laugh which came very easily.[6]

Suddenly Vyvyan's life was transformed. After years of being a 'friendless, haunted creature', who had been taught never to mention his father, he could reclaim his heritage in the company of intelligent and benevolent people from the artistic and literary worlds. Robbie systematically took him to see Oscar's closest surviving friends and supporters, such as Adela Schuster and Ada Leverson. They did more than just reconcile Vyvyan with his past; they also gave him a fresh outlook on life and human nature. 'They broadened my views, broke down my prejudices and inhibitions and gradually drew me out of the shell into which I had tried to retire.'

Robbie was keen to meet Cyril Holland as well, though Vyvyan warned him that he would find his brother more conservative and less 'tractable' than himself. The three met for lunch in the grand but austere surroundings of the Reform Club, of which Robbie had become a member in 1899. He put on his most serious face and kept his impish sense of humour in check. As Vyvyan had warned him that Cyril took a far less charitable view of Oscar than he did himself, Oscar's name was not mentioned once during the meal. Instead, they conversed about literature and art, and although they held widely different views on those two subjects, Robbie and Cyril became friends. Robbie's chameleon-like facility to adjust to differing circumstances had triumphed once again.

Vyvyan came of age in early November 1907; no one was

quite sure of his exact date of birth, as neither Constance nor Oscar had got round to registering his birth until so long after the event that neither of them could remember which day it was. So 3 November was chosen arbitrarily. Robbie organized a splendid dinner for him at Vicarage Gardens, the ten other guests being Cyril Holland, Reggie Turner, More Adey, William Rothenstein, Charles Ricketts and Charles Shannon, Henry James, Ronald Firbank, Sir Coleridge Kennard and the artist Sir William Richmond. Bosie Douglas was not invited, and not just because he would have made thirteen at table.

Relations between Bosie and Robbie were deteriorating fast. Though Robbie once said that the three most important men in his life had been Oscar Wilde, Bosie Douglas and Freddie Smith, by the end of 1907, relations with Bosie were distinctly frosty. This was largely because Bosie had, in Robbie's view, come under the malevolent influence of the man he had appointed as Assistant Editor of the *Academy*, T. W. H. (Thomas) Crosland. Though Bosie had always been a right-wing Tory, he had up until now not usually let that cloud his literary judgement. Crosland, in contrast, was a narrow-minded bigot, and a vindictive one at that. He had a thuggish appearance to match his character. A poet of sorts, he channelled most of his energy into what he saw as moral crusades. Both as a hack journalist and as a litigant in numerous court cases, he never shied away from vituperative invective, and he quickly left his mark on the *Academy*, meaning that the publication soon ceased to be a suitable platform for Robbie's own work. Crosland despised Wilde and all of 'his sort', which meant that Robbie, with his diligence on the late playwright's behalf, would inevitably become a target for some of his attacks. To get a flavour of Crosland, one only has to look at the opening of the poisonous ode that he composed in response to *De Profundis* and published in 1912 under the title 'The First Stone'. This began uncompromisingly, 'Thou/ The complete mountebank/ The scented posturer/ The flabby Pharisee/ The King of Life/ The Lord of Language/With the bad teeth;/The whining convict/And prince of Hypocrites/That slouchest/Out of the shameless slime . . .' The diatribe against Wilde continued in similar vein for several hundred lines.

In June 1908, Methuen at last started to issue the first volumes of its 12-volume set of the *Collected Works of Oscar Wilde*, which, as Harold Child wrote in *The Times*, had been edited 'with self-effacement, with ability, and with scrupulous and loyal care' by Robbie. The books were both a critical and a commercial success, and Robbie got great pleasure in dedicating individual volumes to people who had been loyal friends to Oscar, including Helen Carew, who handed over £2,000 to Robbie to enable him to purchase a plot for Oscar's final resting place at Père Lachaise. A revised and extended version of *De Profundis* was included in the Methuen collected edition, with an extensive introduction by Robbie, though passages that identified Bosie Douglas were still omitted.

No longer writing for the *Academy*, Robbie was delighted to be offered the position of Art Editor of the *Morning Post*, which meant that he became an influential arbiter of artistic taste way beyond the habitués of the Carfax Gallery. As the newspaper's editor, Fabian Ware, made clear at the outset, the appointment was provisional, for a period of three months starting in August, after which Robbie would have to sever his business connection with the Carfax Gallery if the appointment were to be confirmed. That is indeed what happened. However sad Robbie may have felt at leaving the Carfax, he had the satisfaction of knowing that he had made a real impact on the London art scene during his seven years at its helm. He was also aware that the burden of administration that he had had to shoulder at the gallery, despite the efforts of his business partners, had contributed to the exhaustion and periods of ill-health that recurred with depressing regularity.

The year ended triumphantly. On 1 December, at the Ritz Hotel in London, over one hundred and sixty guests gathered at a dinner in Robbie's honour, to acknowledge the work he had done on Oscar's behalf. The proceedings were chaired by the explorer Sir Martin Conway, and the guest-list – which Oscar would have savoured – included the Duchess of Sutherland, Lord Howard de Walden and Lord Grimthorpe, as well as numerous literary figures such as Edmund Gosse and Laurence Binyon, artists, journalists, academics, clergymen and a few whom Sir Martin described as not fitting into any 'definite category', which caused some sniggers among the likes of Oscar Browning and Freddie Smith. The two toasts to 'Our Guest', Robbie, were proposed by Will Rothenstein and H. G. Wells. Frank Harris gave a bravura performance of a speech in which he affectionately mimicked Oscar's conversation. Vyvyan Holland found himself sitting next to Somerset Maugham, while his brother Cyril had Rothenstein as his neighbour. This time Bosie Douglas had been invited, but he declined, later informing Robbie tartly that, 'As to your absurd dinner to meet the Duchess of Sutherland and other people who have nothing whatever to do with Oscar or literature, I certainly did not feel inclined to go to a function to meet Frank Harris, Robert Sherrard and about 20 other people with whom Oscar was not on speaking terms when he died.' It was Bosie's loss.

Robbie spoke movingly and at length about the struggle he had had to get Oscar's estate in order. His tone was characteristically self-deprecating. He acknowledged that every literary executor labours under the suspicion of building his name on the ruins of another's fame. 'Certainly I do, because no one beyond my personal friends would have even heard of me except for my administration of Oscar Wilde's literary estate.' His task had been not just a manifestation of total dedication, but also an act of faith:

Yesterday evening it was exactly eight years ago since Wilde died. A disciple of Mr Wells, I have always anticipated posterity and never doubted for a single moment that time would readjust those small and greater injustices which ethics pursuing conduct invariably impose upon art. I did not, however, anticipate that I should be so generously complimented for the fulfilment of a promise which I made to myself at the deathbed of Oscar Wilde. I was too cognizant of the complications connected with his literary and dramatic estate, though only half-conscious of their extent. A kind-hearted official at the Court of Bankruptcy assured me in 1901, when the creditors had received about three shillings in the pound sterling, that Wilde's works were of no value; and would never command any interest whatever. It was a less kind successor who, with more enthusiasm, relieved me of the first £1000 produced by *De Profundis*. But the receipts from the productions of Wilde's plays in Germany, together with the first proceeds of *De Profundis*, had paid off all the English creditors in full, by the middle of 1906, and there was even a surplus to satisfy in full French creditors in accordance with Wilde's last wishes. You may think it very vulgar of me to go into these details, but in all our hearts we value something which we know has a value.[7]

Robbie paid tribute to Max Meyerfeld's role in ensuring that Wilde's reputation was regenerated. This had contributed to Robbie's becoming pro-German, he revealed; 'those who know me as an espouser of unpopular but not lost causes will not be surprised'. Although, like many other people born in France, Robbie's heart was 'on the other side of the Rhine', he loved the country that had given Europe Dürer, Holbein, Goethe, Heine, Schöpenhauer, Nietzsche and the dramatist Gerhart Hauptmann.

Robbie said he wished to remove a wrong impression from the minds of many personal friends and of people unknown to him that he had been Oscar's single friend during his last years.

There were many others who were not only better friends but in a position to give him more material assistance than I was able to do at the time. Others preferred and still prefer to remain anonymous. It is only accident which made me the symbol of their friendship, and without their assistance Wilde could not have passed the many happy hours which he enjoyed so much even during the last actual year of his life. Without the assistance and friendship of these and others I could never have achieved what I have done.[8]

For many present, the dinner was an emotive occasion. The following morning, Somerset Maugham penned Robbie a note, congratulating him on his speech. 'It was perfectly delightful and very moving, and I'm sure everyone must have been glad to be there to hear you make it. You are a perfect dear and I'm so glad to have known you.'

Robbie commanded great loyalty from most of his friends, who recognized the great value he himself put on friendship; not the superficial camaraderie affected by so many upper middle-class men of his period, but a deep, self-sacrificing sentiment that withstood the storms of temperament and people's bad or thoughtless behaviour. It was a noble quality, but also one that worried some of his friends and admirers, who saw how profoundly he could be affected by emotional strain. As early as 1894, Henry James had confided to Edmund Gosse about 'poor tragic Bobby R., who has taken me (all earnestly sympathetic) into his confidence of his trouble [over the narrowly-averted Dansey scandal], and whose nervous demoralization (which he must, and his friends must, absolutely stand up against in him) affects me as rending the heart . . . B.R. haunts me. What a torture, truly, is the faculty of pity!' Perversely, it was partly Robbie's self-evident vulnerability that made him such an irresistible target to those who now took it into their heads to destroy him.

ELEVEN

Bosie's Vendetta

Considering Robbie was a man with long-standing literary ambitions, as well as genuine talent, it is astonishing that as he entered his fortieth year, he had still not published a single book of his own. It was not as if he would find it difficult to find a publisher. He was well enough established in London, both as a critic and as Wilde's literary executor, and had numerous contacts in the trade; indeed, several publishers had broached with him the idea of writing a biography of Oscar. Almost all that had appeared about the playwright so far were some very subjective and at times unreliable reminiscences by Robert Sherard (dedicated to Robbie, 'in remembrance of his noble conduct towards the unhappy gentleman who is the subject of this memoir, whom in affliction he comforted, in prison he visited, and in poverty he succoured, thus showing an elevation of heart and a loyalty of character'), and a slight volume by Anna, Comtesse de Brémont.

Robbie maintained that he was too close to the subject to be able to tackle such a daunting task properly. Perhaps he was also aware that he did not have the stamina to complete an extended piece of writing. His forte was the review or essay of between 1,000 and 3,000 words; long enough to display his knowledge of the subject, but short enough to be sustained by a lightness of touch and a puckish humour of a kind that charmed Edwardian readers. The same could be said for most of his short stories.

Nonetheless, early in 1909, John Lane at the Bodley Head brought out Robbie's first bound volume: his study of Aubrey Beardsley, with sixteen full-page illustrations of the artist's work, and what was described as a 'revised iconography' by Aymer Vallance. It was an attractively produced little book, whose layout skilfully concealed the fact that Robbie's text was actually less than 10,000 words in length. The dedication was to Sir Coleridge Kennard, in recognition of his role in bringing Robbie and Vyvyan Holland together. The book was quite well received, not least by Beardsley's friends, and it helped strengthen Robbie's reputation as a knowledgeable commentator on art.

Another reason Robbie found it difficult to apply himself to long periods of literary work was that he had become fond of that most Edwardian of institutions, the weekend country-house party. He was popular with hostesses as a single man with considerable social skills, equally at home talking to gruff politicians or to elderly ladies of the kind he had met so often on continental travels with his mother. Margot Asquith was particularly fond of him, and kept him on her guest-list after her husband Henry became Prime Minister in 1908. A woman with considerable independence of spirit and view, Margot was a Tennant by birth, indeed a sister of Sir Edward's, and thereby a distant relative of Bosie Douglas's by marriage. This did not stop Bosie attacking her husband in print, on religious and other questions.

Olive Douglas tried to keep in touch with Robbie, but in February 1909 he turned down an invitation to lunch at the Douglases' house in Hampstead, having decided to break with Bosie. As he explained to Olive, he harboured no hostile feelings against her husband; 'I know Bosie too well and have known him too long.' But in recent years, whenever they had met, they had invariably had some kind of disagreement, which Bosie soon turned into a violent row. Robbie hated confrontations, or harsh words of any kind, as they put him out of sorts, so he thought it better to relegate their friendship to the past. Olive must have shown Bosie the letter, as he then wrote to Robbie,

As to your determination to forgo my friendship, as you have raised the point, I may say that the boot is very much on the other leg. I gave up going to your house because I disapproved of your views, your morals and most of your friends. My own views have changed and I do not care to meet those who are engaged in active propaganda of every kind of wickedness from anarchy to sodomy.[1]

Bosie then began spreading vicious stories about Robbie. For example, he informed More Adey that Robbie was going around London seducing the staff of various respectable establishments. Robbie was being watched by a detective, Bosie claimed, and among his 'victims' were a waiter at the Royal Automobile Club in Pall Mall and a young man who worked at the Hotel Dieudonné in Ryder Street. Clearly Robbie had grounds for suing Bosie for libel, but he was wisely dissuaded by Oscar Wilde's old friend and legal adviser, Sir George Lewis. Robbie did, however, agree to appear as a prosecution witness in a criminal libel case brought against T. W. H. Crosland by the Hon. Freddie Manners-Sutton, heir to Viscount Canterbury, who was a friend of Olive Douglas's and indeed godfather to the Douglases' little boy, Raymond. Crosland had written in the *Academy* of Manners-Sutton's alleged hypocrisy in being on the one hand the major shareholder of a publishing firm specializing in Christian texts, and on the other being involved with a separate firm producing 'dubious stories of a highly spiced character'. The case was first heard at Bow Street Magistrates

Court, where Crosland was committed for trial at the Old Bailey. The next available session at the Central Criminal Court was not until the following February, when Bosie appeared as a witness for Crosland who won the case with a plea of justification. Even though Robbie did not actually appear in court in the end, from now on he would be seen by both Bosie and Crosland as an enemy.

One element of the hatred Bosie now felt for Robbie was resentment at the way Robbie had endeared himself to Oscar's two sons. Vyvyan, in particular, had become immensely fond of him. They often saw each other in the university vacations, and when Robbie had a business appointment at the Fitzwilliam Museum in Cambridge one day during the summer term – Vyvyan's last – Vyvyan and Ronald Firbank organized a little dinner party for him. Vyvyan ordered the food from the Trinity Hall kitchens, while Firbank provided Moët et Chandon 1884 from his wealthy father's celebrated wine cellar. Notable among the six other guests was the breathtakingly handsome poet from Robbie's old college, King's, Rupert Brooke, as carefully selected for the guest's enjoyment as the food and the champagne.

Immediately after Crosland's appearance at Bow Street Magistrates Court, Robbie travelled with Vyvyan and Coleridge Kennard to Paris, to oversee the transfer of Oscar's body from Bagneux Cemetery to Père Lachaise. Robbie was still smarting from Bosie's abuse and quickly became irritated by all the pettifogging regulations associated with this operation. Numerous forms had to be completed, then signed and counter-signed, and fiscal stamps obtained. Then the cemetery authorities informed him that the luxurious coffin he had ordered at great expense could not be used, as the Bagneux rules stated that the body had to be transferred in a casket manufactured in the cemetery's own workshop. Vyvyan later recalled:

The Bagneux coffin was of plain oak, with a silver plate on the lid on which was engraved OSCAR D WILDE 1854–1900. This was the last straw and I thought that Ross was going to explode. However, the undertaker produced a chisel and hacked out the intrusive D, making a bad mess of it but correcting the error.

When the ceremony was over and the vault closed, the undertaker approached Robert Ross and, in an ingratiating manner, suggested that, pending the erection of the Epstein monument, he might put on '*une petite inscription*'. Robbie recoiled from him and, raising his hands in horrified protest, cried in his rather drawling Canadian French: '*Oh, ma foi! Assezz d'inscriptions!*'[2]

Lunch at the Café Weber, which had been one of Oscar's old haunts, managed to restore Robbie's spirits. Vyvyan was impressed how some of the waiters still remembered his father with affection. Then Robbie took him up to see the view from the top of the Eiffel Tower, pointing out all the places that had been so important to Oscar, as well as his own favourites.

Robbie had heard that the Hôtel d'Alsace, where Oscar had died, was capitalizing on its resultant fame; Jean Dupoirier, the proprietor in Oscar's day, had left, but his successor was charging people a franc a time to see Oscar's bedroom. Out of curiosity, Robbie went incognito to see for himself, joining three American tourists and a German at the entrance. The new patron gave a sensational account of Oscar's death, and lauded the role of Oscar's devoted friend, the 'Vicomte de Rosse', a scion of one of the oldest families in Middlesex, who had been with him at the end. The little group of visitors was then ushered into the wrong room, and shown the wrong bed, on which '*le pauvre poète*' was said to have died. As Robbie confessed in a humorous article he wrote about the incident in an issue of *The*

Bystander the following year, 'It was the best franc's worth I have ever had.'

When Robbie returned to London with Vyvyan, he was satisfied that Oscar had at last found his due resting-place, and that his work on Oscar's behalf was now virtually complete. He could begin to concentrate more single-mindedly on his own projects and interests, the most immediate of which was the appearance in September of his second book, *Masques and Phases*. Published by Arthur Humphreys of Hatchard's, the work was a miscellany of short stories, essays and journalistic articles; Robbie himself referred to it as a patchwork quilt. All the contents had appeared before, in publications ranging from the undergraduate magazine Bosie Douglas had edited at Oxford, the *Spirit Lamp*, to weightier journals such as the *Westminster Gazette*. Many of the pieces had been commissioned for the *Academy* by Harold Child, and it was to him that the volume was dedicated. 'There are essays in my book cast in the form of fiction; criticism cast in the form of parody; and a vein of high seriousness sufficiently obvious, I hope, behind the masques and phases of my jesting,' Robbie wrote. 'The psychological effects produced by works of art and archaeology, by drama and books, on men and situations – such are the themes of these passing observations.'

Complimentary copies were despatched to friends, most of whom found it delightful. William Rothenstein was one of the most enthusiastic recipients, savouring the humour that he found 'so intimate and kindly'. What some critics might decry as shallowness, Rothenstein saw as one of the book's greatest assets.

It is so pleasant in these days when immortality is so fashionable to have some one content to give us literary cartoons dealing with things of the hour. Hours sometimes turn out to be centuries, greatly to people's surprise, and what they took to be a million years was after all only a million seconds.

You at least make the hour shine, and a lovely hour it becomes under your brush; a jolly and ridiculous but very radiant hour, and I am proud to be one of your Aunt Sallies.[3]

The critics were in general kind, though as the anonymous reviewer in the *Times Literary Supplement* accurately judged, Robbie's style was redolent of the 1890s, rather than the post-Victorian age. 'The *Yellow Book*, Aubrey Beardsley, Oscar Wilde, with their limitations, are of yesterday, and it is with them that Mr Ross seems to dwell.'

At the beginning of 1910, André Gide brought out a slim volume of reminiscences of Oscar Wilde in Paris. The text was made up of a memoir and an essay on *De Profundis*, both of which had already appeared in literary reviews, but which were now made available to a much wider public. The style was anecdotal and much of the reported speech attributed to Oscar and to Bosie (who is named simply as 'B') must have been crafted from memory. It could not therefore be taken entirely at face-value. Nonetheless, the recollections of Oscar in France and Algeria gave a vivid picture of their subject, as well as a strong impression of the hold that Bosie exercised over him. Robbie wrote to Gide that the little book was the only true and accurate impression of Oscar that he had ever read. He also mentioned that one day he might publish letters that Oscar had written to him, which would confirm what Gide had described. Robbie continued,

This may one day become necessary in order to refute the lies of Alfred Douglas. You no doubt heard reported in a recent libel action that he swore in the witness-box that he was unaware of Oscar Wilde's guilt, and that he was the 'only decent friend who remained with Oscar Wilde'. You know perfectly well that Alfred Douglas was the cause of Oscar Wilde's ruin both before and after the imprisonment. I would like to have pretended this was not the case, out of old friendship and regard for Douglas: and the fact that I had quarrelled with him personally would not have affected my determination to let the world think he was really the noble friend he always posed as being. But since he has taken on himself, in his new character of social and moral reformer, to talk about Oscar Wilde's *sins* (in most of which he participated) and has betrayed all his old friends, there is no longer any reason for me to be silent.[4]

Robbie was back in Paris himself in March, on a short holiday to clear his head, as a winter of churning out articles for the *Morning Post* and other journalism had left him feeling stale. His sense of malaise was exacerbated by the fact that he found himself increasingly out of step with current artistic fashion. Fellow critics, such as Roger Fry, had become hugely excited by some of the new work coming out of France. But Robbie decried Post-Impresssionists such as Cézanne, Matisse and Van Gogh for allegedly abandoning form, harmony and artistic probity. None of them could draw as well as Augustus John, or paint like Charles Shannon, or teach like the Slade professor Henry Tonks, Robbie argued. When Roger Fry organized a landmark exhibition of Post-Impressionists at the Grafton Gallery in November, to introduce the British public to the work of Cézanne and others, Robbie had the opportunity to air his opinions. The press view was on Bonfire Night, which Robbie thought singularly appropriate; he was almost splenetic in his denunciation of the pictures in the columns of the *Morning Post*:

To my uninitiated eyes they appear sketches or underpainting of pictures by someone who, if he cannot draw very well, sees though he does not seize the true aspects of Nature at rather commonplace moments. We are told, 'that he aimed at design which should produce the coherent architectural effect of the masterpiece of primitive art'. All I can say is that he failed; whether from insufficient knowledge of the manipulation of paint or an entire misunderstanding of the aims or methods of the primitives I do not profess to judge.[5]

He did find praise for Gauguin, 'an artist with a fresh idea, a curious technique, and a fantastic vision'. That vision included obvious types of beauty, Robbie averred, adding that this was 'a rare quantity in modern art'. However, he maintained that 'if Van Gogh belongs to the School of Bedlam, M. Matisse follows the Broadmoor tradition in a predilection for mere dischords of pigment . . . The relation of M. Henri Matisse and his colleagues to painting is more remote than that of Parisian Black Mass or the necromantic orgies of the Decadents to the religion of Catholics.'

Roger Fry could not have asked for better publicity for his bold enterprise. The art world was in uproar, and huge fun was had by all. Sir William Richmond trumpeted, 'Oh Vulgarity, thou hast taken possession of the Bastille but we will dynamite you out of it, or better still you will do it yourself.' Other prominent people, including the Earl of Carlisle, lobbied Robbie in the Post-Impressionists' defence. Despite the highly public disagreement over modern trends, Robbie remained on good terms with Roger Fry and continued to acknowledge Fry's importance as a critic. He also actively supported the aims and activities of the Contemporary Art Society, which had been founded earlier in the year by Fry, Lady Ottoline Morrell, her brother Lord Henry Cavendish Bentinck and Lord Howard de Walden. However, when, in March 1911, Robbie applied for the

Directorship of the Tate Gallery, he was passed over in favour of Charles Aitken, who had been running the Whitechapel Art Gallery. It was a bitter disappointment, though it is easy to understand why the interviewing panel may have considered Robbie's qualifications a little thin.

Domestically, things were more satisfactory. Since his lease on Vicarage Gardens had expired, he had led rather a nomadic existence, latterly based in Hertford Street, Mayfair until he found a more permanent abode at 13 Lower Grosvenor Gardens. His relationship with Freddie Smith was still flourishing, and had become more balanced, not just because of Freddie's growing maturity, but more importantly because he inherited from a distant relative enough money to make him financially independent. He no longer wished or needed to work as Robbie's secretary, so Robbie took on Christopher Millard instead. At times the atmosphere at Lower Grosvenor Gardens must have been quite riotous, especially when Reggie Turner – who had also leased an apartment in the same building – was visiting London from his Paris base.

Reggie had not lost his waspish tongue. Having watched King George V's Coronation procession from a window of the Savile Club, he dropped a note to Max Beerbohm saying that the 'King looked feeble-minded and the Queen like a very unsuccessful mannequin'. Though Robbie still enjoyed his company, at times they got on each other's nerves. Robbie almost screamed at him once over lunch at the Reform Club, when the conversation doubtless turned to Bosie Douglas. Reggie considered himself to be a good friend to both parties in the increasingly acrimonious dispute between Oscar Wilde's lovers. But as time went by, he leaned more and more to Bosie's side. It was not that Reggie had himself renounced homosexuality, though his sexual drive appears to have diminished. Rather, he felt that Robbie had made a mistake in publishing so much of *De Profundis*. Even worse, Robbie had compounded his error by coming to an arrangement with the British Museum to deposit the original manuscript there, on the understanding that it would not be available to scholars for another fifty years. The remaining typescript of the full document he kept for himself.

It was on the basis of his full knowledge of Wilde's terrible epistle, as well as his own experience, that Robbie was able to brief the bohemian young writer Arthur Ransome, who had been commissioned by the publisher Martin Secker to write a biography of Wilde. Though known more to posterity as the author of children's favourites such as *Swallows and Amazons*, at this early period of his writing career, Ransome was more interested in the adult market. A study he had written of Edgar Allan Poe had been quite favourably received. And as he was only sixteen when Oscar died, Secker thought he could bring a fresh eye to his complex and still highly controversial subject. Robbie was keen to cooperate, and seems to have shown Ransome the whole typescript of *De Profundis*. He continued to be hurt by what he saw as inaccurate or ignorant portrayals of Wilde, the latest of which had been in a book called *Ancient Lights*, by Ford Madox Hueffer (later Ford Madox Ford). Hueffer was the son of the music critic of *The Times*, Francis Hueffer, and had been brought up in Pre-Raphaelite circles. Robbie's damning review of *Ancient Lights* in the *Morning Post* was headed 'Pre-Raphaelite Chestnuts'. Hueffer wrote apologizing for hurting Robbie's feelings in his criticisms of Wilde, but added challengingly:

> If the reputation of Wilde were still under a cloud he would have been absolutely unattackable. One could not have done it. It is just because he seems personally secure nowadays that – quite automatically and not thinking of him as 'down' at all – I wrote as I did. Do therefore consider that what I wrote is

the best evidence you could possibly have that Wilde is no longer a figure calling for compassionate handling. And that, in the end, as a friend of Wilde's is what you *ought* to want – not that one should avert one's face or treat him tenderly. I don't like his work: I disliked his personality. But I don't insult his memory by avoiding saying so. That really is a tribute that all that you have with so much self sacrifice done for him.[6]

Ransome's *Oscar Wilde: A Critical Study* came out in March 1912. The author had asked Robbie to read through the final proofs, to check for any mistakes or misinterpretations, but Robbie declined. As he explained to Oscar's loyal friend Carlos Blacker, an English dilettante of independent means, who spent much of his life in France, 'I thought the value of Ransome's opinion (the fresh opinion of a younger generation) would be vitiated if I began to doctor it.' Robbie was also worried he might not like the book, though in the event, he thought Ransome had largely been fair. He was, however, annoyed that Ransome had dedicated the study to him, without asking his permission. This made it appear that he had given the book his imprimatur, which he knew would enrage Bosie Douglas. Though Ransome did not name Bosie in the book, there were unmistakable references to him for anyone who knew Wilde's story intimately, and some of these could be seen as libellous.

Spurred on by T. W. H. Crosland, Bosie did indeed choose to interpret them that way. His acceptance into the Church of Rome the previous year had done nothing to calm his combative nature; indeed, it had merely served to give him new grounds for falling out with people. His father-in-law, now a widower, was horrified by Bosie's conversion, and set about trying to get Bosie's son Raymond away from him, which only increased Bosie's paranoia. No one was safe from Bosie's vicious assaults, which usually came in the form of highly intemperate letters. In the process, he managed to alienate almost all of his family and most of his friends.

Once he had read Ransome's book, Bosie wrote to Robbie demanding to know why he had never made clear to him the exact nature of *De Profundis*, which Ransome had said was 'addressed not to Mr Ross but to a man to whom Wilde felt that he owed some, at least, of the circumstances of his public disgrace'. Bosie maintained, 'Hitherto I have always been under the impression that *De Profundis* was a letter written by Wilde to *you* but containing abusive or scandalous references to me which you suppressed.' Robbie thought it prudent to get his solicitor George Lewis to reply, setting down clearly the circumstances of Oscar's entrusting the manuscript of his prison epistle to Robbie. Bosie found them impossible to credit, protesting to Robbie,

You now ask me to believe that Wilde was so base and so vile as to have left you in the possession of the original letter (of which I burnt the copy) and to have agreed with you that it was to be published in whole or in part after his death, and this at a time when he was on terms of the most affectionate friendship with me and was receiving large sums of money from me. Whether it is true or not that Wilde was a party to your action (and I prefer to believe that it is not true and that in spite of his degradation he was not quite as bad as that) there can be no question as to your part in the matter. You admit it and positively glory in it and you have made a lot of money out of it.[7]

The idea that Robbie had profited financially from the publication of *De Profundis* was only one of the wilful misconceptions Bosie had about the matter. But it was something that particularly enraged Bosie, as his own situation was so precarious that he was on the verge of bankruptcy. Partly in the hope of winning substantial damages, Crosland then urged Bosie to take legal action against the Ransome book, which he did, having writs served on Ransome, the publisher Martin Secker, and the Times Book Club, which had added the book to its list. With any luck, Crosland reasoned, they would concede and come to an agreed financial settlement, without the need of actually going to court. Secker immediately capitulated and offered an apology, but the two other parties accepted the writs. Aware that Ransome, as a young man with a family to support, did not have the means to fight the case, Robbie offered to cover the costs and arranged for Sir George Lewis to represent him. Lest anyone should have any doubt as to who was the real defendant in the libel action, Bosie wrote to Robbie, 'You filthy bugger and blackmailer, my libel action against Ransome henceforth becomes an action against you and it will be so conducted.' Showing himself a true son of the Marquess of Queensberry, Bosie in another letter to Robbie declared, 'It is my intention to give you a very severe thrashing with a horse-whip. I am bound to come across you one day or another when occasion serves and you shall be whipped within an inch of your dirty life.'

They met sooner than Robbie would have wished, at the house of Edward and Pamela Tennant, now Lord and Lady Glenconner, who gave a reception at which the Prime Minister and Mrs Asquith were present. Robbie had only accepted the invitation in the belief that Bosie would not be present, so he was startled when his enemy suddenly appeared. Bosie strode up to him, and shouted 'You have got to clear out of this: you are nothing but a bugger and a blackmailer.' Some of the men present intervened and bundled Robbie into an adjoining room, where Bosie pursued him. Bosie lunged at him across a table, which sent Robbie scuttling into yet another room, where Margot Asquith came to his rescue, making a very public demonstration of her support by leaving the party with him and taking him to 10 Downing Street to recover from his ordeal. Far from being satisfied with his outburst, Bosie wrote to him the following morning:

> I could not make a scene last night at my cousin's house or I would have kicked you out. You may be quite sure that you will *never* be asked to the house again. I shall take care that your true character is made known to everyone I know. It is fortunate in one way that you had the impudence to come to Lady Glenconner's house last night, because my anger was so obvious that a complete explanation was inevitable. This explanation I gave to all and sundry. You will not find many respectable houses open to you in future. There is a bad time coming for you and all your gang.[8]

In fact, in the short term, it was to Bosie that the bad time was coming. In January 1913, he was declared bankrupt, having failed to keep up repayments to a money-lender. He was expelled from White's, that most aristocratic of London clubs, and discovered that the number of people willing to put up with his offensive behaviour was dwindling rapidly. His father-in-law, Colonel Custance, having endured a barrage of offensive letters from Bosie, instituted libel proceedings against him, which the *Star* newspaper gleefully heralded as 'the long-postponed trial of Lord Alfred Douglas'. There was no reason for Robbie to gloat, however. Apart from the fact that such a reaction would have been against his nature, he was aware that worse was to come, and that it could all compromise his own personal and professional standing irredeemably.

He was no longer working as Art Editor of the *Morning Post*. The editor with whom he had got on so well, Fabian Ware, had retired, and Robbie did not see eye-to-eye with his successor, which precipitated his resignation. Fortuitously, other possibilities presented themselves, enabling him to remain at the heart of the London art world. Sir Hugh Lane, the London-based director of the Johannesburg Art Gallery, which was being set up largely thanks to the generosity and drive of the politician and diamond dealer Sir Lionel Phillips and his wife, retired on grounds of ill-health. He suggested that either Henry Tonks or Robbie would be a suitable replacement, but as the Johannesburg Municipal Council took so long in moving the project forward, Tonks was soon no longer available. Frustrated by the lack of progress, Lady Phillips decided off her own bat to appoint Robbie, even paying him a modest salary from her own resources. She was a woman of considerable will-power, despite indifferent health, and she had a particular flair for fund-raising. She extracted thousands of pounds from benefactors; it was Robbie's job to spend the money on purchases of significant sculptures, paintings and books. Lady Phillips had her own view of what was or was not suitable, which did not always accord with Robbie's. His first major purchases, made with some assistance from Henry Tonks, were Pre-Raphaelite works by Millais, Rossetti and Ford Madox Brown. Robbie was solicited incessantly by artists and dealers, as well as by the owners of private collections, who hoped he would buy what they had to offer. Fortunately, his years at the Carfax had made him an experienced negotiator, as well as an astute judge of quality, however mistaken he may have been about the Post-Impressionists.

It was largely because of this artistic judgement, as well as his awareness of market values, that he was invited to sit on the Executive Committee of the National Art Collections Fund, which raised money to purchase important works so they could be seen by large numbers of ordinary people. Encouraged by this honour, in August 1912 he applied to become Valuer of Pictures and Drawings for the Board of the Inland Revenue. Testimonials had to be provided for this post, which was technically in the gift of the Prime Minister. This provided several friends and professional colleagues with an opportunity to express their appreciation of Robbie's talents. The Scottish artist and art historian D. S. (Dugald) MacColl, who had become Keeper of the Wallace Collection the year before, declared that Robbie was not only a learned student of the history of painting and an excellent judge, but also 'a man of the most scrupulous and delicate sense of honour, and I know no one who could be more completely trusted to give their due weight to all the considerations on which a decision should depend'.

Robbie duly got the appointment, which involved a great deal of travel, visiting great houses to assess pictures for the purposes of death duties. Despite the professional and sometimes distressing nature of these visits, the position offered him further entrées into the highest echelons of British society.

Reports of Robbie's success only served to fuel Bosie's jealous rage. Edmund Gosse urged Robbie to ignore Bosie's rantings. 'He is a criminal, but not a dangerous one, because his mind is loose and ragged.' Even more sensibly, Gosse advised Robbie to avoid a confrontation with Bosie in court, if at all possible. 'Your unhappy fondness for litigious struggles and fightings, sometimes, if you will forgive my saying so, causes you to lose a sense of the proportion of things.' Robbie heeded the warning not to sue Bosie himself, but he was determined to press ahead in openly backing Arthur Ransome's libel defence.

The hearing was scheduled to begin in mid-March 1913, but had to be delayed for five weeks because of Bosie's bankruptcy summons. Mr Justice Darling presided over the Ransome case, in which the Times Book Club was represented by the formidable orator F. E. Smith, a Conservative Member of Parliament and future Lord Chancellor as Lord Birkenhead. Pitted against him, in an uneven battle, was Bosie's counsel Cecil Hayes, who had been one of the witnesses at his wedding. The kernel of the case that Cecil Hayes set out was that Ransome's book had damaged Bosie's reputation by asserting that he had been instrumental in bringing about Oscar's disgrace, that he prevented him starting life afresh after his release from prison, and that he had abandoned him in Naples when Oscar's money ran out. The Times Book Club denied this was the intent of the passages quoted, whereas Arthur Ransome's legal team took the tack that the implied criticism of Bosie's behaviour was justified. To prove this, Ransome's junior counsel took everyone by surprise by stating his intention of reading out in court the entire text of the unexpurgated *De Profundis*, which Robbie had supplied.

After some time, Bosie requested that he be allowed to leave the witness box, but the judge refused. Hour after hour, he had to sit listening to his character being dissected and destroyed from beyond the grave. Eventually, on the second day, the foreman of the jury intervened to say that they had heard enough. In subsequent questioning, Bosie further antagonized almost everyone in the court, including the judge, who had to rebuke him for impertinence. Mr Justice Darling's summing up was predictably hostile to Bosie. The jury's verdict was that parts of Ransome's book were indeed libellous, but that they were also true, which meant that Ransome had been justified in publishing them, and that the Times Book Club was justified in circulating them. Costs were awarded to the defendants. Robbie had sat in the well of the court throughout the proceedings, but had not been called as a witness. The defence counsel was aware that under cross-examination he might say something that would put their strategy at risk. Cecil Hayes queried why Robbie had not been called, saying he believed 'Mr Ross is well equipped to prove all my client's charges to be true.' But the judge pronounced that Robbie was merely Wilde's literary executor, and that it was his duty to protect him.

Robbie went to dinner with Edmund Gosse that evening, to celebrate the outcome. Over the next few weeks, he received numerous letters of congratulation. One of the most welcome was from Cyril Holland, who had joined the army and was currently hiking in Tibet:

> First, a most heartfelt cry of joy that the last cause célèbre is at an end. I trust it is the last indeed. I know nothing of the details, which were I have no doubt of the customary futility. I fear that the affair must have worried you terribly. I wish I could share a portion of your burden – but that would deprive you also of much of the glory. Well, something too much of this. You require no words of mine; what I think and feel you know.[9]

Robbie was conscious of the fact that this was unfortunately unlikely to be 'the last indeed'. Bosie was threatening to appeal, and as Sir George Lewis warned Robbie, fighting such a case would be an expensive business. Robbie railed to William Rothenstein about how unjust it was that Bosie was able to call on financial support from affluent relations such as George Wyndham. 'Loyalty to a relative is one thing: but to supply a bankrupt relative with the means of blackmailing and persecuting other people is a singular comment on English social life.'

At least Robbie had some potential backers of his own. Both his brother Aleck and Edmund Gosse promised that they would help out if Bosie went to appeal. Indeed, George Lewis was impressed by the number of others who indicated that they could be called on if necessary. This did little to reduce the strain on Robbie, however; one of the worst things was not knowing when and how the enemy would strike. What was certain was that something was being hatched.

In reality, Bosie and his lieutenant Crosland had devised two lines of attack, which they hoped would make an appeal against the Ransome verdict superfluous, thereby avoiding both great expenditure and risk. The first stratagem was to provide an alternative view of Wilde and his relationship with Bosie to that given in Ransome's book. They noted that the controversy surrounding the libel hearings had generated great interest in the subject. Methuen quickly brought out a second edition of Ransome's biography, having removed the specific passages to which Bosie had objected in Martin Secker's original version. Then a publisher called John Long approached Bosie and offered him £500 if he would write a book, which would become *Oscar Wilde and Myself*. The problem was that Long wanted the book within a couple of months, before the interest in the libel case waned. Bosie knew that there was no way he could complete anything that quickly. But Crosland had a facility with words honed by years of popular journalism. Moreover, he would not let the facts get in the way of a good story. Though Bosie provided most of the content, Crosland shaped and coloured it to fit his own agenda, which was to expose the 'perfidy and vileness' of Oscar Wilde and his apologist, that well-known sodomite and seducer of young boys, Robert Ross.

The second stratagem in Douglas's and Crosland's campaign to bring down Robbie was far more underhand and dangerous. For some months prior to the Ransome libel case, Robbie had been aware that he was being watched and followed. More Adey had warned that Bosie had told him he had set detectives on to Robbie, although at first they tended to treat this claim as mere bluff. But when in January 1913, Robbie approached a man lurking in the shadows near his home, the man confirmed that he had indeed been in Bosie's employ for the past six months, monitoring Robbie's and Freddie Smith's movements. The private detective proved to be unexpectedly forthcoming, as he was in dispute with Bosie about his pay and expenses. So it was from him that Robbie learned that Bosie had had an anonymous statement drawn up, accusing Robbie and Freddie of unnatural offences. The document had already been sent to Scotland Yard and Bosie was savouring the prospect of Robbie's being arrested at any moment.

TWELVE

New Beginnings

An invitation from the Moscow Arts Theatre to attend the first Russian production of Wilde's *Salomé* provided Robbie with temporary escape from his worries. Armed with letters of credit and what proved to be rather unreliable travel tips from Thomas Cook's, he set out at the beginning of September 1913, in a spirit of adventure. The twilight years of Tsarist Russia were a fascinating time to visit, as the country was in ferment. The Tsar and Tsarina in St Petersburg had become remote from the people, while wild rumours had been circulating about the exact role and powers of the peasant mystic Rasputin, who was cherished by the Tsarina for his apparent ability to reduce the suffering of the haemophiliac heir to the throne. A small elite enjoyed great wealth and looked westwards for their cultural inspiration, whereas the masses toiled in a system that was still largely feudal, despite Nicholas II's half-hearted reforms.

Frustratingly, when Robbie arrived in Paris on 5 September, he discovered that no sleeper was available on the trains to Moscow for another ten days. The weather was hot and the city was crowded; he had some difficulty finding a reasonable room. Fortunately there were plenty of exhibitions to see. He ran into a couple of friends from London, who kept him amused over meals together. But in letters to his brother Aleck and to his secretary Christopher Millard, who was looking after his affairs while he was away, he complained how expensive Paris had become. Not previously one to harp on about living costs – except when trying to curb the profligate Oscar Wilde, or complaining in the Reform Club's suggestions book – Robbie had developed a deep anxiety about money, doubtless provoked by a concern over possible future expenditure in a legal showdown with Bosie Douglas. He had even given up drink, as he informed Aleck, 'though my nerves are all on edge. I have come to the conclusion that Paris is a bad place for nervous people: and it is fearfully exhausting, though I have been living a model life and going to bed early, my only dissipation being museums.'

From Paris to Berlin, Robbie shared a compartment with a charming German Jew, who took one look at Robbie's luggage label and declared, 'Ah, Oscar Wilde!' The man was a Wilde enthusiast, and wanted to invite Robbie to his house in Berlin to meet his wife. For a moment, Robbie thought of denying that he was *that* Robert Ross, but then he recalled St Peter, and kept the man happy with stories of Oscar, while insisting that he must press ahead for Warsaw. At Berlin, the Jew was replaced by a bluff Afrikaner tradesman, who regaled Robbie with tales of his exploits in the Boer War, as well as sharing his unflattering impressions of the Germans. It was as well that Robbie had such a garrulous travelling companion for the latter part of his journey, as he found the countryside from Warsaw to Moscow deeply depressing. 'It is like Canada only more monotonous,' he complained to Aleck.

The Director of the Moscow Arts Theatre, Michael Lykiardopulos, and several colleagues were at the station to greet him. He was taken to check in at the Hotel National, then whisked off to a music hall where entertainment and a lavish supper had been laid on. It was three o'clock in the morning before he got back to his room, exhausted. He had not been allowed to pay for anything that first evening, but he soon discovered that everything in Moscow was alarmingly expensive, including cigarettes, which he virtually chain-smoked. It also seemed to be the custom to hand out tips on every occasion, though the servants looked permanently melancholy. The city itself he considered provincial, and he was frustrated that his lack of Russian meant that he had to rely on his hosts to facilitate everything as the locals were not quick at anticipating the most obvious wants of foreign visitors, such as hot water for morning coffee. Yet the hospitality was overwhelming, as he told Aleck:

> My room is a mass of expensive flowers sent me by various enthusiastic 'femmes'. I feel like a popular prostitute, and the papers have long and sometimes imaginary interviews with me. I am glad to say that the almost absurd interest in poor Oscar is really because they admire his work not, as is so often the case, merely for his 'unimpressioniste' tastes. Grave and white haired professors are trundled up to me and make long speeches. Their names are all unpronounceable, and their French is only a trifle more intelligible than mine.[1]

To Christopher Millard he decried the apparent absence of any gay life in Moscow. 'Among the multitude of people I have met here I have not seen any purple people or any who avowed they were or looked in the least like it. Nor does one see them in the streets. It is rather depressing.'

Plans to visit St Petersburg were abandoned, partly because of the expense, but also because the weather had suddenly turned cold, and Robbie had no heavyweight formal attire with him. Moreover he was feeling below par from a cold he had picked up in Paris. Much as he enjoyed visiting some of the Old Believer Churches in Moscow, where the singing was sublime, or chatting with Russian Liberals, who were unanimously condemnatory of the Tsar, he was beginning to find the city oppressive.

It was therefore with a degree of relief that he embarked on the long train journey home, via Ostend, reaching London on 5 October.

During his travels, Robbie had had plenty of time to analyse his present situation, both domestically and in relation to the threat of action by Douglas and Crosland. On the home front, he had decided to terminate his relationship with Freddie Smith, who had failed to give him the sort of loving support he had needed during his recent troubles. Although he knew Freddie would feign enthusiasm at his return, he was conscious that the passion had gone out of their union, and that more disappointment and heartache would lie ahead if he did not bring things to an end. He specifically asked Christopher Millard not to tell Freddie exactly when he was returning, which would make it more likely that Freddie would not be there when he got home. This proved to be the case, which gave Robbie the opportunity to work calmly through the great pile of letters and administrative papers that Millard had prepared for his return.

When Robbie and Millard next met, however, Millard imparted some disturbing news. During Robbie's absence, he had frequented a rent-boy by the name of Charlie Garratt. Late one night, as young Charlie was leaving Millard's apartment, he was arrested and charged with importuning. Millard nobly but foolishly spoke up for the boy at his appearance in the Magistrates' Court, though this did not prevent Garratt being sent to jail. Both their names appeared in a story about the case in *Reynold's News*. Aware that his link with Millard could prove dangerously compromising, Robbie reluctantly felt he had to dispense with his services, even though he had been an excellent secretary and would remain an amusing friend. What is more, Millard had proved his loyalty by rejecting an offer of money from one of Bosie Douglas's agents in exchange for stealing some of Robbie's personal correspondence.

The piece in *Reynolds* inevitably came to Bosie's attention. He cut it out and sent it to George Lewis with a covering note renewing allegations against Robbie of sodomy and anarchy. Clearly his intent was to provoke Robbie to sue him, but for the time being, Robbie did not rise to the bait. Noting that Robbie had sardonically included 'litigation' amongst his hobbies in his entry in *Who's Who*, Edmund Gosse stressed once more how disastrous any legal action initiated against Bosie might turn out to be. Instead, Gosse arranged for Robbie to see the Lord Chancellor, Lord Haldane, on a personal basis, to get some advice about handling this delicate situation. Haldane proved to be highly sympathetic, as indeed he had been to Oscar in prison. He asked Robbie to write a complete account of the persecution he had been suffering from Bosie over the preceding four years, and to submit it to him along with copies of any abusive letters he had kept. Though Haldane could not promise any official protective measures on Robbie's behalf, he said he would do all he could in a personal capacity.

In mid-December 1913, Robbie moved yet again, this time to a service apartment in Bury Street, where a few days later he was served with a writ from Charlie Garratt's mother, charging him with improper conduct and demanding damages. The following week, there was an even more alarming development when he learnt that Bosie Douglas had moved into the same building and had tried to bribe one of the service staff to steal any papers he could lay his hands on in Robbie's apartment. Fortunately, the building's proprietor quite understood Robbie's predicament, when Robbie explained it to him, and made Bosie leave. The question now was what Bosie would do next. Robbie was afraid he might turn up and make a scene at Vyvyan Holland's wedding, which was due to take place in the New Year. As Robbie informed Gosse, 'Detectives disguised as guests and members of the theatrical profession are to be both at the

Church and the House in case Douglas had organised a demonstration.'

In the event, Bosie did not show up at the wedding, and before long he left for France. His father-in-law, Colonel Custance, had reactivated libel proceedings against him and was trying to get him arrested and sent to prison, which made it prudent for him to get away from English jurisdiction. As Crosland soon joined Bosie in France, having himself sent Robbie a number of libellous letters, Robbie decided that this was the moment to move against them both, in the hope that they would not feel able to return to England. Accordingly, on 24 March 1914, he filed a suit of criminal libel against Douglas, as well as issuing writs for criminal conspiracy and perjury against Douglas and Crosland jointly. Bosie did indeed decide to stay well away, but Crosland defiantly returned from France on 12 April and was promptly arrested. When he was charged at a police station, on fourteen counts of conspiring to make false accusations against Robbie of gross indecency with Charlie Garratt, he responded defiantly, 'Why don't you arrest Robert Baldwin Ross? We gave you all the information about what these fellows did to the boy Garratt.'

At the Magistrates' hearings, Garratt's mother was called as a witness. She said that Crosland had visited her after her son's imprisonment and told her it was Robbie and Millard who ought to be in jail, not Charlie. On a later occasion, Crosland had offered her ten shillings a week to have her son back home when he was released, as he would then be easily accessible as a witness, if required. It was on Crosland's and Douglas's instructions that the writs for damages against Robbie had been issued and signed by her, though these were later withdrawn as she did not wish to pursue the matter.

Robbie took advantage of a weekend adjournment in the proceedings to go to Paris for the official unveiling of Jacob Epstein's

Wilde memorial. This bulky but impressive monument, featuring a winged messenger, had taken the sculptor three years to complete. But when the French authorities viewed the finished work in 1912, they were scandalized by the messenger's obvious genitalia, and insisted that the monument be covered by a tarpaulin. Controversy raged about this on both sides of the Channel, with Robbie writing cheekily in *The Pall Mall Gazette* that the censorship showed that the French were worthy partners of the English in putting propriety before everything. 'I hesitate to say that the rest lies in the lap of the gods, because that is precisely the part of the statue to which exception is taken.' Aleister Crowley, writer and master of the occult, who spent much of his adult life on the Continent, later tried to take matters into his own hands by conducting an informal, unauthorized unveiling with a group of British artists and poets.

Maurice Gilbert, Oscar's faithful little sailor friend, accompanied Robbie at the official ceremony. He had met Robbie at the Gare du Nord when he arrived in Paris and handed him a letter that he had received from Reggie Turner, criticizing Robbie for allegedly provoking Bosie into taking action against him. Robbie was furious at what he saw as an act of betrayal and wrote to Reggie that he now considered that their friendship had ceased. Friends who 'are precious are those with whom one has *not* been too intimate,' he declared. Though they later patched up the quarrel, they were never very close again.

Back in London, Charlie Garratt was called as a witness in the case against Crosland. When Robbie was pointed out to him in the court, he maintained that he had never seen him before, though under hostile cross-examination he became less emphatic. He spoke of visits that Crosland's and Douglas's solicitors had made to him while he was in Pentonville jail, where they tried unsuccessfully to make him state that he had had sexual relations with Robbie. Immediately he was released from

Pentonville, he went round to see Millard and told him everything that had happened. Shortly afterwards, he was again arrested for importuning and sent to prison for a second time.

When Robbie appeared in the witness-box at the Crosland hearings, he read extracts from a letter Bosie had sent him in December 1912, accusing him of keeping a copy of *De Profundis* for the express purpose of blackmailing him. The letter contained an unambiguous threat that he would 'smash you all inevitably and finally because I have right on my side and because I am a decent man fighting a lot of filthy rats'. Another of Bosie's letters, quoted by Christopher Millard when he was called to give evidence, was even more explicit, describing Robbie as 'probably the foulest and most filthy beast drawing the breath of life'.

However, it was Crosland, not Douglas, who was before the court. He declared that he believed Garratt, Millard and Robbie were all lying. Men had been hanged on less evidence than he had against Robbie, he claimed. Far from being penitent over the distress he had caused Robbie, he was happy that at last matters were coming out into the open. In the face of his uncompromising attitude, he was duly committed for trial at the Old Bailey.

During the course of the hearings at the Magistrates' Court, Robbie received considerable emotional support from Margot Asquith and her family. She invited him to dinner at 10 Downing Street, and he accompanied her step-daughter Elizabeth to the theatre. Lady Phillips in Johannesburg also expressed concern. Robbie had tendered his resignation as London Director of the Johannesburg Art Gallery the previous year, as he feared the legal battles he was being driven into would consume too much time and perhaps harm his reputation. There was still outstanding work to be completed for the Gallery, but Lady Phillips was indulgent, and most of Robbie's well-placed friends saw him as the victim of persecution and therefore worthy of sympathy and support, much to Bosie's indignation.

F. E. Smith led the prosecution's case against Crosland at the Central Criminal Court on 27 June, once again pitted against Cecil Hayes. Smith outlined the outcome of the Ransome libel case for the jury's benefit. But the conduct of the defence in the current trial was more reminiscent of the prosecution against Oscar Wilde almost twenty years earlier – a point that would not have been lost on the judge, Mr Justice Avory, who had by coincidence been a junior prosecution counsel on that occasion. Cecil Hayes produced a copy of *The Picture of Dorian Gray*. Echoing the proceedings of 1895, he asked Christopher Millard whether he considered it to be an immoral book, to which Millard replied simply that he did not. Later, Robbie added a moment of levity when he was asked whether he considered there was such a thing as an immoral book, and he responded in the affirmative: 'Lord Alfred Douglas's poems, for instance.'

It soon became obvious that it was not so much Crosland who was on trial but Oscar Wilde and all that he had stood for. Crosland portrayed himself as a decent, upright man who was fighting a moral crusade against those who were trying to whitewash Wilde and legitimize filthy practices. F. E. Smith wrong-footed him by forcing him to admit that he had left his wife and children and was now living with a mistress. But such was the hypocrisy of the age that this was considered by the jury to be a minor misdemeanour in comparison with the excesses of Wilde, Robbie Ross and their coterie. In his summing up, the judge informed the jury that they were not there 'to convict anybody merely because Mr Ross had the good fortune to secure the services of one of the most eminent and most eloquent of the counsels at the English Bar'. Moreover, they should be aware that if they acquitted Crosland, this would not imply that Robbie was guilty of any offence. The direction was clear, and the jury's verdict was rapid, enabling Crosland to leave the court a free man.

Robbie felt devastated. The verdict was humiliating, and confirmed the depth of prejudice that still existed among ordinary people despite all the work he had done towards Wilde's rehabilitation. He could not bear the thought of being talked about, criticized or even pitied in London, so sought refuge at his sister Mary's home at Pangbourne in Berkshire. Conscious that he might have become stigmatized in the eyes of some of the grand people whose houses he had to visit in his work as Assessor of Picture Valuation for the Inland Revenue, he resigned rather than cause embarrassment, or worse still, be asked to stand down. Dugald MacColl was dismayed and wrote to Asquith's Private Secretary, Maurice Bonham-Carter, suggesting that Robbie be appointed Administrator of the National Gallery. Bonham-Carter raised the matter with the Prime Minister, who said he would consult with the Gallery's Trustees, though nothing came of this.

The outbreak of War on 4 August 1914 provoked a development that Robbie had subconsciously feared more than anything else: Bosie Douglas's return to England. When Bosie landed at Folkestone a month later, he was greeted with two warrants, one from his father-in-law Colonel Custance, and the other from George Lewis on behalf of Robbie. Christopher Millard was delighted by the news of Bosie's arrest, but Edmund Gosse was appalled when Robbie intimated that he would proceed with legal action against him. For Gosse, it was a foolhardy rerun of Oscar's prosecution of the Marquess of Queensberry. He had a blazing row with Robbie over the matter, leaving Robbie feeling more isolated than ever. However, just as Oscar had felt it necessary to bring things to a head in 1895, after two years of harassment from Queensberry, so Robbie felt he had to act if he was to remain sane.

Bosie quickly dealt with the outstanding libel action from Colonel Custance, by offering a full apology in court, and promising not to repeat the libels against him. Bosie was warned that he faced imprisonment if he broke his word, but this did little to make him feel penitent. His sights were firmly set on the fight ahead with Robbie. He entered a plea of justification for what he had said about Robbie, citing four cases of alleged gross indecency: with Biscoe Wortham's Bruges pupil, Dansey, two decades before, Freddie Smith, Charlie Garratt and a boy called William Edwards. The last-mentioned was the strangest allegation, not least because Bosie later claimed that his favourite saint, Anthony of Padua, had intervened to give him the evidence. According to his autobiography, Bosie had heard reports of Robbie's being involved with young Edwards, but when he visited the address he had been given for the Edwards family in Kensington, not far from Robbie's former home in Hornton Street, the people living there said they had never heard of them. Bosie prayed to St Anthony, and a beautiful young boy materialized. The angel took Bosie by the hand, leading him to the Edwardses' current home, and then evaporated.

Had Bosie recounted this preposterous tale at his trial, which opened at the Old Bailey on 19 November, the jury might have viewed him less favourably than it did. Instead, they were presented with William Edwards' father, who recalled that his son had come home one day in 1908 with the name Ross on his collar and shirt-band, these presumably being gifts from Robbie. It was sometime later before the upright Mr Edwards read a newspaper article which mentioned Robbie's connection with Oscar Wilde and jumped to the conclusion that Robbie had seduced the boy.

Thirteen other witnesses were produced in Bosie's defence, including a young woman who had taken part in amateur dramatics with Freddie Smith. She testified that she had seen Robbie hug Freddie and call him 'my darling'. A priest, whom Freddie had served as an acolyte, spoke of his revulsion when he had seen Robbie's lover with make-up on his face. H. G. Wells, who was one of four character witnesses called by the prosecution, mentioned that he had met Freddie Smith several times at Robbie's home and never noticed anything of the sort. Wells had become very friendly with Robbie, and had recently asked him to become his literary executor. Now, suddenly, he found his own work being attacked in court by Bosie's counsel, who accused him of constantly advocating the view that 'the ordinary ideas of marriage are nonsensical'.

Edmund Gosse fared somewhat better. He said Robbie had been a dear and loyal friend to him and his wife for nearly fifteen years. There was nothing in Robbie's conduct that indicated that he was in any way immoral; if he was guilty of anything, it was an occasional lapse of judgement about other people. He had worked tirelessly to help other people, Gosse underlined, not least Oscar Wilde's two sons. Vyvyan Holland, as another of Robbie's character witnesses, confirmed this. He said he saw Robbie as a kind of second father and he strongly refuted claims from Douglas and Crosland that Robbie had made money out of Wilde's estate. Aleck Ross loyally spoke on Robbie's behalf, but was obliged by the defence counsel's questioning to admit that Robbie had been known to have periods of mental instability, which at one time had led to his being sent to Davos to convalesce.

The judge, Mr Justice Coleridge, made no secret of where his sympathies lay when he noted sourly in his summing up that Robbie had never given any indication that he viewed homosexuality with disgust. This contrasted starkly with Bosie Douglas's active campaigning against the 'vice'. Yet when the jury retired, it was unable to reach a verdict. A retrial was ordered, to open on 11 December, when Mr Justice Avory, who had been the judge at the Crosland trial, would preside. Rather than go through the whole painful business again, Robbie decided, in consultation with Sir George Lewis, to withdraw. Bosie Douglas, not content with this partial victory, pressed to ensure that the papers relating to the case were sent to the Director of Public Prosecutions. There was little substantive evidence in them to show that Robbie had indulged in gross indecency, however, so the DPP decided not to pursue the matter.

Bosie continued to maintain that the allegations he had made against Robbie were true. He wrote to the Prime Minister, demanding that the Asquiths stop receiving Robbie at Downing Street and at their country home, The Wharf. Otherwise, Bosie warned, he would take his campaign against Robbie to the newspapers, which would embarrass the government. Asquith had no intention of being cowed by the ravings of a man he considered mad and did not deign to reply. Bosie then targeted Robbie's professional and personal acquaintances, even writing to the Committee of the Reform Club insisting that Robbie should be asked to resign. As Asquith himself was on the Committee, along with other men who held Robbie in high esteem, they treated Bosie's letter, and a childishly offensive verse that accompanied it, with the contempt they deserved.

Despite such support Robbie's public standing did not remain unscathed. After the latest trial, he had been phoned by a senior official at the Inland Revenue, who suggested that Robbie write asking whether his resignation as Assessor of Picture Valuations had yet been formally accepted, as he believed there was a good chance Robbie could be reinstated. Robbie duly wrote, only to receive a hurtful reply that the resignation had been accepted, and the matter was now closed.

Determined to rescue Robbie's reputation, his most loyal friends finalized plans they had been discussing for some time to raise a subscription and testimonial to him. A committee was set up, with Edmund Gosse in the chair. The joint secretaries were Dugald MacColl and his fellow art expert Robert Witt, while the Earl of Plymouth took on the role of Honorary Treasurer. A letter was sent out to potential subscribers, offering them the opportunity of 'testifying publicly to their admiration and regard for one who has been unfailingly at the disposal of any who claimed either his sympathy or his help. The calls that have thus been met with rare loyalty and courage will never be fully known, but in our time there has been no friendlier influence in the world of Art and Letters.'

Over three hundred people responded positively. The Prime Minister headed the list of distinguished politicians, while from the world of literature George Bernard Shaw, Thomas Hardy and H. G. Wells were among the most prominent. Friends from the various periods of Robbie's life contributed, raising a considerable sum that was sufficient to endow a scholarship at the Slade School of Art. An annual prize of £25 would be awarded to the student who had completed three successive years and who showed the most promise in the field of drawing, painting, sculpture or architecture. Robbie insisted that the bulk of the money should go to this worthy cause, rather than directly to himself, though he was presented with an inscribed pocket watch. A stipulation of the scholarship that Robbie imposed was that it should only be available to males. The restriction was understandable considering the way he had stood up for what the Keeper of the Department of Prints and Drawings at the British Museum, Sidney Colvin, had described, in refusing to subscribe to Robbie's testimonial, as 'Oscar Wildeism – the most pestilent and hateful disease of our time.' Paradoxically this meant that Robbie would never see the award made, as most healthy young men would be on active service on the Continent for the duration of the war.

Both Cyril and Vyvyan Holland were serving in France. Vyvyan was working with ammunition convoys, trying to persuade recalcitrant mules to pull wagons laden with shells down narrow lanes bordered with deep ditches full of water and mud, all in the inky blackness of night. As he wrote to Robbie on 14 May 1915, 'it is hair-greying work, particularly as I had a horrible horse who was frightened of the dark'.

That same week, Cyril was reported killed in action, shot by a sniper's bullet at Neuve-Chapelle. Knowing how much Robbie would feel the loss, Charles Ricketts wrote on behalf of Charles Shannon and himself that 'we sincerely trust that you may find consolation in the knowledge of your splendid devotion to Oscar's son; and, I am sure, if there was time for remembrance at the end, that Cyril must have thought affectionately of you as the one generous and kindly influence he had met in his life'.

Every day, the newspapers carried details of the dead and the missing in action: artists, poets, the scions of famous families, as well as tens of thousands of ordinary young men, whose names meant nothing to Robbie, but whose sacrifice angered and upset him. Far from being carried away by the jingoism associated with the conflict, Robbie was revolted by the war, its futility and its callous decimation of a whole generation. As Arnold Bennett noted, 'whenever Ross talks about the war his whole face changes'. At the same time, Robbie was frustrated by the lack of purpose to his own existence. His poor health precluded any form of humanitarian work or any other form of non-military service. But unlike the invalid Ronald Firbank, who had just published the novel *Vainglory*, Robbie was not even writing anything substantial. Instead, he produced two slight volumes of intellectual parlour games, *The Connaught Square Catechism or Confessions to Mrs Robert Witt*, and *Really and Truly: A Book of*

Literary Confessions: Designed by a Late Victorian, both published in 1915. Players of these games were invited to name the greatest living draughtsman, or the worst deceased European painter. Pat answers, such as 'The Bible' or 'Shakespeare', in response to a question on favourite books or authors, were excluded. It was harmless stuff, designed to provide light but stimulating entertainment in a pre-television world, for people who might otherwise be preoccupied by the war.

Most of Robbie's own limited energies were being expended on his ongoing private battles with Bosie Douglas and T. W. H. Crosland. Crosland was pursuing Robbie for malicious prosecution, relating to the trial of the previous year. The case opened on 15 April 1915, at the Old Bailey, in front of Mr Justice Bray, who proved to be a far more impartial figure than Mr Justice Avory had been. Crosland was represented yet again by Cecil Hayes. Hayes asserted that Robbie had devoted the preceding fifteen years of his life to promoting the work of a man who had been imprisoned for advocating unnatural practices. Crosland particularly objected to the way that Robbie's successful negotiation of a cheap, collected edition of Wilde's works had meant that Wilde's pernicious doctrines could be spread among the 'cheap public, the street public, office boys and others'. When Mr Justice Bray inquired whether that justified him calling Robbie 'opprobrious names', Crosland asserted that Robbie had 'an ulterior interest in booming Wilde's works, not a literary interest'.

On the fourth day of the trial, Mr Justice Bray declared that the case rested essentially on whether there was any substantial corroboration of the allegations about Robbie's intimacy with Charlie Garratt, as that would determine whether an accusation against Robbie had been justifiable. Moreover, without actually dismissing the jury, the judge announced that he alone would decide the verdict. He pointed out that it was hard to credit that

Crosland could have believed Garratt's original, supposed accusations against Robbie – which he had subsequently denied – when at the time of the alleged act of gross indecency, Robbie had been in Russia. In his summing up, Mr Justice Bray said that there was no evidence that Robbie was guilty of the charges made against him, and that therefore he must assume that he was innocent. Accordingly, he gave judgement in Robbie's favour, with costs. Christopher Millard, who had sat through the whole trial, wrote to Walter Ledger, 'It was good to hear the whole story of the vile conspiracy exposed before a just Judge who made no bones about saying that C. and D. were both trying to blackmail Robbie . . . I now hope that Robbie will be left in peace.'

For a while, Robbie did enjoy a tranquillity that had been notably lacking in his life in recent years. Since the early summer of 1914, he had been living in rooms at 40 Half Moon Street, near Shepherd Market, which he was now able to enjoy properly as a snug home. The landlady of the house was his mother's old lady's maid, Nellie Burton. She only took in single gentlemen, as she was suspicious of young women, whom she described as 'fair to the eye and rotten to the core'. Dubbed Dame Nellie by her bachelor tenants, she was a squat, stout figure who added height by wearing her hair piled on top of her head. One good friend of Robbie's, Squire Sprigge, likened her to a bad character out of Hogarth. She had a penchant for elaborate clothes, which belied her sometimes gruff manner. As a memorial article about her in the *Manchester Guardian* noted, she was firmly of the belief that 'it is in the nature of gentlemen to err and behave strangely'. How much this attitude resulted from her experience with the young Robbie while she was working for Eliza Ross cannot be known; what is certain is that it made her ideally suited to oversee the last years of Robbie's life.

In *Siegfried's Journey*, the poet Siegfried Sassoon, whom

Robbie had first met at a party at Edmund Gosse's in the summer of 1913, left a vivid picture of Robbie's sitting-room at Half Moon Street, where he entertained a number of young writers, most of whom, like Sassoon, had joined the army:

> The tones of the room were mellow and subdued, half Italian and half Oriental, yet essentially imbued by London homeliness. There was a richly-looming Roman landscape by Richard Wilson. A few small Chinese prints and pieces of faience, refined and delicate in colour, harmonised with the Persian carpet and the curtain at the tall windows which opened out onto a balcony.[2]

Robbie himself, his face tired and old before its time, his breathing rasping from asthma, would stand, 'in his loose grey alpaca jacket, wearing a black silk skull-cap and smoking his perpetual cigarette in its jade-green holder, emphasizing his lively pronouncements with controlled gestures of the left hand, on the third finger of which was a fair-sized scarab ring'.

Robbie now discovered a new vocation, part literary midwife, part agony uncle, to Sassoon and several other men in uniform. In March 1916, Sassoon came over to England on leave from France, and stayed with Robbie at Half Moon Street. There is no reason to think that any physical contact ever took place between the two, though like many people, Robbie did find his twenty-nine-year-old guest, with his dark, almost Mediterranean looks, strikingly handsome. Their conversations often centred on literature and the war. Whereas other friends of Sassoon's, such as Edmund Gosse and Eddie Marsh, appreciated what he called his 'idealized soldier-poems', Robbie was more likely to be attracted by his first satirical efforts. As Sassoon noted in *Siegfried's Journey*, Robbie hated the war so much that he 'was unable to be tolerant about it and those who accepted it with civilian bellicosity and self-defensive evasion of its realities'. It was Robbie who spoke contemptuously of 'screaming scarlet Majors', a phrase that Sassoon would incorporate so effectively into one of his own poems. And it was into Robbie's hands that Sassoon entrusted the manuscript of his most recent work, before returning to the Front. Robbie and other friends saw him off at Waterloo Station, little realizing that he would first acquire celebrity for his heroism, followed by notoriety because of his revulsion at the carnage around him.

THIRTEEN

Worn Down by Cares

Even in wartime, there were oases of calm, such as Garsington Manor near Oxford, the country home of the Liberal MP Philip Morrell and his statuesque wife, Lady Ottoline. A passionate woman, in every sense of the word, Ottoline counted the Prime Minister, Augustus John and the pacifist philosopher Bertrand Russell amongst her lovers. She was an extravagant hostess, both at Garsington and at the Morrells' town house in Bedford Square. A flamboyant dresser, six feet tall and with striking features, she was forever on the lookout for new literary and artistic talent. Many were the young novelists who enjoyed her hospitality, only to caricature her cruelly later in their work. Her energy and studied eccentricity could be overwhelming. But she was essentially a kind woman, who was happy to provide a haven for men like Robbie who were distressed by the realities of the war.

Robbie and Ottoline had first come into contact through the Contemporary Art Society, but their friendship flourished thanks to Herbert Asquith. This was despite an unfortunate incident on 21 May 1916, when for once Robbie's dignified façade crumbled. He had been spending the weekend with the Asquiths at The Wharf, when the Prime Minister suggested a drive over to Garsington. Elizabeth Asquith and Mrs George Keppel, mistress of the late King Edward VII, accompanied them. It was a hot Sunday afternoon, and as Ottoline was having a picnic in the grounds with the painter Dorothy Brett and some of her Bloomsbury Group friends, Clive Bell, Lytton Strachey and Dora Carrington, she had given permission for the maids and a girl groom called Lucy to have a swim in the pond. Spying the sudden arrival of the Prime Minister and his party, Lucy let out a scream. She then splashed about as if drowning, causing Robbie to plunge fully clothed into the pond to rescue her. His knees hit the bottom, as the pond was no more than four feet deep, and he was left feeling extremely foolish as the Prime Minister and others roared with laughter. Hurrying to see what the commotion was about, Ottoline missed the dramatic action itself but commented wittily, 'He's always jumping into the water to pull people out, isn't he?' Philip Morrell lent Robbie a set of dry clothes and he became a regular, favourite visitor from then on.

In August, Siegfried Sassoon, who had been awarded the Military Cross for bravery, succumbed to trench fever and was sent home on sick leave. He was billeted at Somerville College, Oxford, where Robbie went to see him. 'My heart went out to his careworn face, lit up by pleasure at seeing me home from the war in an undamaged condition,' Sassoon later recorded. As Sassoon was looking so surprisingly robust, Robbie suggested that they go over to Garsington so he could introduce his friend to Ottoline. They arrived by taxi and found Ottoline in the studio, where Dorothy Brett was painting her portrait. According to Sassoon, the first sight he had of his hostess was of a pair of voluminous pink Turkish harem trousers descending a ladder. Above these, Ottoline was wearing an orange tunic, with a purple hat topping her purple-dyed hair. In her memoirs of Garsington during the war years, Ottoline recalled that she sat watching Sassoon as he talked to Robbie and her husband Philip. 'Perhaps it was his way of turning his head, and the lean face with green hazel eyes, his ears large and rather protruding, and the nose with the wide nostrils, that was not exactly *farouche* but he seemed very shy and reserved, he was more *sauvage*; and, as I looked at his full face I said to myself, "He could be cruel".' Obviously, this prospect rather thrilled her, as she soon fell deeply in love with him, not realizing that he was in love with a fellow officer in France. Although later Sassoon did marry, and fathered a son, his nature was predominantly homosexual. Sometimes Robbie's candour on the subject dismayed him, however, which was one reason why sometimes he stayed at a London club, rather than at Robbie's when he was in town. Nonetheless, he remained grateful to Robbie for his hospitality and advice.

So, too, did their mutual friend Robert Graves, who had been wounded, and indeed posted as dead, during the Battle of the Somme that July. Graves was invalided home to England and spent a couple of days at Robbie's before moving on to stay with Sassoon at his family home in Kent. At this period of his life, Graves also considered himself predominantly homosexual, though he later 'converted' vigorously to heterosexuality, partly because a gay friend of his committed suicide and the prospect of such despair ahead filled him with horror.

The news from the Front was increasingly depressing, as one after another, friends and acquaintances fell. On 7 September 1916, Robbie's nephew Edward Jones was killed; though Robbie had never forgiven him for his intervention over Freddie Smith, he was upset by the distress the loss caused his sister Mary. Then, only a few days later, news came of the death of the Prime Minister's brilliant eldest son Raymond. As Violet Asquith told Robbie, 'it is very hard to see Father suffering so – though he has been wonderfully brave. Raymond's life was a romance to him – which he watched unfolding with a thrilled expectancy he never felt about his own.'

To add to Herbert Asquith's problems, there was unrest in Ireland. The troubles there were partly why Robbie turned down an offer to become Keeper of the National Gallery in Dublin. As he explained to Lady Gregory, the nationalist soulmate of W. B. Yeats and co-founder of the Abbey Theatre, 'politics enter into everything in Dublin and I am too much of a partisan not to be dragged into the vortex'. Nonetheless, in the autumn he agreed to make representations to Asquith about a contested bequest of an important collection of Impressionist paintings. The pictures belonged to Sir Hugh Lane, who had been instrumental in getting the National Gallery in Dublin set up. Sir Hugh drowned when the passenger liner, the *Lusitania*, was sunk by enemy action. In his original will, he had bequeathed his pictures to the National Gallery in London, but in a codicil had changed the beneficiary to the Dublin gallery. The codicil had not been witnessed, however, and the London gallery refused to acknowledge Dublin's claim. Robbie took advantage of one of his weekend stays at The Wharf to raise the matter with his host. But, as he reported back to Lady Gregory, although the Prime Minister was personally sympathetic to the Irish claim, he confirmed what Robbie had been told by lawyers, that the matter would require parliamentary legislation to enable the Trustees of the National Gallery in London to act. The dispute was only finally sorted out over forty years later, when the collection was divided up between London and Dublin.

Robbie was more successful with commissions he had been given on behalf of the Johannesburg Art Gallery, which was due to open in April 1917. Though he had long since resigned as London Director, and was not receiving any honorarium, he arranged for all the works of art and books that had been bought for the gallery and temporarily stored at the Tate to be shipped out to South Africa. Lady Phillips offered to pay him for this assistance, but he declined.

He did, however, accept an offer from the National Gallery of Victoria in Melbourne, Australia, to become its paid adviser for purchases. He wanted to travel out to Australia, to see the gallery for himself and to meet its Trustees, but wartime restrictions and his own indifferent health made that inadvisable for the time being. Instead, he set about acquiring significant oil paintings and watercolours by artists as diverse as Blake, Burne-Jones and Canaletto on Melbourne's behalf. This burst of activity coincided with his appointment by David Lloyd-George, who had succeeded Asquith as Prime Minister, to be a Trustee of the Tate Gallery. On the Tate's board, he was truly among friends, as his colleagues included Dugald MacColl, Robert Witt, the Earl of Plymouth and Ottoline Morrell's brother, Lord Henry Cavendish-Bentinck. Robbie was immediately invited to sit on a sub-committee that was charged with drawing up a list of painters who should be represented in the Tate's growing collection of contemporary British art.

Siegfried Sassoon, back with the British forces in France, kept Robbie informed of life on the frontline. 'I loathe the sacrificial imbecility of war,' he had written in February, while recuperating from German measles, 'and the whole scheme of things as one sees it out here. I could never have believed that things could be so meaningless and so contemptible.' Yet he showed himself to be a courageous, even reckless, fighter, oblivious to personal danger and fiercely loyal to his men. In April, at the Battle of Arras, he was shot by a sniper, which meant he had to be evacuated once again to England. He was thus able to be in the country when an important volume of his verse came out, *The Old Huntsman*. Robbie was enthusiastic about some of the collection's abrasive war poems, though many other critics, including Edmund Gosse, found their hostile tone offensive at a time when the nation was concentrating on the war effort. This was nothing, though, compared with what

Sassoon was mulling over: an open protest about the conduct of the war.

Conversations he had had with pacifists within Lady Ottoline Morrell's circle heightened his determination to take a stand. But he was wary about letting even his closest friends in on his plans. One day he called in at the Reform Club, on the off-chance of finding Robbie there. Robbie was soon located, up a step-ladder in the gallery that overlooks the imposing reception hall, cleaning a murky portrait of the Victorian Prime Minister Gladstone. 'He was wearing his black silk skull-cap and looked small and somehow touching as his tired face brightened to greet me.' But Sassoon could not pluck up the courage to let Robbie in on his secret, though Robbie sensed that there was something on his friend's mind. When he asked if anything was wrong, Sassoon muttered merely that he was sleeping badly.

Robbie was on a visit to Brighton on 8 July 1917, when he received a copy of Sassoon's anti-war statement, which he had sent with a covering letter to the Commanding Officer at Litherland, where he had been ordered to report for duty now he was well again. Robbie's heart sank as he read the uncompromising open sentences: 'I am making this statement as an act of wilful defiance of military authority because I believe that the War is being deliberately prolonged by those who have the power to end it. I am a soldier, convinced that I am acting on behalf of soldiers. I believe that this War, upon which I entered as a war of defence and liberation, has become a war of aggression and conquest.' It was not that Robbie disagreed with the sentiments Sassoon was expressing but rather that he was alarmed at the possible consequences. He immediately sent off a note to Sassoon, saying, 'I am appalled at what you have done. I can only hope that the C.O. at Litherland will absolutely ignore your letter. I am terrified lest you should be put under arrest. Let me know at once if anything happens.'

Fortunately, one of the first things Robbie did was to inform Robert Graves of what Sassoon had done. Graves then wrote to the Sergeant-Major at Litherland imploring him not to let the Colonel take Sassoon's statement seriously. He was clearly in need of further convalescence, Graves argued, and ought to be given a special Medical Board. That is indeed what happened, resulting in Sassoon being sent to Craiglockhart, a nursing home outside Edinburgh that specialized in the treatment of the shell-shocked. Robbie and Graves were immensely relieved, though they felt bitter towards pacifists such as Bertrand Russell who, they believed, had put Sassoon up to what seemed to them to be a foolhardy gesture, without realizing the possible outcome or having to shoulder any of the consequences themselves. Sassoon went along with the charade of his 'treatment' at Craiglockhart, entering into a particularly close and challenging relationship with the specialist who was assigned to him, Dr William Rivers. Sassoon reported regularly to Robbie on how he was getting on, one of his earliest letters being headed 'Dottyville'.

A number of his fellow patients were indeed in a seriously deranged state, though one stood out as being exceptional: a young, aspirant poet by the name of Wilfred Owen, who nervously showed Sassoon some of his work. Sassoon enjoyed being the young man's mentor, though it is not certain whether he realized that Owen was starting to fall in love with him. When Owen was discharged in October, Sassoon provided him with a letter of introduction to Robbie, who was more than happy to add him to the band of soldier-poets who frequented his rooms in Half Moon Street. Moreover, Robbie was not the sort of person to keep new 'discoveries' for himself, as Osbert Sitwell and many others were also to discover to their benefit. Early in November, he took Owen to the Reform Club, where he introduced him to Arnold Bennett and H. G. Wells. Later in the month, Sassoon himself left Craiglockhart and came to stay with Robbie for a few days. London had been experiencing the unpleasant novelty of German air-raids, about which Robbie discoursed wryly, aware that they were as nothing compared with the misery that soldiers were enduring in the trenches.

On 12 December, the indefatigable society hostess Mrs Sybil Colefax held a charity poetry reading attended by a distinguished and well-heeled audience. She had twisted Edmund Gosse's arm to be Master of Ceremonies, while Robbie was roped in to organize the programme. The poets and writers who performed included T. S. Eliot, Edith and Osbert Sitwell, Aldous Huxley and another of Robbie's coterie of young, new talents in the armed forces the idiosyncratic and demanding Robert Nichols. Gosse was dreading the event, but in the end it proved a great success. As he enthused to Robert Graves, in the camp tone that he sometimes adopted in letters, 'What perfect dears the Sitwells are, and R.N. is a portent of tragic splendour.' Nichols never managed to achieve the success he aspired to, either as a poet or as a novelist, but Robbie viewed him with the affection a bachelor uncle might feel towards a spirited, reckless nephew.

By the beginning of January 1918, Nichols was back in action, writing to Robbie on the 9th from 'Wipers' (Ypres). 'War has not desecrated it,' he declared, 'has sanctified it and as an emblem has put upon it a beauty higher than that of any city I've ever seen. Oxford can't hold a candle to these glorious ruins and the finest russets and buffs you ever saw.' At the end of his rather forced jocular missive, with shells falling around him, Nichols hoped that Robbie was feeling better than when he'd heard from him last. 'Wish you were as plein des haricots as I am here.'

But Robbie was not full of beans. He was physically run-down, his constitution weakened by frequent illnesses and the aftermath of the removal of his kidney. The mental stress caused by his friends' problems only served to debilitate him further.

The same day that Nichols wrote his letter, Christopher Millard was arrested on charges of gross indecency. Both he and Robbie had long realized that this might happen again one day; indeed Millard, though in his forties, had joined up earlier in the war, precisely in order to escape that eventuality. He served for two years in France, before being wounded and sent home. He had hoped that the authorities would leave him alone from then on, but he underestimated the continuing British obsession with 'perversion'. If anything, in wartime conditions, the prevailing culture became even more relentlessly 'manly' and intolerant. Millard was found guilty as charged and sentenced to a year's imprisonment, though without hard labour.

One unfortunate side-effect of Millard's conviction, and the fact that it gave the press the opportunity to remind people of his connection with Robbie, was that it helped reactivate Bosie Douglas in his vendetta against his former friend. Another important element in Bosie's re-emergence was the appearance towards the end of January 1918 of a sensational article in a publication called the *Vigilante*, penned by a right-wing independent Member of Parliament, Noel Pemberton Billing. In the article, Billing claimed that there existed in Germany a 'Black Book' compiled by the Kaiser's Secret Service, and based on reports from German agents in Britain, 'agents so vile and spreading such debauchery and such lasciviousness as only German minds can conceive and only German bodies execute'. In that book, so Billing maintained, were the names of 47,000 'perverts', including well-known people in the government and society.

Three weeks later, the *Vigilante* ran another exclusive exposé, startlingly headlined 'The Cult of the Clitoris'. This referred to private performances of the Dance of the Seven Veils, from Oscar Wilde's *Salomé*, by Miss Maud Allan, a well-established but *risquée* dancer who had often appeared before royalty. The

Vigilante article pointed out that one had to apply for a special membership to attend one of Miss Allan's performances, adding, somewhat incoherently, that 'if Scotland Yard were to seize the list of these members I have no doubt that they would secure the names of several of the first 47,000'.

F. E. Smith, who was now Attorney-General, looked into the possibility of bringing some sort of prosecution against Pemberton Billing, but the only legal recourse appeared to be for Maud Allan and her impresario Jack Grein to sue the maverick MP for libel. Robbie, who, as Wilde's executor, had granted Grein permission to stage the extracts from *Salomé*, urged them not to, given his own experience of the viciousness of those who opposed 'the cult of Oscar Wilde' and the strength of the populist chord that they struck. But the prosecution went ahead. Billing conducted his own defence when the trial opened at the Old Bailey on 29 May 1918. Mr Justice Darling presided.

The proceedings were a travesty of justice. Billing had packed the court with his supporters, strategically placing a line of maimed soldiers at the front of the public gallery. Both Billing and his witnesses played to anti-German hysteria, and the alleged involvement of senior Liberals in debauchery. One witness was produced who claimed to have seen the Black Book. When Billing asked her if Margot Asquith's name was in it, she replied that it was. So too was Mr Asquith's. And Lord Haldane's. Even Mr Justice Darling's. The public gallery went berserk as the revelations continued. Much was made of the Asquiths' link to Robbie, and of his to Oscar Wilde. But Billing was unable to subpoena Robbie to appear as a witness, as he had hoped, because Robbie was by now seriously ill. Instead, Bosie Douglas featured as Billing's star witness. He declared that Oscar had had a diabolical effect on everyone he met. 'I think he is the greatest force of evil that has appeared in Europe during the last 350 years.' Robbie was not immune from Bosie's righteous wrath either. 'If I were still on Oscar Wilde's side, I should be getting praise from judges and Prime Ministers, and praise from greasy advocates,' he thundered. 'Like Ross, I should get a testimonial from Asquith and £700 given to me from people in society saying what a fine person I was. Asquith and all these people presented Ross with a testimonial and £700 because he was a sodomite.'

Counsel for Maud Allan and Jack Grein tried to counter such tirades by reading out letters that Oscar had written to Bosie at the height of their relationship, hoping to undermine his testimony by showing that he, too, had practised the love that dare not speak its name. But Bosie refused to be drawn, denying categorically that he had any sodomitic tendencies now. When the trial ended, and the jury declared Billing not guilty, the public stood up and cheered. A few minutes later, Bosie joined Billing on the steps of the court building, to acknowledge the acclaim of the crowd gathered outside.

Despite his physical weakness, Robbie vented his fury at the outcome on the Director of Public Prosecutions, Sir Charles Matthews, directly accusing him in a letter of conniving with Bosie Douglas in his campaign against Robbie and the Asquiths. 'Now I understand what Shakespeare intended in presenting so vividly the venom and snobbery of a bastard, particularly the bastard of a mummer;' he added, with uncharacteristic ferocity. Yet in reality, he was not surprised by what had happened. He knew from the start that Billing would be acquitted, because the British populace was entirely on his side. As Robbie lamented to Cecil Sprigge, Squire Sprigge's son, 'Kicking the corpse of Wilde has also been a pleasure to the English people even if they disapprove of Billing's methods.' As for himself, 'I have been used as a piece of mud.' Charles Ricketts was not alone among Robbie's friends in noting with concern that both his physical and mental state had been adversely affected.

Nonetheless, with the end of the war now in sight, and the easing of travel restrictions, Robbie turned his mind to his postponed project of visiting Australia to see the National Gallery of Victoria. Siegfried Sassoon, who had returned to active service, only to get shot in the head by one of his own junior officers who mistook him for a German, arrived back in London at the end of September 1918, and accompanied Robbie over the next few days, as he bid farewell to various friends prior to his long journey. There was lunch with Arnold Bennett and Maurice Baring one day, then with Edith Sitwell and Clive Bell the next. Ottoline Morrell came for tea at Half Moon Street. On 3 October, Sassoon and Robbie planned to spend a quiet evening together but the Scottish translator Charles Scott-Moncrieff turned up unannounced, to introduce to Robbie a new discovery of his, Noël Coward. Sassoon left early, pleading a headache, but as he opened the front door, Robbie came downstairs quickly and stood beside him. 'He said nothing, but took my hand and looked up at me for a long moment. His worn face, grey with exhaustion and ill-health, was beatified by sympathy and affection.'

Two days later, on 5 October 1918 Robbie returned home from a long lunch with friends. He complained to Nellie Burton of chest pains, suspecting indigestion. She helped him up to his bedroom to have a lie-down, but when she returned to wake him to dress for dinner, she discovered that he was dead. He was aged just forty-nine. It is true that he had outlived Oscar by three years, but like Wilde, he was old before his time. Sassoon noted fittingly, in *Siegfried's Journey*, 'While resting before dinner, he died of heart failure. It seems reasonable to claim that this was the only occasion on which his heart failed him.'

Postscript

Robbie's sudden death was a shock to many friends, who shared their grief and their condolences with his brother Aleck. Vyvyan Holland wrote from France, where he was serving in the army, 'You know without my telling you what it means to me. Robbie has always been my dearest friend, and I have always looked to him when I wanted sincerity and advice.' Edmund Gosse, who was on holiday in Scotland, confided:

> I and all my family suffer a loss which can never be repaired – we shall not again meet such a compound of loyalty and affection, of shrewdness and enthusiasm, of originality mainly directed to the help and encouragement of others. Robbie's character was nobly unselfish: his intellect, excellent as were its evidences, never did complete justice to itself. He was capable, I always felt, of the highest critical developments. All he needed was calm, and this was denied him and that denial killed him.[1]

The obituary that appeared in *The Times* acknowledged that Robbie had been a far more substantial figure than he often appeared. 'It was his foible to pretend to be a trifler in all things and to gibe at the greatest reputation; but he knew more and did more than many solemn people and, in acts of kindness, he was always in earnest.'

An autopsy had to be carried out on Robbie's body, followed by an inquest, which was held at Westminster Coroner's Court on 9 October. Any suspicion of suicide was firmly ruled out, with the coroner finding that the cause of death had been a loss of consciousness 'caused by chronic bronchitis and gastritis', which was too much for Robbie's system to sustain, as he was already weakened by many years of poor health. In accordance with Robbie's will, he was cremated at Golders Green, with the ordinary burial offices of the Catholic Church. Another stipulation in the will was impossible to accomplish immediately, namely that 'I direct that my ashes shall be placed in a suitable urn and taken to Paris and buried in the tomb of . . . Oscar Fingal O'Flahertie Wills Wilde.' Referring to the difficulties he had had with cemetery authorities at the time of the transfer of Oscar's body from Bagneux to Père Lachaise, Robbie added that if it proved impossible to obtain the necessary licence from the authorities, then his ashes should be scattered at Père Lachaise instead.

It was only on 30 November 1950, the fiftieth anniversary of Oscar's death, that Robbie's wishes were fulfilled. Marjorie Ross – the wife of Robbie's nephew William Jones, who had changed his name by deed-poll to Ross, as neither Jack, Aleck nor Robbie had left an heir – conveyed the urn to Paris. In a simple ceremony, she placed it in the dedicated cavity that Robbie had asked Jacob Epstein to incorporate into the monument, confident that one day, he would find his rightful resting-place.

Notes

Prologue
1. Oscar Wilde [OW], *De Profundis*, in Rupert Hart-Davies (ed.), *The Letters of Oscar Wilde [Letters]*, London, 1962, pp. 459–60.

Chapter 1: A Legacy to Live Up To
1. Quoted in Graham Robb's *Balzac*, London, 1994, pp. 67–8.
2. Also sometimes spelled 'Alec', although his family, including Robbie, called him 'George', and his friends called him 'Augustus'.
3. 'The Literary Log', *Bystander*, 2 November 1910.

Chapter 2: Reckless Youth
1. Quoted in H. Montgomery Hyde's *The Other Love*, London, 1970, p. 134.
2. OW to RR, circa 13 October 1888, *Letters*, p. 225.
3. OW to OB, October 1888, Rupert Hart-Davis (ed.), *More Letters of Oscar Wilde [More Letters]*, London, 1985, p. 75.
4. OW to W. E. Henley, September 1888, *Letters*, p. 224.
5. *Granta*, 1 March 1889.
6. Quoted in Ian Anstruther's *Oscar Browning*, London, 1983, pp. 133–4.
7. OW to RR, July 1889, *Letters*, p. 247.

Chapter 3: In Oscar's Shadow

1. RR to OB, September 1889, KCC.
2. W. E. Henley to RR, 20 December 1889, Margery Ross (ed.), *Robert Ross: Friend of Friends [RRFF]*, London, 1952, pp. 19–20.
3. *Truth*, 2 January 1890.
4. OW to the Editor of *Truth*, January 1890, *Letters*, pp. 253–4.
5. W. E. Henley to RR, 28 February 1890, *RRFF*, p. 20.
6. RR to OW, no date 1890, William Andrews Memorial Library, University of California, Los Angeles.
7. *Scots Observer*, 5 July 1890.
8. OW to the Editor of the *Scots Observer*, 9 July 1890, *Letters*, p. 266.
9. Reprinted in Robert Ross, *Masques and Phases*, London, 1909, pp. 49–51.
10. Walter Besant to RR, 12 July 1891, *RRFF*, p. 22.
11. Walter Besant to RR, 3 December 1891, *RRFF*, p. 23.

Chapter 4: Catastrophe Averted

1. RR to Edmund Gosse [EG], 16 March 1892, Brotherton Library, University of Leeds.
2. OW to RR, ? May/June 1892, *Letters*, p. 314.
3. OW to RR, ? November/December 1892, *Letters*, p. 323.
4. EG to RR, 22 December 1892, *RRFF*, pp. 24–5.
5. OW to Lord Alfred Douglas [BD], ? January 1893, *Letters*, p. 326.
6. Robert Ross, *Aubrey Beardsley*, London, 1909, p. 15.
7. OW to Campbell Dodgson, 23 February 1893, *Letters*, p. 333.
8. Quoted in David Cecil's *Max, a Biography*, London, 1964, p. 64.
9. Max Beerbohm to Reggie Turner [RT], 19 August 1893,

Rupert Hart-Davis (ed.), *Max Beerbohm's Letters to Reggie Turner*, Philadelphia and New York, 1965, pp. 52–3.

10. Quoted in Ian Anstruther's *Oscar Browning*, London, 1983, p. 134.
11. Ibid., p. 135.
12. RR to OB, 16 October 1893, King's College, Cambridge [KCC].
13. Biscoe Wortham to OB, 25 October 1893, ibid.

Chapter 5: Oscar's Downfall
1. RR to BD, ? November 1893, quoted in Maureen Borland, *Wilde's Devoted Friend: A Life of Robert Ross*, Oxford, 1990.
2. Aubrey Beardsley [AB] to RR, ? December 1893, *RRFF*, p. 28.
3. Quoted in Borland, *Wilde's Devoted Friend*, p. 38.
4. Ibid., p. 39.
5. AB to RR, December 1893, *RRFF*, p. 30.
6. OW to BD, ? August 1894, *Letters*, p. 363.
7. OW to George Ives, 22 October 1894, *Letters*, p. 375.
8. OW to RR, c. 25 January 1895, *More Letters*, pp. 128–9.
9. OW to RR, 28 February 1895, *Letters*, p. 384.

Chapter 6: Standing by Oscar
1. OW to RR and More Adey, 9 April 1895, *Letters*, p. 390.
2. Lord Alfred Douglas's *Autobiography*, London, 1929, p. 108.
3. Quoted in Richard Ellmann's *Oscar Wilde*, London, 1987, p. 435.
4. OW to BD, May 1895, *Letters*, p. 397.
5. Max Beerbohm to RT, 3 May 1895, *Max Beerbhom's Letters*, p. 102.
6. EG to RR, 17 May 1895, *RRFF*, pp. 36–7.

7. Quoted in Ellmann, *Oscar Wilde*, pp. 448–9.
8. RR to OB, 21 October 1895, KCC.
9. BD to More Adey, 25 November 1895, quoted in Douglas Murray, *Bosie: A Biography of Lord Alfred Douglas*, London, 2000.
10. RR to More Adey, no date, *RRFF*, pp. 39–41.
11. OW to RR, 23 or 30 May 1896, *Letters*, p. 400.

Chapter 7: An Uncomfortable Triangle
1. Ada Leverson's *Letters to the Sphinx from Oscar Wilde and Reminiscences of the Author*, London, 1930, pp. 48–9.
2. More Adey to OW, 23 September 1896, *Letters*, p. 407.
3. OW to RR, *Letters*, p. 413.
4. BD to RR, undated 1897, quoted in Murray, *Bosie*, p. 102.
5. OW to More Adey, 15 May 1897, *Letters*, p. 550.
6. RT to OW, May 1897, *Letters*, p. 557.
7. OW to RR, 19 May 1897, *Letters*, pp. 565–6.
8. More Adey [ed.], *After Berneval: Letters of Oscar Wilde to Robert Ross*.
9. OW to RT, 27 May 1895, *Letters*, p. 575.
10. OW to RR, 28 May 1895, *Letters*, pp. 576–7.
11. OW to RR, 24 August 1897, *Letters*, pp. 634–5.
12. OW to BD, ? 31 August 1897, *Letters*, p. 637.
13. OW to RR, 21 September 1897, *Letters*, p. 644.
14. OW to RR, 1 October 1897, *Letters*, p. 649.
15. OW to Leonard Smithers, 30 November 1897, *Letters*, p. 688.

Chapter 8: Competing Demands
1. RR to Leonard Smithers, April 1898, quoted in Ellmann, *Oscar Wilde*, pp. 532–3.
2. OW to RR, July 1898, *Letters*, p. 755.
3. Max Beerbohm to RR, 19 December 1898, *RRFF*, p. 54.

4. OW to RR, April 1899, *Letters*, p. 794.

5. William Rothenstein to RR, 14 September 1899, *RRFF*, pp. 56–7.

6. RR to William Rothenstein, 27 November 1899, Houghton Library, University of Harvard.

7. OW to RR, ? 28 February 1900, *Letters*, p. 817.

8. OW to RR, March 1900, *Letters*, p. 819.

9. Reprinted in Robert Ross, *Masques and Phases*, London, 1909, p. 24.

10. OW to RR, 1 September 1900, *Letters*, p. 833.

Chapter 9: Life after Oscar

1. RR to Adela Schuster, 23 December 1900, *RRFF*, pp. 67–8.

2. RR to William Rothenstein, 11 December 1900, Houghton Library, University of Harvard.

3. Cyril Holland to RR, no date, quoted in Vyvyan Holland's *Son of Oscar Wilde*, London, 1954, p. 153.

4. RR to Roger Fry, 30 April 1903, KCC.

5. RR's *Aubrey Beardsley*, p. 32.

6. E. V. Lucas to RR, November 1904, *RRFF*, p. 88.

7. 1905 Methuen edition of *De Profundis*.

Chapter 10: New-Found Stability

1. Compton Mackenzie's *My Life and Times*, Vol. 3, p. 225.

2. RR to the Editor of the *Sphere*, 20 July 1905, *RRTF*, p. 116.

3. RR to the Editor of the *Academy*, published 23 December 1905.

4. RR's 'Mr Arthur Symons' Morality', the *Academy*, 21 April 1906.

5. RR to EG, 19 April 1907, *RRFF*, p. 138.

6. Holland, *Son of Oscar Wilde*, p. 186.

7. *RRFF*, p. 154.

8. Ibid, p. 156.

Chapter 11: Bosie's Vendetta

1. BD to RR, 1 March 1909, quoted in Murray, *Bosie*, pp. 165–6.
2. Vyvyan Holland, *Son of Oscar Wilde*, pp. 196–7.
3. William Rothenstein to RR, 3 October 1909, *RRFF*, p. 163.
4. Quoted in André Gide's *Si le Grain ne meurt*, translated by Dorothy Bussy, p. 288.
5. RR's 'Post-Impressionists at the Grafton', *Morning Post*, 7 November 1910.
6. Ford Madox Hueffer to RR, 27 March 1911, *RRFF*, p. 211.
7. BD to RR, 9 March 1912, quoted in Murray, *Bosie*, pp. 171–2.
8. BD to RR, 30 November 1912, ibid., pp. 174–5.
9. Cyril Holland to RR, 1 July 1913, *RRFF*, p. 244.

Chapter 12: New Beginnings

1. RR to Aleck Ross, 26 September 1913, *RRFF*, p. 254.
2. Siegfried Sassoon, *Siegfried's Journey*, p. 32.

Postscript

1. EG to Aleck Ross, 7 October 1918, *RRFF*, p. 340.

Bibliography

Amor, Anne Clark, *Mrs Oscar Wilde: A Woman of Some Importance*, Sidgwick & Jackson, London, 1983

Anderson, Garrett, *'Hang Your Halo in the Hall!': A History of the Savile Club*, The Savile Club, London, 1993

Anstruther, Ian, *Oscar Browning*, John Murray, London, 1983

Bennett, Daphne, *Margot: A Life of the Countess of Oxford & Asquith*, Victor Gollancz, London, 1984

Bentley, Joyce, *The Importance of Being Constance: A Biography of Oscar Wilde's Wife*, Robert Hale, London, 1983

Borland, Maureen, *Wilde's Devoted Friend: A Life of Robert Ross*, Lennard, Oxford, 1990

Brooke, Christopher, *A History of the University of Cambridge, Volume IV 1870–1990*, Cambridge University Press, Cambridge, 1993

Brown, George W., *Building the Canadian Nation*, J. M. Dent & Sons, London, 1942

Brown, W. Sorley, *The Life and Genius of T. W. H. Crosland*, Cecil Palmer, London, 1928

Cecil, David, *Max, a Biography*, Constable, London, 1964

Charteris, Hon. Evan, *The Life and Letters of Sir Edmund Gosse*, William Heinemann, London, 1931

Croft-Cooke, Rupert, *Bosie*, W. H. Allen, London, 1963

Croft-Cooke, Rupert, *Feasting with Panthers*, W. H. Allen, London, 1967

Douglas, Lord Alfred, *Oscar Wilde and Myself*, John Long, London, 1914

Douglas, Lord Alfred, *The Rossiad*, Robert Dawson & Son, Galashiels, 1921

Douglas, Lord Alfred, *Autobiography*, Martin Secker, London, 1929

Ellman, Richard, *Oscar Wilde*, Hamish Hamilton, London, 1987

Fryer, Jonathan, *André & Oscar: Gide, Wilde and the Gay Art of Living*, Constable, London, 1997

Gide, André, *Oscar Wilde*, William Kimber, London, 1951

Gide, André, *Si le Grain ne meurt*, trans. Dorothy Bussy, Secker and Warburg, London, 1950

Harris, Frank, *Oscar Wilde*, Robinson, London, 1997

Hart-Davis, Rupert (ed.), *Max Beerbohm's Letters to Reggie Turner*, J. B. Lippincott Company, Philadelphia and New York, 1965

Hart-Davis, Rupert (ed.), *The Letters of Oscar Wilde*, Rupert Hart-Davis, London, 1962

Hart-Davis, Rupert (ed.), *More Letters of Oscar Wilde*, John Murray, London, 1985

Hoare, Philip, *Wilde's Last Stand: Decadence, Conspiracy & The First World War*, Duckworth, London, 1997

Holland, Merlin, *The Wilde Album*, Fourth Estate, London, 1997

Holland, Vyvyan, *Son of Oscar Wilde*, Rupert Hart-Davis, London, 1954

Housman, Laurence, *Echos de Paris: A Study from Life*, Jonathan Cape, London, 1923

Hyde, H. Montgomery, *Lord Alfred Douglas*, Methuen, London, 1984

Hyde, H. Montgomery, *Oscar Wilde*, Eyre Methuen, London, 1976

Hyde, H. Montgomery, *Oscar Wilde: The Aftermath*, Methuen, London, 1963

Hyde, H. Montgomery, *The Other Love*, Heinemann, London, 1970

Jenkins, Roy, *Asquith*, Collins, London, 1964

Lago, Mary M. and Beckson, Karl (ed.), *Max & Will: Max Beerbohm and William Rothenstein*, John Murray, London, 1975

Leacock, Stephen, *Baldwin, LaFontaine, Hincks*, Morang & Co., Toronto, 1907

Leverson, Ada, *Letters to the Sphinx from Oscar Wilde and Reminiscences of the Author*, Duckworth, London, 1930

Mackenzie, Compton, *On Moral Courage*, Collins, London, 1962

Mackenzie, Compton, *My Life and Times, Vol. 3*, Chatto & Windus, London, 1963

Masters, Brian, *The Life of E. F. Benson*, Chatto & Windus, London, 1991

Melville, Joy, *Mother of Oscar: The Life of Jane Francesca Wilde*, John Murray, London, 1994

Murray, Douglas, *Bosie: A Biography of Lord Alfred Douglas*, Hodder & Stoughton, London, 2000

Page, Norman, *An Oscar Wilde Chronology*, Macmillan, Basingstoke, 1991

Palmer, Geoffrey and Lloyd, Noel, *E. F. Benson As He Was*, Lennard, Luton, 1988

Pearce, Joseph, *The Unmasking of Oscar Wilde*, HarperCollins, London, 2000

Pearson, Hesketh, *The Life of Oscar Wilde*, Methuen, London, 1946

Raby, Peter (ed.), *The Cambridge Companion to Oscar Wilde*, Cambridge University Press, 1997

Ransome, Arthur, *Oscar Wilde*, Martin Secker, London, 1912

Robb, Graham, *Balzac*, Picador, London, 1994

Ross, Margery (ed.), *Robert Ross: Friend of Friends*, Jonathan Cape, London, 1952

Ross, Robert, *Aubrey Beardsley*, John Lane, The Bodley Head, London, 1909

Ross, Robert, *Masques and Phases*, Arthur L. Humphreys, London, 1909

Sassoon, Siegfried, *Siegfried's Journey*, Faber and Faber, London, 1945

Sewell, Brocard, *Olive Custance: Her Life and Work*, The 1890s Society, London, 1975

Sherard, Robert Harborough, *Oscar Wilde: The Story of an Unhappy Friendship*, The Hermes Press, London, 1902

Sturgis, Matthew, *Aubrey Beardsley*, HarperCollins, London, 1998

Sturgis, Matthew, *Passionate Attitudes: The English Decadence of the 1890s*, Macmillan, London, 1995

Symonds, John Addington, *The Memoirs of John Addington Symonds*, edited by Phyllis Grosskurth, Hutchinson, London, 1984

Thwaite, Ann, *Edmund Gosse: A Literary Landscape 1849–1928*, Secker & Warburg, London, 1984

Von Eckardt, Wolf, Gilman, Sander L. and Chamberlain, J. Edward, *Oscar Wilde's London*, Michael O'Mara, London, 1988

Weintraub, Stanley, *Reggie: a Portrait of Reginald Turner*, George Braziller, New York, 1965

Wilson, Jean Moorcroft, *Siegfried Sassoon: The Making of a War Poet*, Duckworth, London, 1998

Index

277